Why was the European Monetary System in 1992–93 swept by waves of disruptive speculative attacks? And what lessons emerge from that episode as regards the future of the European Monetary Union?

A blend of theoretical and policy-oriented analysis, this book provides a comprehensive assessment of the causes and implications of the 1992–93 crisis of the exchange rate mechanism of the European Monetary System. Cogent factual presentation – including new details on the crisis – original theoretical analysis, and an interpretation rooted in the theory make this treatment essential reading to understand the process toward economic and political integration in Europe.

The authors first sketch the history of monetary cooperation in Europe from Bretton Woods to Maastricht. A step-by-step account of the 1992–93 events follows, including a discussion of the extent to which financial markets anticipated the crisis. A survey of the recent literature on the subject introduces the authors' center-periphery model of currency crises. The authors argue that the vulnerability of Europe to financial crises was – and still is – the result of the lack of concern with the systemic dimensions of monetary policy-making, both in terms of the international spillovers of domestic policies and the strategic interaction among monetary authorities.

Financial markets and European monetary cooperation

Financial markets and European monetary cooperation

The lessons of the 1992–93 Exchange Rate Mechanism crisis

WILLEM H. BUITER
University of Cambridge

GIANCARLO CORSETTI
University of Rome, III

PAOLO A. PESENTI
Princeton University

CAMBRIDGE
UNIVERSITY PRESS

PUBLISHED BY THE PRESS SYNDICATE OF THE UNIVERSITY OF CAMBRIDGE
The Pitt Building, Trumpington Street, Cambridge, CB2 1RP, United Kingdom

CAMBRIDGE UNIVERSITY PRESS
The Edinburgh Building, Cambridge CB2 2RU, United Kingdom
40 West 20th Street, New York, NY 10011–4211, USA
10 Stamford Road, Oakleigh, Melbourne 3166, Australia

First published 1998

Printed in the United States of America

Typeset in Times Roman

Library of Congress Cataloging-in-Publication Data
Buiter, Willem H., 1949-
Financial markets and European monetary cooperation : the
lessons of the 1992–93 Exchange Rate Mechanism crisis /
Willem Hendrik Buiter, Giancarlo Corsetti, Paolo Arturo Pesenti.
p.   cm. – (Japan-U.S. Center monographs on international financial markets)
ISBN 0-521-49547-4
1. European Monetary System (Organization)   2. Foreign exchange rates–
European Union countries.   3. International finance.   4. Monetary
policy–International cooperation.   I. Corsetti, Giancarlo.   II. Pesenti,
Paolo A.   III. Title.   IV. Series: Japan-U.S. Center Sanwa monographs
on international financial markets.
HG3942.B85   1997
332.4′56′094–dc21   97-1241
                                                                  CIP

A catalog record for this book is available from
the British Library

ISBN 0 521 49547 4   hardback

Contents

Foreword

The Sanwa Bank established The Sanwa Research Endowment Fund on International Financial Markets at The Center for Japan–U.S. Business and Economic Studies, Leonard N. Stern School of Business, New York University to provide continuing support for research on international economics and financial markets. One of the activities supported by the endowment is an annual financial award to write a monograph based on original research. The first monograph, "International Financial Integration: A study of interest differentials between the major industrial countries," was written by Richard C. Marston, of the Wharton School of the University of Pennsylvania and published by Cambridge University Press in 1995.

The second award went to Professor Willem Buiter of the University of Cambridge, Giancarlo Corsetti of University of Rome III, and Paolo A. Pesenti of Princeton University. Each researcher gets two to three years to complete the monograph and three monographs are under preparation.

I am delighted that the second Monograph draws lessons that have much wider relevance than the 1992–93 crisis in European Rate Mechanism. The Bretton Wood System that established a period of considerable stability in exchange rates in the post-World War period ended with the Smithsonian Agreement of 1971. While the relatively higher rate of inflation in the United States made it impossible for many nations to pursue price stability and dollar parity at the same time, it was not clear that the fluctuations in exchange rate that followed were desirable. So Europe then moved to the Exchange Rate Mechanism with narrow bands for exchange rates.

The dollar–yen rate has fluctuated dramatically in the last twenty years, creating hardship for Japan's exporters and accentuating political tensions between the two countries. This has prompted the suggestion that Japan should establish a Yen currency area with its neighbors. The monograph, by exploring the problems that arose within ERM, alerts us to difficulties in establishing such a currency area. The discussion of the need for policy coordination – not only between the center and the periphery economies but among the periphery countries themselves – should be carefully considered before any attempt is made elsewhere to replicate the European arrangement.

I would like to express my gratitude to the distinguished members of the Selection Committee of the Sanwa Monograph – Professors Ryuzo Sato of

New York University (Chair), Akiyoshi Horiuchi of the University of Tokyo, Merton Miller of University of Chicago, James Tobin of Yale University, and Richard Zeckhauser of Harvard University – for their careful deliberation. I also thank Dean George Daly of the Stern School for his support to the program, and Professor Ryuzo Sato, C. V. Starr Professor of Economics and Director of The Center, Professor Rama Ramachandran, Associate Director of The Center, for making the monograph series such a success.

Kenji Kawakatsu
Senior Advisor, Sanwa Bank Limited

Financial Markets and European Monetary Cooperation examines the crisis of the exchange rate mechanism (ERM) of the European Monetary System (EMS), interpreting the 1992 and 1993 events through an analysis of the strengths and weaknesses of systems of fixed exchange rates. The authors describe and document thoroughly the historical antecedents and the actual events of the ERM crises on the basis of all available sources.

The book is focused on the crisis of the ERM within a narrow margin of fluctuations (1979–1993). Nonetheless, the analysis of the basic weaknesses that plague systems of fixed exchange rates sheds light on several other examples of such systems. The authors channel their commendable ambition towards the formulation of a "center-periphery model." On the basis of the differentiation – which is helpful for analytical purposes – between the "center" and the "periphery" of fixed exchange rate systems, the authors emphasize that cohesion among the partner countries is indispensable. Therefore the willingness must exist to undergo realignments in due time, without waiting until adjustments are forced by the markets.

The history of the ERM shows that great dilemmas may occur between political objectives and market expectations. Such dilemmas tend to be more disruptive in a system with narrow margins of fluctuation than in the system with wide margins that has been adopted in Europe since mid-1993. The rather positive experience of the ongoing exchange rate arrangements can only be touched upon briefly in a book completed in 1996 on the 1992–1993 ERM crisis.

The reader will find the chapter on the planned European monetary union particularly useful. It discusses in a suitably detached manner the pros and cons of a union designed to last forever. It also clarifies the difference between monetary union and exchange rate system with fixed but adjustable parities. In particular, emphasis is placed on the requirement of jointly designed and stability-oriented monetary and fiscal policies that is an inherent characteristic of a monetary union.

Because monetary union is not likely to include all member states of the European Union at its start and an exchange rate mechanism will have to be devised for the countries out of the EMU (a sort of ERM II), the core experience of the ERM I described in this book may prove to be especially useful. Thus, this book can contribute to reduce the discrepancy between the current barbed and often polemical political debate, on one hand, and the actual policy process determining the changeover from an EMS fraught with tensions to a clearly defined and stable monetary union on the other.

Helmut Schlesinger
Former President, Deutsche Bundesbank

Acknowledgments

In the aftermath of the 1992 speculative episodes in the European Monetary System, we planned a research project focusing on an assessment of the interpretations and "lessons" of these events, as a contribution to the ongoing debate on monetary unification and financial integration in Europe. In 1993, our proposal was chosen by the selection committee for the second edition of the Sanwa Foundation Monograph Award in International Finance. This monograph represents the end product of the research program outlined in that proposal. We gratefully acknowledge support and encouragement throughout this project from Mr. Kenji Kawakatsu, Chairman of Sanwa Bank Limited; Professor Ryuzo Sato, Director of the Center for Japan-U.S. Business and Economic Studies; and Professor Rama Ramachandran of New York University.

The list of persons to whom we owe an intellectual debt of gratitude is long indeed. We would particularly like to thank Dr. Helmut Schlesinger, former President of the Deutsche Bundesbank and Visiting Professor at Princeton University in the fall of 1994. His thorough comments and remarks were crucial in shaping our reconstruction and interpretation of the 1992–93 events. Peter Kenen of Princeton University, Guido M. Rey of University of Rome III, and three anonymous reviewers offered countless helpful suggestions that improved both the substance and the presentation of the arguments in the monograph.

Among our colleagues and friends, special thanks for valuable comments go to Ben Bernanke, Michael Bordo, Jorge Braga de Macedo, Bill Brainard, Bill Branson, Alessandra Casella, Lilia Cavallari, Marcello De Cecco, Barry Eichengreen, Raquel Fernandez, Jeff Frankel, Jeff Frieden, Georg von Furstenberg, Peter Garber, Mike Gavin, Rex Ghosh, Vittorio Grilli, Koichi Hamada, Pierre-Yves Hénin, Yves Hervé, Karen Lewis, Richard Marston, Jacques Mélitz, Bill Nordhaus, Maury Obstfeld, Peter Orszag, Arvind Panagariya, Ken Rogoff, Nouriel Roubini, Chris Sims, Lars Svensson, Guido Tabellini, Aaron Tornell, Niels Thygesen, Jim Tobin, Bart Turtleboom, Andres Velasco, and Casper de Vries.

We thank seminar participants at the University of Amsterdam, Banca d'Italia, Bank of England, Berkeley, University of Bordeaux, Cambridge, Danmarks Nationalbank, European Monetary Institute, Harvard, Innocenzo Gasparini Institute for Economic Research, London School of Economics, University of Nantes, NBER Summer Institute, New York University, Princeton,

University of Rome, Rutgers, Tinbergen Institute, World Bank, and Yale for helpful remarks and suggestions on early versions of Chapters 2, 3, 6–8, and 10.

We thank Mariagiovanna Baccara and Ning Zhang for excellent research assistance. While working on this book, Giancarlo Corsetti visited the Departments of Economics at Columbia University and Yale University, which offered him an extremely productive research environment. Paolo Pesenti thanks the IGIER in Milan, the Tinbergen Institute in Rotterdam, and the EPRU in Copenhagen for warm hospitality and intellectual encouragement.

Last but not least, we thank Jean, Trui, and Mette for their continuing support, as well as patience and tolerance, throughout the project. With affection and gratitude, this book is dedicated to them.

CHAPTER 1

Introduction

Since 1979, the Exchange Rate Mechanism (ERM) of the European Monetary System (EMS) has represented the cornerstone of monetary policy strategies in Europe and the most ambitious experiment in international monetary and exchange rate cooperation of the post-Bretton Woods era.[1] Over the past decade, the nature of the ERM has changed drastically, from a system of fixed but adjustable rates with limited international capital mobility – as originally intended – to the "hard" mechanism implicitly ratified by the Basle-Nyborg agreement in 1987, characterized by stable and narrow target zones and the removal of capital controls.

By the end of the 1980s, the prima facie satisfactory performance of the "hard" ERM enhanced the general appeal of a further transformation of the system toward complete monetary harmonization and eventual unification. The successful conclusion of this transition was heralded as the permanent solution to the problem of inconsistency among national monetary policy objectives under free mobility of commodities, persons, and capital.

Starting in early 1992, however, a sequence of adverse developments of increasing severity seemed to compromise past achievements, as well as to undermine the process towards European Monetary Union (EMU). The crisis and revamping of the ERM between 1992 and 1993 represent the key events in the recent monetary history of Europe. Their origins, consequences, and implications are at the core of the current academic and political debate, both in Europe and elsewhere.

The literature offers different readings of the ERM crisis. A first set of explanations focuses on the behavior of macroeconomic and political fundamentals in Europe. Specifically, a popular interpretation of the 1992–93 events emphasizes the consequences of German internal reunification, and the monetary/fiscal policy mix adopted by that country in the early 1990s, for the stability of the ERM. Other explanations stress the divergent developments of national prices and costs, presumably reflecting divergent national monetary and fiscal

---

1. As the EMS consists of an agreement among the central banks of *all* member States of the European Community to manage exchange rates and finance currency interventions, the ERM represents only one aspect of the EMS and involves only a subset of the EMS countries. In March 1979, the ERM countries did not include the United Kingdom. By the end of November 1996, the ERM countries did not include the United Kingdom, Greece, and Sweden.

policies during the "hard" ERM years; the liberalization of international financial movements under the Single Act; and the perceived weakening in national policy makers' commitment to fixed exchange rates in the aftermath of the Danish referendum in June 1992. These views of the crisis are, to a large extent, complementary to each other.

A second set of explanations downplays the role of fundamentals, pointing out instead the possibility that the ERM was hit by a wave of disruptive, self-fulfilling speculative attacks. According to this view, at the root of the crisis was a sudden and essentially arbitrary shift in market participants' expectations.

The question we address in this book is whether these theories, individually or collectively, offer a reasonable picture of the ERM crisis. We believe that in the present stage of international debate on EMU, when European policy makers are about to give shape to the future by (one hopes) drawing lessons from the experience of the past, an incorrect or even incomplete assessment may have costly repercussions. In addition to the German unification shock, competitiveness problems, a perceived fall in the commitment to exchange rate stability after the first Danish referendum, and disruptive self-fulfilling speculative attacks, which other aspects should be taken into account in a comprehensive interpretation of the 1992–93 episode?

In our view, the literature has paid insufficient attention to a crucial element. The ERM crisis was the crisis of an exchange rate *system*, not the collapse of a collection of unilateral pegs pursued by each country on its own. The literature on the crisis has rightly focused on the policy conflict between Germany and the rest of the ERM in the aftermath of German reunification. It has, however, ignored the role played by structural policy spillovers and strategic interactions in the system as a whole. We believe that the nature and the extent of coordination (or lack thereof) of monetary and exchange rate policies among the countries facing the German reunification shock is a key factor in the analysis of the causes and consequences of the monetary earthquakes that shook the European monetary construction in the recent past.

In this book, we build a model of international cooperation and currency crises that adds the rules of the international monetary game to the conventional list of fundamentals in the economic system. We develop our interpretation of the crisis both in a historical perspective and in the light of the current debate on monetary union and financial integration in Europe. Also, we present a reconstruction of the 1992–93 events that emphasizes important factual evidence corroborating a systemic interpretation of the crisis. Our analytical framework is able to encompass several theories and explanations of the ERM demise. We will therefore revisit the existing literature, showing directions for possible extensions and generalizations.

This introductory chapter presents an overview of both the theoretical and policy-related aspects of our analysis. First, we look back at the root of the

European consensus on limiting exchange rate flexibility. Next, we review the logical and empirical weaknesses of a fixed exchange rate as nominal anchor. After a brief analysis of the current state of the debate on the ERM crisis, we outline the main results of our reconstruction and interpretation of the 1992–93 events.

1.1 The roots of the European consensus on limiting exchange rate flexibility

The evolution of the Exchange Rate Mechanism – from the pre-1987 flexible system of adjustable target zones, through the "hard" regime between 1987 and 1992, and up to the crisis and near collapse of 1992 and 1993 – is but an episode, albeit a crucial one, in what Giavazzi and Giovannini (1989) refer to as the "quest for exchange rate stability in Europe". The term *quest* seems indeed appropriate. The dictionary definition of quest as "a journey in search of adventure, as those undertaken by knights-errant in medieval times" fits well the complex web of events in the European currency markets, from the early fights in defense of the monetary Snake up to the more recent battles against successive waves of speculative attacks in 1992–93.

It seems appropriate to begin our study of the origins and implications of the ERM crisis by focusing briefly on the rationale underlying the widespread agreement regarding currency stabilization in Europe, and by analyzing its evolution over time. Needless to say, opinions diverge radically as regards both the technical validity and the political relevance of the arguments in favor of limiting exchange rate flexibility. Nevertheless, there is a general consensus that, from a historical perspective, the political drive toward exchange rate stability in Europe has been bolstered by two widely shared perceptions about the way the economy functions.

First, European political leaders have traditionally held the view that the completion of an internal market for goods, factors, and assets requires an orderly development of the European Community (EC) monetary system. With the abolition of tariffs, subsidies, and other barriers to trade, commercial policy disappears from the set of policy tools available to individual national authorities. In the presence of nominal rigidities of goods and factors prices, national policy makers may be tempted to use exchange rate policy in order to gain competitive advantage over the other members of the Community.

To the extent that a nominal devaluation can be translated into a devaluation of the real exchange rate (even if only temporarily), this form of competition has long been regarded by Europeans as inconsistent with free and fair trade. Furthermore, if adversely affected countries were to resort to conventional trade-restricting measures in order to retaliate against unfair exchange rate competition, the single market could be permanently impaired.

In addition to this European aversion to "beggar-thy-neighbor" exchange rate policies, there is the belief that uncoordinated national macroeconomic policy is increasingly ineffective (because of large international spillovers) in a steadily more integrated European economy. The inefficiencies stemming from neglecting international spillovers, together with the potential danger of the use of exchange rate policy as a competitive tool, motivate the insistence at Community level on the need for closer policy coordination among member countries within a framework of stable exchange rates.

Second, the traditional resistance to freely floating exchange rates in Europe is a specific manifestation of a general skepticism about the operation of unregulated financial markets. In this view, a regime of flexible exchange rates is subject to two kinds of inefficiencies. The first is severe and persistent misalignments of international relative prices (overlooking the fact that persistent misalignments can occur under a fixed exchange rate regime as well). The second concerns excess volatility of exchange rates – with its possible trade and investment-deterring consequences – and other manifestations of speculative "bubbles" in the foreign exchange markets.

From this standpoint, speculative financial markets not only reflect and process exogenous, "fundamental" noise generated elsewhere in the economic system; they are themselves an independent generator of nonfundamental noise. Financial markets, including the foreign exchange markets, are seen as potential destabilizers of the international trade system and of the "real" economy in general.[2]

In the last thirty years, an additional reason for the unpopularity of price flexibility in the exchange market could be found in the Common Agricultural Policy (CAP).[3] While the share of the Community budget devoted to this policy may contribute to the strength of Brussels' aversion to flexible exchange rates, it is worth stressing that the political consensus that created the CAP in its present form has been eroding over time, and the role of the CAP as an independent motivation for exchange rate stability may diminish further as far-reaching reforms of the system are implemented. Other political-economy considerations, such as the distribution of international seigniorage away from the United States through the institution of a European reserve asset and vehicle currency, may have received some attention in the past,[4] but they do not

2. This mistrust of the allocative efficiency of financial market prices underlies Keynes' position on the reform of the international monetary system. He emphatically rejected the notion that financial asset prices fully reflect fundamentals, and assumed and recommended that the Bretton Woods international financial system should be characterized by extensive capital controls.

3. See Chapter 2. The havoc created in the CAP by significant exchange rate variability is often mentioned as an argument in favor of irrevocably fixed exchange rates or a common currency. On the other hand, it also could be argued that anything that helps undermine the CAP cannot be all bad.

4. See Giscard D'Estaing (1969) and the brief discussion in Chapter 10.

seem to play any significant role in the current debate and decision-making processes.

Technical economic considerations have certainly been relevant in the different attempts to shape the process of European integration. Nonetheless, a full understanding of this process is impossible without paying proper attention to the general political movement for greater unity of Western Europe. Historically, German leaders keen on European economic integration have been concerned with strengthening the ties of Germany to the Western allies. A perception that the world political order was changing (reflecting the secular decline in the relative economic strength of the United States, as well as doubts about the ability and/or willingness of the United States to assume leadership in the post-Vietnam era[5]) motivated the political initiative by Giscard d'Estaing and Schmidt that led to the creation of the European Monetary System and the exchange rate management system at its core, the ERM. Ongoing transformations in Eastern Europe provided the stimulus for advocating an ambitious leap forward in West-European integration in the second half of the 1980s and the early 1990s.

1.2   The ERM and the logic of nominal anchors

In addition to the traditional motivations underlying the "quest for exchange rate stability" in Europe, a relatively novel view gained widespread attention during the 1980s, in parallel with the progressive increase in the degree of asymmetry in the European Monetary System. For several countries, participating in the ERM was increasingly viewed as a politically acceptable, institutionally painless way of "importing" disinflation and "borrowing credibility" (according to the famous characterization by Fischer, 1987) from the Bundesbank through the stability of the exchange rate. The intellectual case for reducing exchange rate flexibility often hinged upon the argument that, for an open economy, a fixed nominal exchange rate was the preferred *nominal anchor*, that is, the most effective way to pin down market expectations and stabilize nominal prices of goods, services, and factors of production.[6]

The logic of using a fixed exchange rate as a nominal anchor is straightforward. With perfect capital mobility, by setting a publicly observable, readily verifiable exchange rate target vis-à-vis a key currency or a basket of currencies,

---

5. The strong personal animosity of Chancellor Schmidt towards President Carter is often mentioned as an additional relevant factor.
6. Bill Branson has pointed out that use of the term *nominal anchor* reveals the economics profession's ignorance of things nautical, as every ship has two anchors. The adoption of two nominal anchors (such as the nominal exchange rate and the money wage) would in fact amount to one real anchor (the real exchange rate in our example) and the absence of any nominal anchor. Anne Sibert has added the further observation that, while every ship has two anchors, a second is used only in special circumstances.

the policy makers in the inflation-prone country give up the ability to conduct independent national monetary policy. Neither nominal interest rates (except for default risk premia) nor monetary aggregates can any longer be influenced by the domestic policy makers in the inflation-prone country, the *Periphery*. To the extent that the peg is reliable, inflation expectations of the public in the Periphery are influenced by the commitment to follow the monetary stance of the (supposedly more conservative) central bank of the *Center* country or countries.

In assessing the performance of the European Monetary System, a crucial question that was frequently overlooked during the ERM years is whether a fixed exchange rate represents the best choice of nominal anchor for a Periphery country, relative to any other nominal anchor, such as a monetary aggregate, the inflation rate (or the price level), or the level or growth rate of nominal GDP.

A first argument in favor of an exchange rate anchor is that it has a direct impact on prices and costs. This is obviously an advantage when we compare the exchange rate with a monetary aggregate. It is clearly not a source of superiority when we compare the exchange rate with a price level nominal anchor. Targeting the price level itself as the nominal anchor, however, would not give any specific guidelines as to how the actual instruments of monetary, financial, and fiscal policy should be used in the pursuit of the objective.

From the standpoint of ranking alternative nominal anchors in terms of their contribution to the ultimate objective of reducing price fluctuations, monetary targetry[7] effectively died during the 1980s as any trace of a stable relationship between every previously used monetary aggregate and any reasonable definition of the general price level vanished. The stability of the relationship between the exchange rate and the general price level (roughly, the stability of the real exchange rate) is, however, not one of the great success stories of empirical open-economy macroeconomics either.

Is an exchange rate commitment more easily established or more credible than a commitment to other nominal anchors? The short answer is that we have no satisfactory theoretical arguments or empirical evidence to argue convincingly on either side of this issue.

An argument in favor of an exchange rate anchor is that it is a natural "focal point" because it is more highly visible in everyday life than the other nominal anchors. The idea that the exchange rate may be a superior commitment device because it is more easily monitored and verified than the other candidate nominal anchors has some prima facie plausibility. When there is a unified exchange rate and financial markets are well developed, the value of the exchange rate can

---

7. Monetary targetry, that is, the use of monetary growth as a nominal anchor, is of course consistent with a wide range of operating procedures for monetary policy and with the use of a variety of actual monetary and financial instruments (including discount rates, reserve requirements, open market operations, and sterilized and unsterilized foreign exchange market intervention).

be continuously and instantaneously monitored 24 hours a day. Observations on monetary aggregates are rarely available more frequently than weekly, and representative price level data are hard to find at smaller than monthly intervals. While all this is true, it is not self-evident that the differences in observation frequencies in question (continuous versus discrete, daily versus weekly or monthly) really make much of a difference from the point of view of establishing and maintaining credibility.[8]

National or personal political prestige costs often are alleged to be associated with the abandonment of a fixed parity, especially if the abandonment takes the form of a devaluation rather than a revaluation. Why the exchange rate should be an index of national prestige is hard to establish from the conventional first principles that are assumed to motivate *homo economicus*. There is no doubt, however, that one reads and hears "macho talk" about the external value of the currency of a kind that one does not encounter about national monetary or price level targets. The perception of devaluation as national humiliation has at times been a real political factor, although, in view of the extensive list of devaluations that occurred nevertheless, its importance should not be exaggerated.

Indeed, while monetary targets have more often been honored in the breach than in the observance, it is clear that exchange rate commitments also have been broken with remarkable regularity in both industrial and developing countries.[9] No exchange rate commitment (with the possible exception of full monetary union) is absolute or unconditional, whatever the language with which it is introduced. Judging from the official public statements before and during the ERM crisis, Pinocchio would not make a good minister of finance.

1.3   Escape clauses and financial stability

From the vantage point of an inflation-prone country, even taking the argument in favor of the exchange rate as nominal anchor at face value, there is still the problem of designing an efficient exchange rate policy targeted at reducing the inflationary bias in domestic policy making. Exchange rate rules, like policy rules in general, are subject to an inherent tension between two desiderata: flexibility (the ability to respond to unexpected shocks) and credibility (the ability to renounce opportunistic violations of prior policy commitments).[10]

At one extreme, the implementation of an irrevocable, unconditional peg – one that locks in the conversion rate between two currencies under all circumstances – would lower expected inflation but also force the government

---

8. After all, the Bundesbank maintains anti-inflationary credibility despite (a) pursuing explicit monetary (M3) targets, (b) frequently violating the monetary targets, and (c) occasionally over-shooting even its (implicit) inflation objectives, as was the case in the aftermath of reunification.
9. See for instance Obstfeld and Rogoff (1995b).
10. See for example Buiter (1981) and Minford (1995).

to a painful defense of the existing parity in the presence of sizable macroeconomic disturbances. Perfect credibility of the nominal anchor would be achieved at the expense of any flexibility of the nominal interest rate and the nominal exchange rate in implementing stabilization policies.

At the other extreme, the adoption of a float would guarantee exchange rate flexibility when needed, but it would not in and of itself provide any monetary (and/or fiscal) discipline. A high degree of flexibility could indeed be argued to aggravate the credibility problem.[11] As an intermediate step between fully discretionary monetary policies (contingent rules without credible precommitment) and fixed exchange rates (rules providing commitment without flexibility), realignment rules in a fixed exchange rate regime have been proposed as a way of retaining some of the advantages of a contingent rule, while reducing "discretion" in policy making and its associated inflationary consequences.

Such an argument provides the logical underpinnings of the ERM as a system of flexible or adjustable pegs, that is, a fixed exchange rate regime with implicit escape clauses allowing for the possibility of realignments in the presence of relatively large, publicly observable, and verifiable shocks. Since the welfare consequences of a realignment depend on both the gains from flexibility and the costs of reduced credibility, escape clauses ideally should allow governments to devalue without also signalling to the private sector that persistently inflationary economic policies have been adopted. To the extent that the market participants have information on the state of the economy, the reliability of the government's commitment to defend the new parity need not be reduced by a devaluation if this is a response to a severe adverse contingency.

Is it possible to design a fixed exchange rate regime with an option to realign that would be exercised only under clearly specified, understood, and verifiable contingencies and that does not impart an inflationary bias to the economy? In practice, it will be very difficult to distinguish between an abandonment of the parity that reflects the legitimate exercise of the escape clause and one that represents a discretionary breach of the contingent rule.[12] But, in addition to

11. There are two reasons for this. First, imperfect and asymmetric information may make it difficult for the private sector to infer from the government's observed behavior whether the government is responding to an unexpected shock in the manner prescribed by the (contingent) policy rule, or whether it is exercising discretion and departing from its pre-announced policy rule for opportunistic reasons. Second, bounded rationality provides strong arguments in favor of simple, unconditional rules (such as a fixed exchange rate) that are intrinsically less complex and easier to monitor than flexible, contingent rules. It should be stressed, however, that in a world with unbounded rationality, fixed, unconditional rules would be subject to the same kind of credibility (or time-consistency) problems as fully flexible, contingent rules. See Chapters 6 and 7.

12. It is worth emphasizing that monetary targets are not immune to the same problem of interpretation. The violation of the monetary target could be the proper exercise of an (implicit) escape clause permitting departure from the norm in the face of unexpected developments in velocity.

these practical considerations, there exists an argument against escape clauses that has acquired increasing importance since the crisis. This argument is based on implications for financial stability.

Consider a world where the policy norm is given by a fixed, unconditional rule such as a fixed exchange rate. Departures from that norm (the exercise of an escape clause) are feasible, but they involve a political "sunk" cost, say a loss of anti-inflationary reputation. The recent literature has frequently pointed out that, in the presence of such an escape clause and in the absence of credible precommitment, the interplay between private sector expectations and optimal public policies may generate "multiple equilibria" that would not exist without the escape clause (or indeed in a world with fully credible commitment). For unchanged fundamentals, there could be either low expectations of devaluation (the good equilibrium) or high expectations of devaluation (the bad equilibrium).[13]

Thus, when measuring the level of social welfare in terms of the objective function of the policy makers, "flexible pegs" such as the ERM will typically generate some equilibria that welfare-dominate the equilibrium under a fixed rule, as well as some equilibria that are welfare-inferior. Exogenous, arbitrary mechanisms will determine whether market participants (including financial intermediaries and currency speculators) coordinate on one equilibrium or another.

These theoretical results have generated considerable skepticism about the efficiency of escape clauses in a fixed exchange rate regime, and even about the effectiveness of any unilateral peg policy. In the academic literature and the popular press, the crisis of the ERM has often been interpreted as the requiem for fixed exchange rate policies among industrial economies. The Mexican peso crisis two years afterwards has, according to this interpretation, sealed the coffin for emerging economies as well.

1.4   The debate on the ERM crisis

In the post-mortem interpretations of the 1992–93 events, unilateral peg models with multiple instantaneous equilibria have provided theoretical foundations for the analysis of self-fulfilling speculative attacks in the foreign exchange markets. According to this approach, an exchange rate crisis due to self-fulfilling speculative behavior consists of a sudden (unexpected) shift from an equilibrium with zero or low expectations of devaluation to another equilibrium with high expectations of devaluation, for unchanged fundamentals. If a crisis is triggered by such a shift in expectations, the familiar macroeconomic indicators would not give any early indication that a period of exchange rate instability is approaching. Right up to the instant the crisis hits, forward-looking asset

13. We survey this literature in Chapter 7.

prices in the financial markets would reflect expectations of a persistence of the good equilibrium.

In the case of the ERM, financial markets indeed did not anticipate the magnitude of the crisis. The interest differentials between ERM countries and Germany fell on average in 1992; in the summer, there was some worsening of credibility, but to a very limited extent.[14] According to this view, the unanticipated (and essentially arbitrary) shift in market participants' expectations appears to have had permanent effects: Since the 1992 crisis, endemic monetary and financial instability is the original sin that marks the ERM after the fall.

In contrast to this "multiple equilibria" interpretation, the literature has provided at least three interpretations of the ERM crisis based on fundamentals. The first one stresses the role of the German reunification shock and of the fiscal-monetary policy mix that accompanied it. The basic elements of this story are well known. The German domestic demand boom, partly fueled by the sustained fiscal transfers from the West to the Eastern regions of the country, put upward pressures on the German real exchange rate. Given the Bundesbank's commitment to containing inflationary pressures, a D-mark real appreciation would have required either a nominal devaluation or a deflation in the rest of the ERM. The employment and fiscal costs of such a deflation undermined the stability of the exchange rates of the Periphery currencies vis-à-vis the Center.

The focus of the second "fundamental" interpretation of the crisis is on the policy makers' commitment to exchange rate stability. At the beginning of the 1990s, the perceived political benefits from participating in the ERM were high. Price stability being a national priority, governments tended to base the credibility of their anti-inflationary policies on their ability to maintain a stable exchange rate vis-à-vis the D-mark. The first Danish referendum revealed that the popular consensus over Maastricht was much weaker than previously believed. The social costs of deflationary policies, exacerbated by the regime of high interest rates following German reunification, suddenly became less bearable. The temptation to correct domestic imbalances through a devaluation grew stronger. This temptation was strengthened by the pronounced fall of the US dollar in the summer of 1992, in line with the (imperfectly understood) empirical regularity that a low dollar weakens some European currencies with respect to the D-mark.

The third "fundamental" explanation points to an inherent weakness of any price stabilization policy based on pegging the exchange rate. If inflation has inertia or if the new exchange rate regime is not perfectly credible, the policy initially results in an appreciation of the real exchange rate. Worsening competitiveness affects the trade balance, production, and employment. In or-

14. See Chapter 4.

der to offset the initial real appreciation, the country must push its domestic rate of inflation below that of the Center country. Since the costs of the required deflation are generally high, the commitment to maintain the exchange rate parity may not be credible.

1.5   Understanding the crisis: The missing elements

1.5.1   Theory...

In the context of the current debate on the recent difficulties of the ERM, the novelty of this book consists in modelling the crisis of a system of exchange rates based on international agreement, rather than the crisis of a collection of unilateral pegs, pursued individually by a number of countries. We cast our interpretation and reconstruction of the 1992–93 events within a theoretical model that allows both for structural spillovers and for policy interactions among the countries in the system.

In specifying our model, we maintain the traditional view of the ERM as a disinflation mechanism based on the exchange rate as nominal anchor. The system consists of a set of Periphery countries that peg their currencies against the currency of the price-stabilizing Center country. The Center has an uncompromising attitude towards its own price stability objective, reflected both in its objective function – which does not exhibit any inflationary bias – and in its unwillingness to compromise by cooperating with the Periphery. This makes it the natural candidate to receive the mandate of guaranteeing price stability in the system. Conversely, the policy makers' commitment to a fixed exchange rate in the Periphery countries is credible only up to a point. There are contingencies under which the escape clause will be exercised, because the costs associated with reneging on announced policies can be swamped by the cost of not responding to a sufficiently large shock.

Periphery countries have, in general, a welfare incentive to coordinate their monetary policies among themselves and to internalize their reciprocal spillovers (that is, the impact of domestic policies on other Periphery countries' inflation and employment). Coordination, however, may not be feasible, for two reasons. First, the cooperative equilibrium requires an effective enforcement mechanism (to prevent unilateral deviations from the agreement) that may not available to the Periphery as a whole. Second, there may be lack of consensus and agreement on how the costs and benefits from Periphery-wide policies should be distributed among the individual Periphery countries.

In addressing this second issue of feasibility, we argue that, based on the EMS experience, special weight should be given to a principle of *national horizontal equity* in cooperation. The principle states that national authorities accept to cooperate only to the extent that their joint actions preserve their relative welfare.

No scheme is acceptable that causes one country to benefit or lose from the common policy more – in relative terms – than the others. As for exchange rate policies, national horizontal equity implies that no country is willing to bear a disproportionate share of the cost of a coordinated realignment, or even to accept an unfair distribution of its benefits, even though such a "sacrifice" might be efficient for the system as a whole.

In principle, national horizontal equity is consistent with a very large set of Community-wide policy decisions (and of realignment schemes) provided that countries can use appropriate side-payments to compensate the losers for such decisions. It is sometimes argued that if a compensation mechanism existed, transfers contingent on asymmetric devaluations should be used to compensate the countries that do not devalue for their declining competitiveness. It is worth stressing that such a view neglects the costs associated with the loss of reputation and anti-inflationary credibility that accompanies a realignment. It may well be that, under a national horizontal equity constraint, transfers would run in the opposite direction, that is, from countries that keep the exchange rate fixed (and thus gain in terms of disinflation) to those that give up the exchange rate parity.[15]

Clearly, either kind of transfer (the latter in particular) is unrealistic, politically questionable, and difficult to implement. It does not come as a surprise that transfers contingent on devaluations never represented an institutional reality in the EMS.[16] Thus, in our model we postulate national horizontal equity but rule out side-payments among countries. These considerations provide the basic building blocks of our analysis.

Consider the impact of a large asymmetric shock in the Center hitting all Periphery economies contemporaneously; the German demand boom associated with internal reunification is the natural example. The Center country is not willing to implement any coordinated action that may jeopardize its price level stability objective. In our analysis, we characterize the policy responses of the Periphery countries by comparing two alternative scenarios. In the first scenario, Periphery countries coordinate their exchange rate policies in order to maximize a common additive social welfare function. As explained above, cooperation is subject to the "constraint" of national horizontal equity. In the alternative scenario, there is no cooperation, and each country unilaterally maximizes its own national objective function.

---

15. This is consistent with "the prediction of Otmar Emminger, who in the early 1980s had foretold the advent of an era of competitive revaluations among currencies seeking to import stability" (Padoa-Schioppa, 1994, p. 17).
16. In the history of the European Community, the only evidence of such transfers consists of the monetary compensatory amounts of the CAP. Considerations related to agricultural taxes and subsidies played no significant role in the process leading to the devaluations of 1992–93.

The model we present in Chapter 8[17] shows that the optimal coordinated response by the Periphery (that is, the one that maximizes Periphery-wide welfare) is a set of small devaluations by a large number of countries (with an important exception to this result, which we will discuss shortly). Conversely, if the Periphery countries do not coordinate their monetary and exchange rate policies against the Center, we will observe large devaluations by a small number of countries. In the aggregate, coordinated exchange rate policy generally is more expansionary than uncoordinated policy actions.

The intuition underlying these results is rooted in the sign of the structural international spillovers. The econometric literature on policy multipliers and international linkages in Europe[18] shows that a devaluation by one country (say the United Kingdom), all other things being equal, affects the rest of the system through two channels. First, a fall in the price of imports from the United Kingdom decreases other countries' CPI inflation and reduces the demand for their output. Second, by devaluing, the United Kingdom contributes to loosening the stance of the ERM-wide monetary policy, lowering real interest rates and increasing aggregate demand in the system. Our analytical model incorporates both these channels. The empirical evidence also supports our key assumption on the relative importance of these two channels, that a devaluation by one Periphery country increases output and employment in the rest of the Periphery, despite the switch in demand from the strong-currency countries to the country that has devalued.

Such policy spillovers imply that the coordinated policy response by the Periphery to a sizable shock in the Center calls for "doing more", by implementing a larger monetary expansion, compared with the uncoordinated response. The large monetary expansion that characterizes coordination translates into a generalized realignment including many currencies. Because of the national horizontal equity constraint (the expression of the requirement of political fairness in the Periphery), to the extent that Periphery countries are "similar", they will jointly devalue at a common rate. Given the strong impact that such a joint action has on system-wide interest rates, the individual countries' devaluation rates do not need to be high to have the desired stabilization effect.

Instead, in the alternative scenario with no cooperation, some countries may avoid a realignment, helped in this by the devaluations of the other currencies in the system. In equilibrium, the average monetary stance is less expansionary than in the cooperative case. Because of the less pronounced fall in the system-wide real interest rate, for each devaluing country the equilibrium depreciation rate will be large.

17. See also Buiter, Corsetti, and Pesenti (1995).
18. See Chapter 8.

It is worth noting that in our setup, a coordinated realignment by the Periphery is also in the interest of the Center. This is because a cooperative devaluation that takes into account international spillovers raises the magnitude of the Periphery's policy interventions towards their optimal level for the system as a whole. In particular, in response to a positive aggregate demand shock in the Center, the cooperative policy action results in a large appreciation of the Center's currency against the Periphery. This permits the Center to be more successful in achieving its price level objective.

1.5.2   ...and policy

What is the contribution of our model of systemic currency crises to an understanding of the 1992–93 events? Consider again the explanation stressing the role of the German reunification shock. According to this view, the ERM currency crisis stems from the conflict between a Center that is willing to bear the inflationary consequences of its unification up to only a (very limited) point, and Periphery countries that dislike the idea of a nominal realignment but are not willing to sustain the cost of a deflation. It is worth pointing out that the protracted conflict among policy makers on this issue was apparent on several occasions; it climaxed at the Bath meeting of EC finance ministers and central bank governors on September 5 and 6, 1992, a few days before the crisis erupted.

By itself, the identification of an important source of tensions calling into question the existing ERM parities does not tell us much about the likely adjustments of these parities. Clearly, the response to the Center shock will depend on the degree of intra-Periphery cooperation. To clarify this point, recall that in our model the same shock could trigger either a set of small devaluations by a large number of countries (under cooperation) or a set of large devaluations by a small number of countries (without cooperation).

In the light of our results, to the extent that market participants expect a coordinated response by the Periphery to the mounting tensions in the system, they will forecast a generalized realignment involving small devaluations. Consistent with this interpretation, although the credibility of the ERM was falling in August 1992, expectations of bilateral devaluations vis-à-vis the D-mark – as measured by interest rate differentials – were not high by historical standards.[19] Indeed, during the weekend preceding the lira devaluation, Germany and Italy formulated a realignment scheme that would have validated market expectations. It included a D-mark nominal revaluation of 3.5%, coupled with a 3.5% devaluation of the lira, so the lira would have been devalued by 7% against the D-mark.[20]

19. See the survey in Chapter 4.
20. See Chapter 3.

In our interpretation, the realignment of the lira on September 14 – or rather the fact that only the lira was realigned – gave the private sector a strong (and largely unexpected) signal about the lack of policy coordination in the ERM, revealing to the markets what kind of strategic game the central banks were playing. As soon as market participants understood the implications of the solitary realignment of the lira, they revised their beliefs according to a new scenario of uncoordinated policy behavior, which pointed to a relatively tight average monetary stance.

Market expectations of devaluation jumped upward. The sudden shift in expectations after the devaluation of the lira need not be interpreted as the manifestation of arbitrary self-fulfilling prophecies. Rather, it is predicted by a "fundamental" theory of currency crises focusing on the role of international cooperation in exchange rate policy. The theoretical predictions of our model imply that, without monetary coordination, restoring equilibrium requires large devaluations by a subset of countries. Consistently, the perception of a regime switch in monetary policy making (from cooperation to noncooperation) was in itself a disruptive fundamental shock in the system leading market participants to revise their beliefs on the persistence of high real interest rates in the system and to anticipate sizable realignments in several ERM countries.

Presumably, in the absence of cooperation, the equilibrium depreciation of the lira should have been higher than the initial 7% implemented on September 14, 1992. Recall that 7% is the same figure that had been proposed in the context of a general realignment two days earlier, which would have had all Periphery countries joining Italy in devaluing their currencies. Also, there was the additional question of whether other countries should have devalued in the new noncooperative environment.

It should be stressed, however, that according to the systemic logic of our model, a "healthy" domestic performance (as measured by the standard set of macroeconomic indicators) is no guarantee against the possibility of a currency crisis. Restoring international equilibrium after a sizable shock to the Center requires a sizable fall in the system-wide real interest rate. This requires a sufficiently large real appreciation of the Center's effective exchange rate against the Periphery. What matters is the average size of the realignment in the Periphery, that is, the average monetary stance in the system. Without cooperation, if too few countries have already devalued by a sufficient amount, both "weak" currencies (such as the pound and the peseta) and "strong" currencies (such as the French franc) are potential candidates for speculative attacks.

Why were the ERM countries unable to act in a coordinated fashion and jointly devalue, implementing some scheme similar to the German-Italian proposal? Our model points to the further possibility that no coordinated realignment might have been politically acceptable under the "national horizontal equity constraint". In other words, it is possible that there existed no common realignment scheme that would compensate for the common loss of anti-inflationary credibility. This is the important exception to the result we have previously stated. Under these circumstances, countries can only coordinate on a painfully deflationary defense of the existing parities. Clearly, insofar as uncoordinated behavior loosens up the average monetary policy in the system (through large, uncoordinated devaluations by a few Periphery countries), it is both individually and collectively rational to switch from (constrained) cooperation to noncooperation.

The model offers an analytical key to interpret the evolution of European exchange rates starting in September 1992, provided we define the Center to include both Germany and other countries, like the Netherlands, that have long delegated their monetary policies to Germany. The exit of the lira and the pound from the ERM, the recurrent speculative attacks against the French franc, and the devaluations of peseta, escudo, and punt were to a large extent the reflection of a low degree of intra-Periphery cooperation, and of each country's subsequent attempt to restore macroeconomic equilibrium in the new international environment.

1.6   Lessons for the future

As a new chapter of European monetary history is being written, the academic debate on the 1992–93 crisis has been increasingly focussed on its lessons for the choice of the appropriate nominal anchor. In the mid 1990s, it appears rather hard to find the same enthusiasm for fixed exchange rate policies that characterized the late 1980s. Svensson (1994) offers a quote that is representative of the new view that virtue begins at home:

> Fixed exchange rates now seem much less effective as means to price stability than many of us thought before. Therefore, monetary stability and credibility has to be built at home with other means. A move to flexible exchange rates makes it no less essential for a price stability policy to build monetary credibility. This should not be interpreted as an argument that flexible exchange rates are always to be preferred to fixed exchange rates. There are other arguments than price stability for fixed exchange rates, for instance, the reduction of relative price variability in order to promote trade, foreign direct investment, and general economic integration. Fixed exchange rates may be a complement to monetary stability and credibility at home, as they appear to be for Austria and the Netherlands, although they are certainly not a substitute. They are simply neither necessary nor sufficient for credible price stability.[21]

Within both the political and intellectual milieu, we have witnessed something of a shift of support from target zones (and other forms of exchange rate management) to inflation or price level targeting, optimal contracts, and central bank independence as stabilization instruments, reputation-building schemes,

---

21. Svensson (1994, p. 467).

and anti-inflationary devices. The crucial turning point for intellectual opinions and policy priorities is the crisis of the ERM in 1992–93.

However, it is a source of some discomfort that, as argued earlier, we have no hard factual or analytical foundations for selecting among competing nominal anchors on the ground of either the relative ease of establishing and maintaining policy credibility or their contribution to price stability. Whether the ERM crisis represents the ultimate proof of the unsustainability (or undesirability) of fixed exchange rates, and whether alternative nominal anchors in Europe would have performed better, are not answerable issues and perhaps not even interesting ones. What the 1992–93 events have painfully revealed is the intrinsic fragility of the European monetary architecture.

What should replace the system that cracked up in 1993? The Center is currently showing an uncompromising attitude towards monetary stability in a monetary union. The traditional debate between the "monetarist" and "economist" approach[22] to European monetary issues has long made us aware of the fact that, for the Center (the home of the economist approach), the "convergence" process is virtually a goal in its own right, rather than a means to the end of monetary union. The transition towards monetary union, rather than monetary union itself, is the crux of the process.

Note that any convergence-centered approach to the transition to EMU reflects a view of monetary union as a coming together of countries that effectively are (or have become) replicas of each other, rather than as a process of integration of heterogeneous economies. There is a further slant given to this approach by the Center that makes the convergence process asymmetric: Monetary union is to be achieved through the addition of homogenized Periphery regions to a preexisting core on the terms of the core. Repeated statements along these lines by German fiscal and monetary authorities in 1995 and 1996 leave no doubt about their stance on these issues.

Is it possible to replace effective and active policy coordination among European countries with the kind of mechanical constraints on national policy autonomy implied by numerical ceilings on public sector debts and deficits and by targets for inflation rates, exchange rates, and interest rates? Despite the well-known objections to the logic and effectiveness of the Maastricht convergence criteria, such tests of prudent macroeconomic behavior may be useful in fostering good policy management, provided that they are applied sensibly and flexibly. After all, public sector solvency, low inflation, and financial stability are reasonable prerequisites for a country that wants to join a monetary union (and indeed for a country that does not).

An obsessively mechanical reading of the Maastricht criteria, however, is harmful. It glosses over the key issue of the appropriate Europe-wide monetary-fiscal policy mix and thus creates the risk of a deflationary bias in the run-up to

---

22. See Chapter 2.

the EMU deadline. It focuses the attention exclusively on domestic problems and thus denies the relevance of reconstructing a system of European monetary cooperation. One key lesson from the 1992–93 crisis is that in the absence of effective internalization of the policy spillovers, nominal or real macroeconomic convergence between Center and Periphery do not insulate the system from currency crises. Even if a country were able to satisfy the Maastricht criteria exactly, it could still be vulnerable to speculative attacks.

In conclusion, this book develops the view that the key event that triggered the collapse of the ERM was (a shift in) the attitude toward exchange rate and monetary policy coordination among European policy makers, and the perception of this shift by market participants. With most of the existing literature, we share the view that the oxymoron-like nature of a "flexible peg" is in itself destabilizing and that it contains the seeds of its own destruction. We do not believe, however, that asymmetric disturbances per se are necessarily disruptive of international monetary arrangements. Almost by definition, a crisis of an exchange rate system is a symptom of insufficient or ineffective policy coordination.

In historical perspective, political cohesion has been the engine of progress in European economic and monetary integration. Political cohesion is what has traditionally overcome the skepticism of markets as well as the objections of the "experts". The insufficient and solitary realignment of the lira in 1992 revealed to both the markets and the experts that European policy makers were no longer able or willing to give a coherent, coordinated response to monetary tensions. A renewed ability to do so will be the first important indicator that the Maastricht design has not been swept away on waves of speculative frenzy.

CHAPTER 2

Exchange rate stability in Europe:
A historical perspective

2.1   From Bretton Woods to the Treaty of Maastricht

2.1.1   The Bretton Woods days

Throughout the history of the European Community, both the political and the intellectual leaders of the movement towards European integration have shared a pronounced aversion to exchange rate fluctuations. One after the other, the political initiatives undertaken to strengthen the process of European integration have led to attempts to lock European currencies into systems and mechanisms that limit the flexibility of their conversion rates. Even during periods when the tide of European integration was at a low ebb, the idea and ideal of exchange rate stability never completely disappeared from the institutional architecture of the Community.

In the first fifteen years after the Treaty of Rome created the European Economic Community (EEC) in 1958 (with the aim of developing a common market for goods, services, labor, and capital), it was the Bretton Woods system that provided the institutional framework for exchange rate stability. The Treaty of Rome did not go beyond characterizing exchange rates as a matter of common concern (Art. 107 of the Treaty). In pursuit of the common goals of external equilibrium, full employment, price stability, and confidence in members' currencies (Art. 104), individual countries were authorized to take appropriate actions whenever exchange rates appeared to be inconsistent with these overarching objectives (Art. 107).

No mention was made of the desirability, let alone the possibility, of a European monetary union, since within the framework of an Atlantic strategic alliance, no form of monetary cooperation independent of the United States dollar was considered feasible at the time. Yet, as soon as most European currencies became fully convertible for current account transactions, member countries felt compelled to strengthen the provisions of the Bretton Wood system by reducing the margins of fluctuation of each EEC currency around its dollar parity, from 1.00 to 0.75 percent. As a consequence of the European Monetary Agreement of 1958, European currencies could deviate from each bilateral parity only within a 3 percent band.

In the mid 1960s, the EEC initiated the Common Agricultural Policy. Its purpose was the Community-wide stabilization of food prices and the support of agricultural producer prices at levels generally above their world market values. In addition to providing protection to the agricultural sector of the Community as a whole, the program was intended to enhance free trade in agricultural commodities within the EEC, while freezing the historical competitive conditions of the agricultural sectors of the individual member states, if necessary through variables levies and subsidies.[1]

Agricultural prices were set in terms of "Green currencies". Changes in the nominal exchange rates not matched by equal proportional changes in the Green rates would give the farmers of a devaluing country a strong incentive to export their output to other EEC members rather than sell it domestically. This is what happened for the first time in 1969, when the French franc was devalued and the French government, fearful of the inflationary effects of an increase in the prices of agricultural commodities, arranged to postpone the devaluation of the Green franc. In order to prevent cheap French exports from swamping its EEC partners' markets, the EEC placed a tax on French exports to the rest of the EEC and a subsidy on French imports from the EEC. These taxes and subsidies were referred to as *monetary compensatory amounts*, or MCAs.

Over time, therefore, the CAP may have provided an independent reason for aversion against intra-European exchange rate flexibility, as the requirement that the effects of exchange rate fluctuations on domestic agricultural prices be neutralized through a complicated system of subsidies and import levies, embodied in the MCAs became generalized.[2] Regardless of the overall historical role of the CAP, the introduction of the MCAs emphasized the European aversion to the disruptive consequences of exchange rate instability for intra-EEC trade.

Within the Bretton Woods system, intra-EEC exchange rates were indeed stable throughout the 1960s. The only deviations from a system of fixed parities were the revaluation of the D-mark and Dutch guilder by 5% in 1961, the French franc devaluation by 12.5% in 1969, and the D-mark revaluation by 9.3% in the same year. Although the United Kingdom did not become a member of the EEC until 1972, the devaluation of sterling by 14.3% in 1967 should also be mentioned. The history of the Bretton Wood system also shows examples of successful management of balance of payments crises, such as the Italian one in 1963–64.

Nonetheless, by the end of the decade it was clear that the system was under unsustainable strain, threatening to jeopardize the stability of the intra-European conversion rates. One of the intrinsic weaknesses of the gold-exchange standard had already been pointed out by Triffin in 1960. The increase in US government

1. The technical features of the CAP can only be understood in the light of the belief, apparently common in those days, that intra-European exchange rate stability was no longer in question (Tsoulakis, 1977).
2. Regarding this argument, see Van Ypersele and Koeune (1985) and Giavazzi and Giovannini (1989).

dollar liabilities – held abroad by official and private agents – relative to US gold, which accompanied the rapid growth of international trade in goods and assets, was bound to generate, sooner or later, a confidence crisis concerning the ability of the United States to convert dollars into gold (Triffin, 1960).

A run on the gold pool early in 1968 ended full convertibility of the dollar into gold. A two-tier gold market was created, with the gold price on the private market left free and the official gold price for transactions between the central banks remaining fixed at $35 per fine ounce. On August 15, 1971, President Richard Nixon closed the official gold window, marking de facto the death of the exchange rate arrangements of the Bretton Woods regime. (De jure the end of Bretton Woods occurred two years later, after the generalized realignment of the central parities against the dollar agreed in the Smithsonian meeting of December 1971, and a further devaluation of the dollar in February 1973.)

There are reasons to believe that the Bretton Woods system could have survived as a gold-exchange standard, had the United States targeted domestic price stability. The golden days of the Bretton Woods system had seen the United States providing both international liquidity and, as the key country in the system, the appropriate framework for monetary stability. With the United States fixing the dollar price of gold, any country could import the US rate of inflation (which was low until the second half of the Sixties) by maintaining a peg against the dollar.

However, the deficit financing of the Vietnam war and the Great Society programs by President Johnson (as reflected in the 2.7 percent of GDP reduction in the full-employment budget surplus between 1964 and 1968[3]) put the United States on a path of increasing inflation. Although the inflation rate in 1968 was only 4.2 percent, this was a relatively high rate by the standards of the preceding fifteen years. In a system of fixed exchange rates centered on the US dollar, this rising US inflation rate soon threatened to turn into a source of world inflation (Commission on the Role of Gold, 1982).

Low-inflation European countries such as Germany became increasingly aware that the objective of domestic price stability, for a European country, was inconsistent with the maintenance of a fixed exchange rate against the dollar. Technically, a revaluation of the D-mark could have resolved the German dilemma, at least for a while,[4] without destroying the exchange rate regime. The inflation-prone European nations had used discrete devaluations of their currencies to correct balance of payments disequilibria without leaving the Bretton Woods system; the 14% devaluation of the pound sterling in 1967 is the most striking example.

3. Economic Report of the President (1971, p. 73).
4. A US inflation rate persistently in excess of the domestic inflation rate desired by the German authorities would have required repeated D-mark revaluations or a crawling peg.

However, it was not clear what the benefits of remaining on the dollar standard were to most European countries, when price stability was no longer obtainable at a fixed dollar exchange rate. A pattern of large, partly sterilized inflows of international reserves and competitiveness cycles, possibly associated with periodic revaluations, did not read like a recipe for economic success.

2.1.2   Monetary union as European long-term goal

In response to the threatening disruption of the international monetary system, the Summit of EEC Heads of State, held in The Hague in December 1969, solemnly declared that a Monetary Union did belong among the long-term goals of the Community. Following a procedure which would again be adopted twenty years later, the 1969 Summit resolved to appoint a special committee with the task of designing a blueprint for the transition to such a Union. This blueprint, the so-called Werner Report, proposed a three-stage approach to monetary unification. The first stage would foster policy coordination; in the second stage, realignments of exchange rates would require agreement among the countries participating in the plan; in the third stage, a unique central bank, similar to the Federal Reserve System in the United States, would take control over European monetary policy.

At the summit in The Hague, the program to speed up European integration was actively sponsored by the German Chancellor Willy Brandt, whose proposals were strongly endorsed by the French government.[5] The initiative by the leader of the new social democrat-liberal coalition in Bonn thus ended a long-standing EEC political crisis, which dated back to De Gaulle's unilateral veto of UK entry into the Community six years before. In the field of monetary cooperation, it is clear that Brandt's initiative to coordinate the European response to the weakening of the dollar was in harmony with German national economic policy goals.

Notwithstanding this strong political support, the process toward monetary unification was brought to a swift halt by the international economic turmoil of the early 1970s. As the world monetary order was disrupted by heavy speculative attacks, Germany and the Netherlands let their currencies float against the dollar in May 1971, while the other European countries introduced severe capital controls in an attempt to fight speculation. After President Nixon officially suspended the gold convertibility of the US dollar in August, few

5. The American response tended to be less favorable. As Robert Solomon (1977, p. 174) put it:

> From a global perspective this effort of the EEC seemed to many of us to be ill-timed. When the world needed greater exchange rate flexibility, the EEC countries were talking about moving in the opposite direction in their relations with each other. But the impulse to narrow EEC margins was basically a political one. When it was implemented in April 1972, the decision was made by prime ministers while many EEC technical experts shook their heads in doubt.

doubted that some specifically European contribution was required to maintain currency and financial stability in the EC.

2.1.3 The Snake

The Smithsonian Agreements in 1971 enlarged the Bretton Woods bands of fluctuation vis-à-vis the dollar from 2.0% to 4.5%. Right away, the width of the implied band for non-dollar currencies – which was as high as 9.00% under the new regime – was deemed unacceptable by European standards. The creation of the "Snake" was the first Community-wide response to the difficulties encountered in setting up a new stable and sustainable global system of fixed exchange rates.

With the resolution of the European Communities on March 21, 1972, and the Basle Agreement among EEC central banks on April 10, 1972, each EEC member country committed itself to limit to 2.25% the fluctuation of its own currency around the dollar parity (implicitly defining a system of 4.5% intra-EEC currency bands). This European currency Snake was thus placed well inside the tunnel represented by the floor and ceiling rates vis-à-vis the US currency, as established in Washington. A notable feature of the agreement was that central banks should employ European currencies when intervening to support bilateral parities involving two Snake members, limiting the use of the dollar to intervention in defence of the external value of the Snake vis-à-vis the US currency.

In addition to the Short Term Monetary Support, which was created in 1970 to meet temporary difficulties in financing balance of payments deficits, member countries could resort to a newly created Very Short Term Financing (VSTF) facility, administered by the European Monetary Cooperation Fund (EMCF, or FECOM) starting in April 1973. In principle, the amount of credit that a central bank could obtain through the VSTF was unlimited, but VSTF liabilities were to be settled within the rather short period of 30 days.

An asymmetry in the operating characteristics of the facility, the same one that had also plagued the Bretton Woods system, was a key feature in the system. In practice, once a weak currency was at the bottom of the bilateral band vis-à-vis some other currency, it was the central bank that issued the weak currency that was held responsible for the defense of the band. Thus when a currency was under pressure, rather than the strong-currency central bank engaging in international reserve accumulation, the central bank issuing the weak currency incurred international reserve losses. Since the amount of credit that could be obtained to bolster international reserves was – de facto, if not de jure – strictly limited, the credibility of the Snake suffered from the limitations of the financing mechanism among central banks.[6]

6. See Thygesen (1979).

Soon after the implementation of the Snake by the six EEC countries in April 1972, the system was joined by the United Kingdom, Ireland, Denmark, and Norway. However, the fragility of the Snake was apparent: UK membership in the system lasted only eight weeks, during which the pound was hit by heavy speculative attacks and a large capital outflow forced the Italian lira out in February 1973. Moreover, as the US authorities had made clear that they would no longer intervene in the foreign exchange markets to support their currency, unilaterally pegging to the dollar appeared neither viable nor desirable.

On March 11, 1973, European central banks stopped defending the dollar parities of their currencies. Freed from the "tunnel", a trimmed "floating Snake" acquired Sweden but soon lost France, which then unsuccessfully tried to re-join. Reduced to a D-mark zone of monetary stability, the "floating Snake" represented an element of continuity between the European monetary agreement of the 1960s and the birth of the EMS in 1979, even if only in a formal sense.

The longevity of the Snake was due to a persistent policy of unilateral pegging vis-à-vis the D-mark by the Benelux countries, Denmark, and two non-EEC countries, Norway and Sweden. The other major EEC countries, France, Italy, and the United Kingdom, tried to join, sometimes more than once, without lasting success. Although formally alive, the Snake could not be considered a European-wide system. "The experts", according to the German Chancellor Schmidt, "had created a climate of resignation in the field of monetary policy."[7] Again, the political arena was where the next thrust toward monetary union originated.

2.1.4   The EMS

On April 7, 1978, at the European Council of Copenhagen, the German Chancellor Helmut Schmidt and the French President Valery Giscard d'Estaing engineered a vigorous revival of the European project by launching the idea of a European Monetary System for all members of the EEC. It took three months to reach a Community-wide consensus on the project (with a resolution by the European Council in Bremen) and six months to elaborate the system in detail. Since the EMS was designed not to require any amendment to the Treaty of Rome, the European Council adopted the conditions of operation of the new system on December 5 and 6, 1978, in Brussels.

Although superficially similar to the Snake – the width of the bilateral bands was maintained at 4.5% (with the exception of a 12% target zone for the lira) – the exchange rate mechanism of the EMS could count on stronger political support as well as more ample financial means. The maturity of the credit obtained through the VSTF facility of the European Monetary Cooperation

7. Quoted in Nölling (1993, p. 49).

Fund, for example, was extended from 30 to 45 days, with an option for a three-month renewal within the limits of the debtor central bank's quota under the short-term monetary support arrangement. Subject to the authorization of the central bank issuing the intervention currency, the VSTF facility could also be resorted to for a source of finance for intramarginal interventions (i.e., discretionary intervention occurring when the exchange rates were well inside the bands, as opposed to the mandatory marginal intervention at the edges of the band).

Moreover, the newly created European Currency Unit (ECU) was intended not just as a unit of account, but also as a means of settlement among EC central banks. The institution of the ECU was coupled with a "commitment" to establish a European Monetary Fund (EMF) no later than two years from the start of the EMS. Such commitment turned out to be ephemeral. Without ever being formally disowned, the EMF project was allowed to die a quiet death of oblivion.

Stripped of the European Monetary Fund, the EMS labored on in an atmosphere of widespread pessimism about its chances of success. Skepticism prevailed as to the feasibility of a system of fixed exchange rates when a low-inflation country such as Germany coexisted with Italy and France, which at the end of the 1970s showed few signs of inflationary rectitude. Indeed, between 1979 and 1985, the cumulative devaluation of the Lira and the French Franc against the ECU turned out to be 20.25% and 9.25%, respectively. Over the same time interval, the cumulative revaluation of the D-mark in terms of the ECU reached 22.25%. In these years, the GDP deflator increased by 85% in Italy, 55% in France, and 21% in Germany.

Between 1979 and 1983, the ERM had little influence on domestic policies. Periodic realignments largely accommodated inflation differentials, with the aim of keeping domestic competitiveness approximately constant. With this strategy understood by the private sector, financial markets could anticipate the timing and size of such realignments, making room for potentially destabilizing speculative behavior. This is the main reason why high-inflation countries kept severe capital controls in place during the first few years of the EMS.[8]

A major change occurred in 1983, when the French socialist government signalled the abandonment of its former policy strategies (aimed at pursuing growth through the expansion of domestic demand) by giving high priority to disinflation within the framework of further European integration. Italy soon followed the French lead. The British government under Mrs. Thatcher, however, reinforced the anti-European stand of the United Kingdom, which did not join the ERM until 1990. Confronted with mixed signals, it took the markets a few years (as well as a few frustrated speculative attacks) to accept

8. See Chapter 4.

the durability of the new monetary course of continental Europe. Inflation differentials narrowed but persisted, despite the increasing stability of the exchange rate system.

2.1.5   Asymmetry in the system

If the intervention obligations of member countries under the EMS had been symmetric regarding deficit (weak-currency) and surplus (strong-currency) countries, the inflation rate in the European Community might have been expected to converge to something like the average of the national inflation rates that would have been achieved under a floating rate regime. Symmetry would have required countries with low inflation and strong currencies to intervene in defense of weak currencies associated with countries with a high rate of inflation. If such interventions had to be nonsterilized to be effective, domestic monetary growth would have been raised in the low-inflation countries, and their low inflation rates would not have been sustainable.

The core of the debate about symmetry in the EMS referred to the intervention rules. Besides an obligation to intervene at the upper and the lower margins of bilateral fluctuations, the EMS also adopted a divergence indicator for each currency with respect to the ECU central rate: 75 percent of the maximum divergence with respect to the ECU central rate in either direction was proposed as the trigger point for intervention. The question was whether intervention should be regarded as obligatory. As pointed out already, an obligation to intervene would impair the ability of a low-inflation country with a strong currency to maintain its low inflation rate, if its currency repeatedly reached the upper limit of its divergence indicator because of the combined weakness (reflecting high inflation) of all other currencies.

It was soon clear that the proposed indicator had the arithmetic property of allowing countries with larger ECU weights to deviate by larger amounts from the bilateral parities before crossing the intervention thresholds defined by their divergence indicators.[9] The arithmetical properties of the indicator thus seemed to guarantee some additional degrees of monetary independence to the low-inflation D-mark and Dutch guilder area, characterized by a combined ECU share of more than 40%. Nonetheless, because of the strong opposition of these countries, the designers of the EMS could not settle on the strong formula of symmetric, "required" intervention at both thresholds. The so-called Belgian compromise consisted in a formulation that included not an obligation to intervene but rather only a "presumption to take action" (Van Ypersele and Koeune, 1985).

9. A given percentage deviation of a currency from a parity defined in terms of a basket containing that currency permits a larger absolute movement of the currency, the larger the weight of the currency in the basket. See Salop (1981) and Spaventa (1982).

While the birth of the EMS was marked by a strong conflict between Germany, which was determined to maintain full control over its domestic price level in the European system,[10] and France, which was concerned with the deflationary bias implied by a Germany-dominated EMS, the early years of the system witnessed the progressive emergence of German monetary leadership. According to the intentions of the architects of the EMS, symmetry should have been achieved by empowering the ECU with the role of Nth currency in the system, against which all other currencies would have been pegged.[11] The compromise on the divergence indicator radically reduced the chances of success of the symmetric view, which then kept losing importance over time, as exemplified by the collective institutional amnesia regarding the European Monetary Fund. The ECU was to be no more than a *numéraire*, instead of becoming the monetary liability of an independent EMF.

In the early 1980s, the D-mark was increasingly perceived as the key currency in the EMS. The strength of the German currency could perhaps have been disruptive of the system, had the dollar kept depreciating at the same pace as during the 1970s. The well-known change in US monetary policy under Paul Volcker, with the ensuing appreciation of the dollar between 1981 and 1985, modified the international environment to such an extent that it is difficult to assess the probability of survival of the EMS in the counterfactual scenario of continued dollar weakness.

In the second half of the decade – in parallel with the new ambitious phase of European integration signaled by the Single European Act (SEA) of 1986[12] – not only was the reality of German monetary leadership universally recognized, but a new vision of the European process was changing both the political and the intellectual evaluation of the desirability of this leadership. An asymmetric system where the low-inflation country sets the pace of system-wide monetary policy was suddenly seen as an opportunity for monetary and fiscal authorities in inflation-prone countries to make an explicit and publicly verifiable commitment to contain and overcome the forces making for domestic inflation (high monetary growth fed ultimately by excessive fiscal deficits) and loss of international competitiveness.

---

10. The strong views of Bundesbank regarding the priority of the defense of the value of the D-mark, relative to *any* form of obligations implied by the EMS, is summarized by the content of the by-now-famous Emminger's letter to the Federal Government in November 1978 (see Chapter 3).

11. The first Chancellor to participate in a meeting of the Bundesbank, "Schmidt claimed that Germany would have a strong position in the new EMS. For precisely this reason the D-mark had to be prevented from becoming the second international reserve currency (alongside the dollar) and the key currency in the EMS. This would pose threats to which Germany should not be exposed." (Nölling, 1993, p. 50).

12. The SEA was the first revision of the Community's founding Treaty of Rome.

Participating in the ERM of the EMS was a way of "borrowing credibility from the Bundesbank" when undertaking a change in the domestic policy regime.[13] The popularity of this thesis, that joining the ERM was an effective means of borrowing anti-inflationary credibility from the Bundesbank, is rather surprising given the paucity of empirical support for its validity as well as the number of logical questions that it leaves unanswered.[14] Notwithstanding these considerations, the proposition undoubtedly dominated the European political and economic debate in the second half of the 1980s and in the early '90s, right up to the collapse of the ERM that started in the second half of 1992.[15]

2.1.6   The "New" EMS

It is customary to draw a demarcation line between the "old" EMS and a "new" (or "hard") EMS starting with the SEA in 1986.[16] For most countries, the SEA mandated the complete removal of all capital controls and exchange controls as early as July 1990. In addition to creating a single market for financial claims, the legislation also aimed to create a single market for financial services.

In the first half of the 1980s, the EMS was a system of de facto adjustable pegs stabilized by the existence of extensive restrictions on financial capital mobility in Europe. After the SEA in 1986, the push towards liberalizing financial markets by 1990 ran into and threatened to expose as inadequate the existing institutional arrangements for surviving large-scale speculative attacks.

13. "Borrowing credibility from the Bundesbank" was obviously not the exclusive prerogative of the EC countries. Although outside the ERM, a few Scandinavian and Eastern European countries started a policy of unilaterally pegging their currencies against the ECU.

14. Besides the issues discussed in Chapter 1, it is worth emphasizing here that, for the dominant ERM country Germany, "lending" credibility could involve some compromising of its domestic inflation objectives. As the Phillips curve of the Center country becomes flatter in a system of fixed exchange rates, the German inflationary bias, if any, is exacerbated by the constitution of the EMS (see the discussion in Fratianni and Von Hagen, 1992, p. 66). However, it could also bring the bonus of a (temporary) improvement in German competitiveness during the transition of the high-inflation countries to German-level inflation rates. The counterpart of any improvement in competitiveness by Germany is, of course, the appreciation of the real exchange rates of the high-inflation countries. One solution to this problem, a period of negative inflation differentials at a fixed nominal exchange rate, is likely to require painful deflationary policies. Only if the borrowing of German credibility changes the nature of the inflation mechanism and reduces the "sacrifice ratio" are the unemployment costs of sustained disinflation likely to be minor. However, the evidence for the presence of important credibility effects on the inflation mechanism is not encouraging (e.g., Blanchard and Muet (1993) have been less than supportive). The other solution to the competitiveness problem, an exchange rate realignment, cannot be anticipated by the private sector without destroying the essence of the policy of borrowed credibility.

15. See Begg and Wyplosz (1993) for a discussion of the intellectual history in the EMS.

16. See Giavazzi and Spaventa (1990).

The encouraging convergence of inflation rates in the 1983–86 period undoubtedly boosted the confidence of European decision makers in the ability of the EMS members to achieve complete convergence by the end of the decade. By 1986, compared to the German zero rate of CPI inflation, the annual inflation differential was not larger than 3% for most European countries; in fact, even for Italy it was down to 5%. A political commitment to disinflation was widely viewed as synonymous with the acceptance of the D-mark as nominal anchor.

Soon after, the emergence of German leadership was to be questioned at an institutional level. When the financing facilities of the European central banks were augmented substantially with the Basle-Nyborg Agreement in 1987, the degree of (formal) symmetry in the EMS suddenly increased.[17] The maturity of debt incurred by resorting to the VSFT facility was further extended from 45 to 75 days, while the limits on automatic renewal were doubled. According to the interpretation of the Agreement favored by the French government but contested by the Bundesbank, the access to VSTF credit for intramarginal interventions was to be considered no longer subject to authorization by the central bank issuing the intervention currency.

This so-called New EMS was set for a relatively long period of European exchange rate stability. No realignment took place between January 1987 and September 1992 (with the exception of a technical realignment of the lira when it joined the narrow band of the ERM in January 1990). Meanwhile, as the idea of complementarity between a single market and a single money received widespread political (but little analytical) support, proposals for a European Monetary Union were back on the European agenda.

At the Madrid Summit in June 1989, the Council endorsed the Delors Report as the official blueprint for monetary unification in Europe. Echoing the Werner Report, the Committee of representatives from EC central banks chaired by Jacques Delors again proposed a three-stage approach to monetary union. Drawing on almost two decades of intellectual and political debate on the issue, the document looked at economic and monetary integration as parallel developments of a unitary process, made precise recommendations regarding the need for policy coordination, and advocated binding rules limiting national government deficits.

While it did not provide a timetable for the three stages, the Delors Report suggested that the decision to enter the process be regarded as a commitment to pursue the goal of monetary unification to the end. At the Madrid Summit, however, the European countries could only agree on starting Stage I of the process in July 1990. Further progress on the road to monetary union required a

---

17. As Kenen (1993) points out, a commitment to rely less heavily on intramarginal intervention when defending the ERM currency bands was part of the agreement. To the extent that this means a heavier use of interest rate policy, the 1987 agreement does not reduce the degree of asymmetry in the EMS.

modification of the Treaty of Rome. Beyond the technical grounds given for this in the Delors Report,[18] it can be argued that revision of the Treaty of Rome was required because of the insistence of some member states (prominently among them Germany) that monetary and economic unification be accompanied by further movements towards political unification and towards greater democratic (i.e., parliamentary) accountability of the EC executive.[19]

2.1.7   Cassandra or Candide: What role for economic analysis?

On the basis of the previous reconstruction, one is tempted to conclude that there is a tendency for political considerations to dominate the timing and the structure of European integration. After all, before launching the EMS, Chancellor Schmidt and President d'Estaing did not bother to notify the EC bureaucrats in Brussels and deliberately left the Bundesbank "out of the loop" in the decision-making process because of that institution's well-known opposition to any European scheme for monetary policy coordination.[20]

The Bundesbank's "D-mark-focused missionary zeal for price stability"[21] explains its distaste for European monetary coordination, as well as its ambiguous attitude toward the German leadership in the process. This dissenting opinion of the Bundesbank was to leave a lasting mark on the concrete development of the initiative. Fratianni and Von Hagen (1992) offer the following instructive quote from Schmidt's memoirs:

> France under Giscard was prepared for the loss of sovereignty which would come at the end of this road; the Bundesbank and many of the German professors of economics, who think of themselves as experts, were not prepared for it (and still are not today).

Of course, a dominant role for political considerations does not need to be a bad thing for keeping the process of European integration moving along. As long as there is a widespread consensus in favor of keeping the process alive, a strong political drive is a powerful force in facilitating the required institutional reforms. It is nonetheless possible that the decision-making process, in responding to political needs, leads to plans that are technically ill-defined or unworkable, or that require substantial amendment before implementation.

The history of European integration provides several examples of political desiderata getting ahead of technical and administrative feasibility. The SEA defines identical rules for all member countries paying no attention to the degree

18. See Committee for the Study of Economic and Monetary Union (1989).
19. The German desire to fill the "democratic vacuum" at the heart of the EC by strengthening the European Parliament did not extend to the European central bank, which was to be independent of all political pressure and oversight, including parliamentary.
20. See, for example, Ludlow (1982) and Fratianni and Von Hagen (1992).
21. Quoted from Chancellor Schmidt memoirs by Fratianni and Von Hagen (1992, p. 19).

of enforcement they can guarantee. Not surprisingly, enforcement-related issues have become a major source of disagreement and conflict in the design and implementation of a common immigration policy. Second, the mandatory removal of capital controls by 1990 immediately raised doubts concerning the compatibility of this aspect of the completion of the internal market with the European monetary and exchange rate arrangements. Third, the fiscal rules advocated by the Delors Report, and subsequently embodied in the Treaty of Maastricht, have little or no economic rationale and can only be explained as the unhappy outcome of a long process of political compromising.

Perhaps bad policy design and bad institutional reforms at times are the reflection of an unspoken desire to not pursue the official, publicly stated goals in earnest. Given the ill-concealed opposition of many of the main players in the game to the mode of European integration opted for in the 1980s, this possibility cannot be ruled out a priori. One is left to wonder about the proper role of economic analysis in European matters, caught as it appears to be between the pessimistic vision of a Cassandra, always warning against the dangers of the built-in inconsistencies in already agreed-upon decisions, and the rosy scenario attitude of a Candide, always ready to demonstrate that any sequence of errors and disasters is nevertheless for the best.

2.2   The Treaty of Maastricht

2.2.1   *Economist and monetarist views of the transition to a monetary union*

The political process that led to the Maastricht Treaty, signed in December 1991,[22] started two years earlier in Madrid. The Strasbourg European Council in December 1989 called for two intergovernmental conferences by the end of 1990, one about monetary union, the other on political union. Both conferences began in Rome in December 1990.[23] In order to understand fully the task faced by the Intergovernmental Conference on Monetary Union, it should be kept in mind that the Delors Report, while dealing at length with the third phase of the unification process, was much less structured regarding the design of the transition, that is, the first two phases.

The three main principles of the Report – irreversibility of the process of monetary integration, flexibility in participation, and economic convergence – needed to be further developed and translated into an appropriate practical

---

22. The ratification of the treaty by the single member states in the following months took different institutional routes, from parlamentary votes to national referendums. The negative outcome of the Danish referendum in June 1992, and its implications for the ERM crisis, are discussed in Chapter 3.

23. The political process leading up to the final draft of the Treaty has been well documented by Bini-Smaghi, Padoa-Schioppa, and Papadia (1994).

normative framework. In addition, the Report intentionally made no reference to the timing of the three stages, with the exception of the starting date, July 1990. The following issues remained for agreement: (1) the nature, design, and functions of the monetary institution (the proto-European central bank) in the second phase; (2) the procedures regulating the passage from the second to the third phase; and (3) the definition of the degree of economic convergence necessary to enter the third phase, as well as the choice of criteria for its assessment.

In the intellectual history of European monetary integration, two schools of thought have been contrasted with each other, at least since the time of the Werner Report. The first school advocates gradualism in the implementation of the institutional reforms and in the change of policy regimes. Gradualism here means that the process of integration is primarily a process of convergence of economic structure and performance in different countries, to be matched by appropriate institutional developments. The second school instead stresses the role of institutional innovations in promoting economic integration, by fostering economic convergence in terms of policy and of economic behavior of the private sector. Perhaps with little semantic justification, supporters of the first school are traditionally labelled "economists", as opposed to the "monetarists" populating the rival intellectual habitat.

According to the economists' view, the Treaty should condition any progress along the road toward monetary union on the existence of appropriate economic conditions. In other words, the Treaty should stress the need for prior convergence among EC countries, before passage from one stage to the next can be contemplated, without specifying a timetable for these events. Progress from one stage to the next should be state-contingent rather than time-contingent. The recipe of the alternative, monetarist school would instead be fixed deadlines and unconditional institutional reforms to lead the behavioral changes required for convergence (that is, a time-contingent rather than state-contingent rule for transition to the next stage).

One of the key points of disagreement in the debate regarded the conduct of European monetary policy during the transition, that is, the transfer of power and responsibility from national authorities to a Community authority. The Delors Report accepted both the principle of independence of national monetary policy and the principle of indivisibility of European monetary policy, calling for close coordination of central bank behavior.

Note that what was at stake was more than the technical issue of monetary policy coordination under fixed exchange rates and free international mobility of capital. The real issue concerned the location of European monetary leadership, and the power to determine the Community-wide level of interest rates and the common external exchange rates. Clearly, the economists' school placed the creation of a European central bank in the third stage, as any attempt to implement early transfers of power and functions would result in the creation of an "empty shell". The opposite view stressed the need to establish a European monetary institution in the second stage of the transition.

Like many other institutional developments in the EC, the Treaty of Maastricht can be read as a set of compromises between the two schools.[24] On the one hand, there are agreed-upon deadlines for the passage from one stage to the other. However, while Stage II began in January 1994, the determination of the starting date of Stage III was left to an EC Council decision – by qualified majority voting – before the end of 1996. In the absence of a decision by the end of 1997 on the date for the beginning of Stage III, Stage III would start automatically after January 1, 1999. The last-minute (after November 1991) inclusion of this "automatism" in Art. 109j of the Treaty was an attempt to reconcile conditionality in the process with the principle of "irreversibility of the Community's movement to the third stage of economic and monetary union", spelled out in the Protocol on the Transition attached to the Treaty.[25]

2.2.2   Nominal convergence

The participation of member countries in the third stage is not unconditional; it depends on the candidate member's satisfying a set of convergence criteria regarding inflation, nominal exchange rates, nominal interest rates, and government debt and deficits. The first convergence criterion states that inflation rates among the member countries should converge to a level not far above that of the three members with the lowest inflation rates.[26]

The Treaty's concession to anti-inflationary rectitude is neither surprising nor harmful. Some doubts have been expressed, however, regarding the relevance of the inflation criterion. First, even in a successful, established monetary union, inflation convergence is restricted to the convergence of the inflation rates of tradable goods. There does not need to be convergence in the inflation rates of broadly defined price indices like the CPI or the GDP deflator, which contain significant shares of nontraded goods. For instance, differences among member states in their internal traded – nontraded productivity growth differentials would lead to sustainable GDP inflation differentials. Second, for a monetary union to be viable, it is not necessary (in principle) that the common inflation rate (of traded goods prices) be a low (or even a stable) one.

24. This is precisely what Bini-Smaghi, Padoa-Schioppa, and Papadia do in their 1994 paper, although without stressing the consequences of the compromises between the two schools.
25. See Kenen (1995, Ch. 2), for a detailed discussion of the schedule for Stage III.
26. It is required that "...a Member State has a price performance that is sustainable and an average inflation rate, observed over a period of one year before the examination, that does not exceed by more than 1.5 percentage points that of, at most, the three best performing Member states in terms of price stability" (Article 1 of the Protocol on Convergence Criteria).

More crucially, by making inflation convergence a precondition for admission to monetary union, the inflation criterion does deny a country that is unable to lower domestic inflation – as long as it has any national monetary autonomy – the option of using the relinquishing of the national currency as an anti-inflationary device. In other words, joining a monetary union can be an effective means for achieving inflation convergence for a country without internal monetary credibility. By ruling this out, the Treaty can be argued to put the cart before the horse.

The second convergence criterion requires the stability of the nominal exchange rate and the absence of persistent pressure to realign for two years before the examination.[27] This criterion, too, is not a logical prerequisite for a credible monetary union. One cannot dismiss the feasibility (perhaps even the desirability) of a coordinated final grand realignment one instant before the disappearance of the national currencies.

The obvious danger is that an uncontrolled and uncoordinated "devaluation endgame" would result in chaotic attempts to gain a (temporary) initial competitive advantage through last-minute devaluations, and/or to achieve a sizeable reduction in the real value of domestic currency denominated public debt. The caution that motivates the exchange rate criterion may therefore seem sensible. However, Eichengreen and Wyplosz (1993) have argued that, perversely, the exchange rate criterion may have the effect of raising the likelihood of a successful speculative attack. This argument is reviewed below.

Nominal long-term interest rates are required to converge to a level not more than two percentage points above that characterizing the long-term rates of the three lowest inflation countries. With a high degree of intra-EC financial capital mobility in the single market, interest rate differentials ultimately depend on four sources: the expected rate of depreciation, a devaluation risk premium, a default risk premium (including sovereign default risk in the case of public debt), and (possibly) national differences in the taxation of interest income. While the first two contributions to the interest rate differential are taken care of (eliminated) by the first two convergence rules, at least in the intention of the Treaty, the desire to eliminate sovereign risk premia may have motivated a fourth convergence criterion, establishing upper limits for the ratios of public debt and deficits to GDP.

The aversion to "excessive deficits" expressed in Maastricht is one of the most controversial features of the Treaty. It is almost impossible to find either

---

27. Article 3 of the Protocol on the Convergence Criteria requires a Member State to respect "the normal fluctuations margins... of the European Monetary System without severe tensions for at least two years before the examination. In particular, the Member State shall not have devalued its currency's bilateral central rate against any other Member State's currency on its own initiative for the same period."

theoretical or empirical support for the upper limits to debt and deficits embodied in the Treaty. Moreover, there are reasons to believe that the active pursuit of these debt and deficit targets in the years leading up to EMU could actually be harmful, by imparting a contractionary bias to the Community-wide level of economic activity. Finally, these criteria could easily be misused for politically motivated inclusion in (or exclusion from) the Union. Even if one shares the worries about a possible systemic bias towards "excessive deficits" in a number of member countries, severe doubts remain regarding the truly unhappy choice of the two indicators in question.[28]

2.2.3 A transition with national monetary sovereignty and free capital mobility

When the Treaty was signed, Stage I had already begun with the removal of capital controls in 1990. Stage II, started on January 1, 1994, is characterized by a set of institutional initiatives preparing the way for monetary union. In this stage, as domestic laws must be modified appropriately to conform to the Treaty, national central banks are to be given formal independence according to the standards agreed upon in Maastricht. While a European Central Bank will not be established before Stage III, the Treaty prescribed the creation of a European Monetary Institute (EMI) as early as January 1994, with the goals of strengthening monetary policy coordination, monitoring the functioning of the EMS, and organizing the preparation of the final stage.

The EMI is chaired by a president nominated by the heads of state and government, acting on a recommendation by national central bank governors. The Institute is endowed with its own resources to finance operations; it is granted the ability to "hold and manage foreign exchange reserves as an agent for and at the request of national central banks"; it has the power to address recommendations to national central banks. The compromise on the EMI preserves to a large extent the view expressed by the German and Dutch delegations at the Intergovernmental Conference about the principle of indivisibility of monetary policy, which during the transition is still under the power and responsibility of national central banks. Once in Stage III, the European Central Bank will pursue the primary objective of maintaining price stability (Art. 105 of the Treaty). It will be granted a degree of independence from the national and supranational governments and legislatures that is, at least formally, even greater than that of the Bundesbank. National central banks will continue to exist as subsidiaries of the European one, however.

The European Council approved the Treaty of Maastricht in December 1991, when capital mobility was already free almost everywhere in the EC. Both

28. See Buiter, Corsetti, and Roubini (1993) for an extensive discussion of these issues.

common sense and economic reasoning warn against the presumption that nationally differentiated currencies can be maintained in a system of fixed exchange rates when financial capital movements are not restricted at all. It seems inconceivable that, as long as the national monetary authorities remain independent, voluntary cooperation can produce the miracle of monetary policy coordination and mutual support required for a multiple currency system to mimic a common currency area.

At best, the length of the transition phase with these unsustainable characteristics should be kept as short as possible. The maximum length of Stage II as allowed by the Treaty is instead rather long: from January 1994 to January 1999. Even taking as given the undue optimism which led the designers of the Treaty to underestimate the possibility of financial instability during the transition, it is hard to understand why some of the features of the Treaty almost seemed designed to make things worse. With free capital mobility, the fixing of deadlines for events that remain uncertain in many important respects[29] may prove to be dangerous. This feature of the Treaty has been criticized increasingly because of the confusion it creates in financial and nonfinancial markets or, more precisely, because it risks destabilizing the exchange market by creating focal dates for likely speculative attacks (see for example Froot and Rogoff, 1991).

Eichengreen and Wyplosz (1993) have argued that the inclusion in the Maastricht Treaty of the exchange rate criterion for full EMU membership may have raised the likelihood of a speculative attack against the currency of a candidate EMU member succeeding, because it reduces the payoff to the policy makers from adhering to anti-inflationary policy in the event that a speculative attack succeeds in forcing the country off its parity. The argument goes as follows. Requiring two years of exchange rate stability in order to qualify for Stage III may provide the private financial markets with a timetable for testing a country's resolve to defend the parity of its currency. A successful attack would jeopardize the country's participation in the union (because it has violated the exchange rate stability criterion and therefore needs at least another two years of exchange rate stability in order to qualify for full membership). Assuming that participation in EMU is indeed seen as a glittering prize by the national authorities, and that the restrictive monetary and fiscal policies required to meet all the Stage III criteria are perceived as costly, the monetary and fiscal authorities will revert to less restrictive policies if the speculative attack succeeds, thus validating the speculative attack ex post.

By the same token, the vague formulation of the fiscal requirements (the fourth convergence criterion) can prevent a country from meeting the interest

---

29. The obvious example is uncertainty about which countries will participate in Stage III at the time of the deadline.

differentials criterion. Consider a high-debt and high-deficit country whose qualifications to join the union are in doubt because they might be judged to not meet the debt or deficit criterion. The uncertainty concerning the future status of this country may put upward pressure on that country's interest rates, and in the process worsen its future fiscal position and endanger its ability to meet the interest rate criterion.

Above all, doubts about the ERM members' commitment to avoid realignment were prompted by the internal and external economic environment that prevailed when the Maastricht Treaty was signed in December 1991. First and foremost, there was the huge, unprecedented asymmetric real and monetary shock of German unification. Second, the bill of past attempts at disinflation with a fixed exchange rate was coming due in a number of EC members, especially Italy, France, and Spain, in the form of growing domestic imbalances (rising unemployment and excess capacity) and unfavorable external competitive positions. While these developments were to varying degrees structural – that is, independent of the nominal exchange rate regime – there is no doubt that contractionary monetary and fiscal policies implemented in defence of the fixed parity put a serious drag on real economic performance. Third, there were the unfavorable international cyclical conditions (a world recession coupled with a steep decline in the value of the US dollar). No favorable wind was blowing from the perspective of the economists school.

CHAPTER 3

The unfolding of the 1992–93 ERM crisis

3.1 Toward the crisis

3.1.1 German reunification

German reunification was an unprecedented economic and political event: the integration of two national economies that had undergone postwar reconstruction under two very different systems, ending up with a substantial gap in productive capacities and standards of living.[1] It would have been a difficult enterprise at the best of times. It was turned into a textbook example of macroeconomic mismanagement, eventually resulting in the adoption of a monetary–fiscal policy mix that was undesirable even for Germany internally, let alone for the EC as a whole.

First, the German Chancellor kept his electoral promise not to finance the massive transfer of resources to the Eastern part of the country by asking Western Germans to pay additional taxes. Nor were there significant cuts in other spending items in the budget. In 1991, the net transfer of West German public funds to East Germany was as high as 139 billion D-mark. To get a sense of this magnitude, it can be compared to West German private saving for that year of 260 billion D-mark. This net transfer reached 180 billion D-mark the following year. The rate of growth of West German public sector indebtedness, which averaged around 5% in the second half of the Eighties, rose to 13.4% and 11.2% in 1990 and 1991, respectively.[2]

Second, with the creation of a Monetary, Economic, and Social Union in May 1990, GDR marks could be converted into D-mark on a 1:1 or 2:1 basis.[3] In the words of Helmut Schlesinger,

> ... the biggest mistake in the transition which has negative consequences to this day began with the wage policy.... Understandably, what people wanted was: one country, one currency, one wage level. But the acceptance of overly

1. See Akerlof et al. (1991), Collier (1991), Dornbusch and Wolf (1992) among others.
2. Bundesbank Monthly Report (1992).
3. To be precise, all debts were converted on a 2:1 basis, and all claims were converted on a 2:1 basis, except bank deposits, which were converted on a 1:1 basis for a limited amount in per capita terms (2000 marks for children under the age of 15, 4000 for adults under 60, 6000 for people over 59). The average rate of conversion, according to the estimates of the Bundesbank (Monthly Report, July 1990, p. 25), was 1.8:1. Wage, price, and pension contracts were converted on a 1:1 basis.

high claims through the entrepreneurs and the government agencies was out of any relation to the low productivity. These maladjustments were costly, and they were largely responsible for

- a relatively high level of unemployment after the closing of a number of enterprises and reducing the overstaffed personnel in existing companies. . . ;
- a substantial need for transfer payments from West to East to compensate for deficits in the budget of the new state and in social security systems and the large losses of inefficient enterprises;
- the need for a relatively restrictive line of monetary policy through the Bundesbank to avoid creating an inflationary spiral.[4]

The chosen conversion rates between GDR Marks and D-mark hit East German production hard (the level of industrial production in the first two months after reunification fell to less than half that of 1989), while the massive budgetary transfers contributed to a sustained high level of consumption demand. In addition, the process of restructuring that began following reunification soon generated a noticeable increase in investment demand. Unless much of the increase in demand from the East was to be directed towards foreign goods, the German reunification scenario pointed to domestic overheating and inflationary pressures in the Western part of the country.[5]

The Bundesbank could not affect this course of action. Their more cautious proposals regarding the conversion rate of the GDR mark were ignored by Chancellor Kohl. Publicly denouncing the "disastrous consequences" of a misguided approach to reunification, as put by its president Karl Otto Pöhl in March 1991, the Bundesbank warned the German government that interest rate increases would result from reunification unless the size of the government budget deficit were reduced drastically.

The idea that reunifying Germany would generate the need for an appreciation of the D-mark in real terms (at least in the short and medium term) motivated much of the debate around and after German unification (see for example Begg et al., 1990). The reasoning is straightforward. In the short run, reunification represented an increase in the demand for German goods relative to non-German goods and in the demand for German nontraded goods relative to German traded goods. An improvement in the German terms of trade and an appreciation of the German real exchange rate are therefore required in the short run. Germany will also run a larger external current account deficit.[6] In the long run, larger external

4. Schlesinger (1994, pp. 6–7). For a discussion of these theses, see Sinn and Sinn (1996).
5. Capacity utilization in West Germany reached 90 percent in 1990, and the unemployment rate fell throughout the period, reaching a level below 7.0 percent during 1990.
6. In these two years the overall current account balance for the United Germany drops from a surplus of 76 to a deficit of 32.9 billion D-mark. The disappearance of Germany's trade and current account surplus since reunification cannot be mistaken for evidence of reduced protectionism in Germany or of improved market access to German markets. It is an obvious reflection of the reduction in the national saving rate associated with the redistribution of income from West to East Germany and with the German government's deficit financing policies, and the capital formation boom (private and public) following reunification.

primary surpluses[7] are required to service increased external debt that results from the initial capital imports. To generate these external primary surpluses, a depreciation (relative to the initial value) of the real exchange rate and a worsening of the terms of trade are required in the long run. All this would be qualitatively true even if reunification had been financed with a balanced government budget. Both the short-run and long-run effects are magnified if reunification is financed by government borrowing.

While few authors have doubted the need for a short-run appreciation of the German *real* exchange rate (but see for example Gros and Steinherr, 1991, and Gros and Thygesen, 1992), the required behavior of the *nominal* exchange rate can be determined only if one knows the behavior of the Bundesbank. The early behavior of the Bundesbank following reunification was in fact quite cautious and difficult to interpret. Only towards the end of 1991 did German monetary policy become severely restrictive.

From the date of reunification until the signing of the Maastricht Treaty in December 1991, German key rates were raised gradually in four steps, and the target range for growth of the M3 measure of the money supply was lowered once without changing the intervention rates. The first increase involved the Lombard rate in November 1990 (from 8.0 to 8.5 percent). This was followed two months later by a move in the opposite direction of the discount rates in the United States. This divergence in the stance of monetary policy did not prevent the Bundesbank from raising key rates again in February 1991.

However, in the first half of 1991, there was some slowing down of German inflation. Also in that period, the appreciation of the dollar accompanying the Gulf war strengthened some of the European currencies against the D-mark, according to a well-established but poorly understood empirical regularity known as dollar-D-mark polarization (see below). As a result, the D-mark weakened within the ERM, leaving some space for a decrease in the interest rate differentials with the European partners. In July, the Bundesbank announced a modest downward revision of money supply growth targets (from 4.0/6.0 percent to 3.5/5.5 percent), and in August, when intervention rates were increased again, the Lombard rise was limited to a quarter point (see Figure 3.1[8]).

Even at the time, the money growth targets appeared overambitious when compared with the expected growth of nominal GDP. The data show a strong increase in the rate of monetary growth after August, with the year-on-year growth rate of M3 as high as 8.0 percent in December 1991.

The rise in inflation in the second half of 1991 mostly reflected changes in indirect taxes and nominal wages during the first half of the year. This adjustment in the price level could hardly be reversed by an ex post tightening of monetary

7. The external primary surplus is the current account surplus minus net foreign factor income, that is, the trade surplus plus net current transfers.
8. Source: Deutsche Bundesbank.

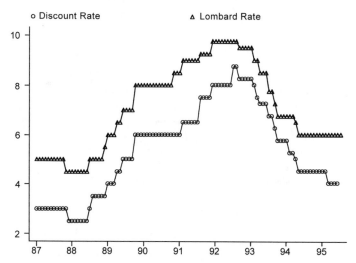

Figure 3.1. Key interest rates in Germany, 1987–1995.

policy, and there were strong doubts about the wisdom of such an attempt. What motivated the strong tightening of monetary policy was rather the intention of the Bundesbank to signal an absolute unwillingness to accommodate further wage inflation and loosening of fiscal policy by the government.[9] At the end of 1991, it became quite clear that in the absence of a realignment in the ERM, the Bundesbank would pursue the goal of monetary stability by using the interest rate instruments regardless of the consequences for the domestic real economy and with utter disregard for the international implications of its policies. A graphical synthesis of these developments is provided by the plot of short-term nominal and ex post real interest rates in Germany, shown in Figure 3.2.[10] The spike in the graph corresponds to September 1992.

The gap between targeted and actual growth of the monetary aggregates kept increasing in 1992, as the target growth rates were held low while the realized growth rates were (surprisingly) rising despite clear signs of a slow-down in real economic activity. No concession was made by the Bundesbank to cyclical considerations in mid 1992, unless one interprets as a concession its decision to limit the response to the increasing distance of M3 growth from its target range to an increase in the discount rate from 8.00 to 8.75 percent, while the Lombard rate was left unchanged at 9.75 percent.

An appreciation of the German real exchange rate in the EMS (at a fixed nominal exchange rate) can be achieved only by an increase in the German

9. Commission of the European Communities (1993).
10. Unless otherwise noted, the source for the time series plotted in the figures of this chapter is Datastream International.

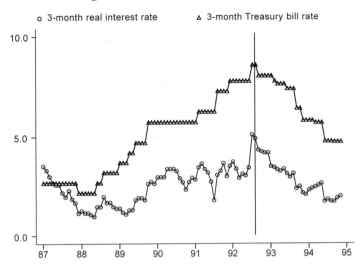

Figure 3.2. Short-term nominal and real interest rates in Germany, 1987–1995.

price level path relative to that in the other EMS countries, that is, by a German rate of inflation that exceeds, at least temporarily, the rate of inflation of the other EMS countries. Notice that to an observer unaware of the economic reasons for expecting an appreciation of the D-mark – or to a professional economist who disagrees with these reasons – the increase in the German rate of inflation in 1990 could have appeared as a relaxation of the nominal constraints on all other members of the ERM, to be welcomed especially by those that had previously suffered a loss in competitiveness. Eichengreen and Wyplosz (1993) carefully explain that the metric of the inflation differential between Germany and the rest of the EMS is changed by the shock of the reunification: Because of the need for a real appreciation of the D-mark, the zero in the scale corresponds to some negative number; that is, for a given nominal exchange rate, the new short-run equilibrium requires a reduction in the inflation rate of the other EMS countries to a level below that in Germany.

The rate of growth of the German GDP deflator increased from 3.3 percent in 1990 to 4.2 percent in 1991. The German regional disparities were huge. The cost-of-living index, reported by the Bundesbank, decreased by 1.1 percent in East Germany in 1990, as opposed to an increase by 2.7 percent in the West. In 1991, these indicators increased by 17.5 percent and 3.5 percent in the two regions, respectively.[11] By German standards, these numbers were more than a nuisance. Replying to those who asked the Bundesbank to loosen up the

---

11. The 1991 figure for East Germany refers to the change in the second half of 1991 compared to the second half of 1990.

strings, German officials must have felt the way many good Christians do when confronted by beggars while leaving church: "We already gave."

3.1.2   Competitiveness problems

A key issue in analyzing the origins of the ERM crisis concerns the effects on competitiveness of the long disinflation processes undergone by a number of countries in the ERM. As shown in Figure 3.3, inflation differentials vis-à-vis Germany had remained persistently positive during five years in the "new EMS", and only in 1991 were they close to zero for several European countries, France and the United Kingdom included.

Nonetheless, erosion of competitiveness as measured by the standard set of price and cost indicators – namely real exchange rates based on labor costs and relative prices – was quite apparent for Spain and Portugal and, to a lesser extent, for the United Kingdom and Italy (see Figures 3.4 and 3.5).[12] It also characterized Sweden and Finland, which, although not formally members of the EMS, had pegged unilaterally to the D-mark.[13]

A first reaction by several European central banks to the accumulating evidence of misalignments in the ERM was a steadfast denial of the relevance of the problem. In 1991, for example, the Bank of Italy stated that the loss of Italian competitiveness since the last realignment was limited to 5 percent,[14] a gap that could be narrowed reasonably by undertaking further efforts of modernization and rationalization of the production process with no need for a nominal realignment. On the contrary, a devaluation was considered counterproductive (since it would undermine hard-earned anti-inflationary gains), would represent a relaxation of the external constraint on domestic fiscal policy, and would generally destroy the credibility borrowed so painfully from the Bundesbank over a number of years.[15]

A problem in carrying out international comparisons of competitiveness using price data is that if tradable goods are close substitutes, their prices cannot diverge much. In the limiting case of perfect substitutes, trading firms either accept the international price or drop out of the market. In such a world, a loss of competitiveness will show up in a reduced profitability of producing tradable goods, not in prices that are higher than those of foreign competitors. This

---

12. See also the discussion in Chapter 7.
13. In assessing competitiveness issues in the Nordic countries, it is worth emphasizing that Finland also suffered from a specific real asymmetric shock – the collapse of trade with the former Soviet Union in 1991 (Söderström, 1993) – while Sweden was hit by an unusual but persistent drop in consumption expenditure at the end of the Eighties.
14. This calculation is based on the change in the index of (multilateral) relative producer prices of manufactures since 1987 (see Banca d'Italia, 1992).
15. This view implicitly advocated a reduction of the profit rate in the externally exposed business sector from the peak reached in 1988. Not surprisingly, the representatives of industry were in favor of a realignment in the EMS.

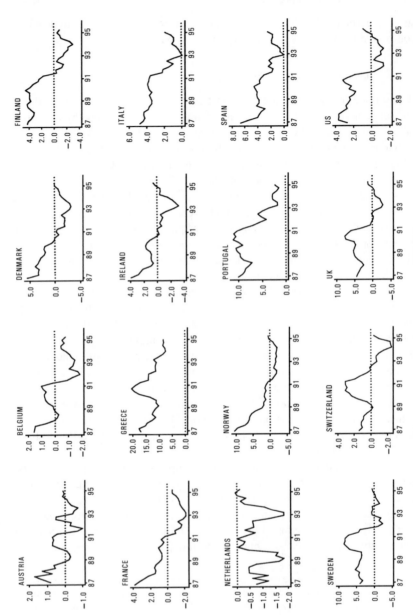

Figure 3.3. CPI inflation differentials against Germany (%), 1987–95.

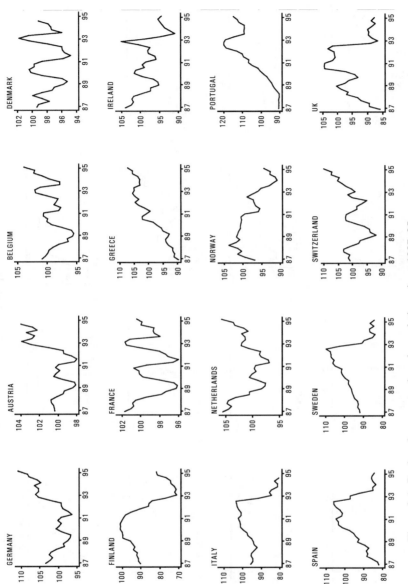

Figure 3.4. Real exchange rates based on relative prices, 1987–95.

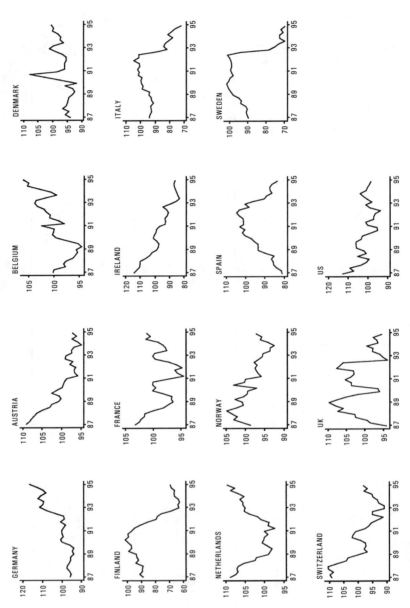

Figure 3.5. Real exchange rates based on labor costs, 1987–95.

46

problem obviously affects the interpretation of terms of trade data as measures of international competitiveness, but it also applies to the use of relative GDP deflators, and of relative CPI or WPI indices that contain a large traded goods component.

The use of information on costs and productivity, such as that summarized in bilateral relative normal unit labor cost figures, may provide more accurate information on the behavior of international competitiveness. Even here, however, the information content of these indicators may not be sufficient to allow a confident resolution of the issue. For example, a case for the existence of a hidden or suppressed competitiveness problem can be made when high unemployment is required to keep domestic unit labor costs in line with those of one's foreign competitors. Tradable goods could be exchanged at the international market price, unit labor costs could be converging, and yet a competitiveness problem may exist in a country where the unemployment rate is steadily increasing over time.

An important case study is provided by the entry of the pound sterling in the ERM in October 1990 at a parity considered overvalued by some (though by no means all) independent observers. From the point of view of the objective of reducing the "sacrifice ratio" (the output cost of disinflation) in the United Kingdom, such a policy choice was motivated with the usual argument of enhancing policy credibility by means of a public international commitment to peg the exchange rate to the D-mark. A few months later, however, the United Kingdom entered what was to become the worst recession in the postwar history of the country, with a record fall in the level of GDP by 4 percent in less than two years and an unemployment rate rising above 10 percent.

Notwithstanding the gradual elimination of interest differentials with Germany, the stance of monetary policy and the level of interest rates required by the ERM obligations soon attracted strong domestic criticism. The hope of speeding up the process of reducing UK interest rates through participation in the ERM – so the argument went – was bound to be shattered by the shift in the German monetary and fiscal policy mix towards tight money and loose budgetary policy.

If we look at the conventional indicators of international competitiveness, we find that almost all of them (including United Kingdom/German bilateral relative unit labor costs) show a slight improvement in the position of the United Kingdom following its entry into the ERM.[16] However, a proper assessment of the competitive difficulties of the United Kingdom cannot be carried out independent of the developments in its unemployment rate in the early 1990s. The United Kingdom suffered from the same recessionary wave that hit the United States in the period 1990–1991. The other European economies, notably

---

16. See for example the discussion in Portes (1993).

Germany, France, Italy, and Spain, started to contract with a significant lag in 1992. The decline in output, although not as deep as for the United States and the United Kingdom, was pronounced. Figures 3.6 and 3.7 display the rate of growth of output and the unemployment rate for a sample of ERM and non-ERM countries in the period 1987–1995.

Some observers have argued that the 1992–93 recessionary episode in Europe was quite independent of the earlier recessionary wave in the United States (see Backus and Galí, 1995). An alternative view stresses the role of the German reunification shock in explaining the two-year time lag between the recessions on opposite sides of the Atlantic Ocean.[17] Nonetheless, from the first quarter of 1992, declining output and rising unemployment clearly exacerbated policy conflicts within the ERM. An interesting issue open to debate is to what extent German and European policy choices (or, rather, macroeconomic mismanagement) contributed to the magnitude of the 1992–93 recession.

Even more serious problems are associated with the use of current account or trade deficit measures (overall and/or bilateral) as measures of competitiveness (see Figure 3.8). The current account deficit is the excess of domestic capital formation (private and public) over national saving (private and public). It therefore reflects in the first instance the intertemporal choices of households, firms, and governments. Considerations relevant to static international trade, such as competitiveness, are only very indirectly (and often in surprising ways) connected with the intertemporal choices that are the proximate determinants of the external deficit. The absence of any simple and unambiguous relationship between the trade balance (or the current account) and measures of competitiveness such as the real exchange rate (both jointly endogenous variables in any serious economic model) should therefore not come as a surprise.

3.1.3   The dollar/D-mark polarization

A popular "model" (really more an empirical regularity in search of a theory) in both the financial markets and the economics profession sees a dollar/D-mark polarization in the European exchange markets. A strong dollar (in effective terms) strengthens the position of some European currencies vis-à-vis the D-mark and vice versa.

An empirical assessment of this regularity and its role in EMS realignments is provided by Giavazzi and Giovannini (1989). They argue that almost all realignments (resulting in an appreciation of the mark vis-à-vis the other currencies in the system) were preceded by a fall in the effective dollar index and

---

17. Schlesinger argues that "the strong demand push which came from the unification in 1990 and 1991 ... happened at a time when the last recession was still in full force in the US, the UK, and some Northern countries. For the continental countries, as well as for Germany itself, the recession was delayed and in the end shortened." (Schlesinger, 1994, pp. 9–10)

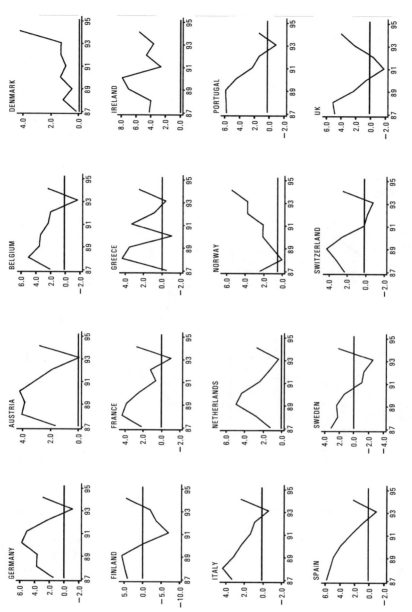

Figure 3.6. Rates of output growth (%), 1987–94.

49

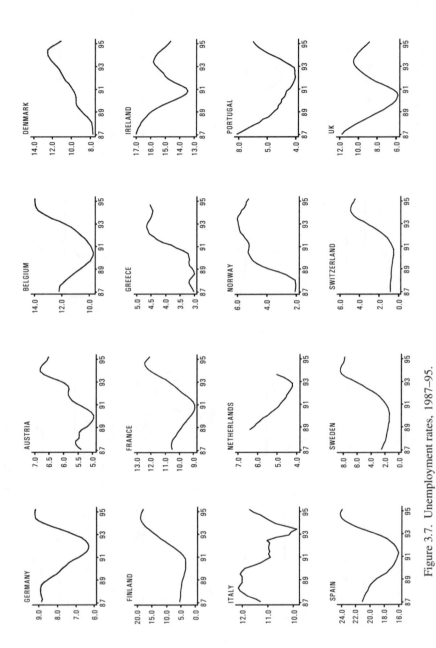

Figure 3.7. Unemployment rates, 1987–95.

50

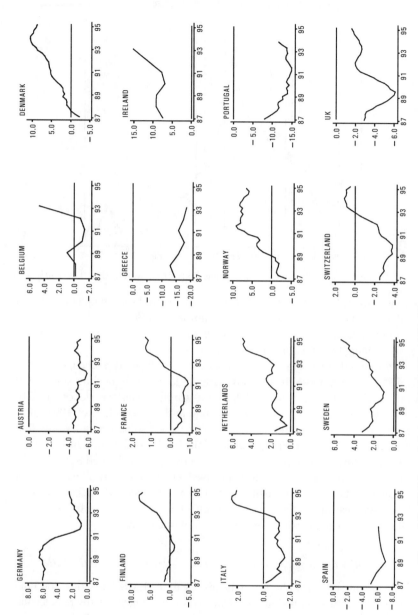

Figure 3.8. Visible trade balance/GDP (%), 1987–95.

51

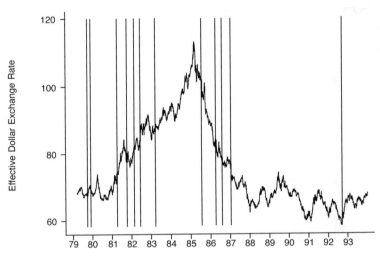

Figure 3.9. Effective dollar exchange rate (trade weighted), 1976–1993.

followed by a recovery of the dollar. Figure 3.9 reproduces an updated version of the plot presented by Giavazzi and Giovannini (1989, p. 138), where the US dollar effective exchange rate index is shown together with vertical spikes corresponding to the realignment dates.

In the period preceding the 1992 crisis, the dollar/D-mark exchange rate was subject to considerable fluctuations. The dollar's steady decline since 1989 came to a halt in 1991, when with the Gulf-war the dollar experienced a sharp rise for a few months. Following a decline in the second half of 1991, after peace had broken out in the Gulf, the dollar gained some strength in the first three months of 1992, when another cut of the US discount rate at the end of the 1991 had boosted the hopes for a speedy recovery of the United States. From April to August 1992, the dollar depreciated again, by almost 20 percent with respect to the D-mark. True to the tradition of benign neglect,[18] the depreciation of the dollar was in part the external side-effect of decisions taken by the United States monetary authorities to engineer a domestic recovery.

3.1.4   *Political consensus and policy makers' commitment to the ERM*

The beginning of a new chapter in the history of the EMS was written on June 2, 1992. In a national referendum, Denmark's voters unexpectedly rejected the Maastricht Treaty by a narrow margin, 50.9 percent against to 49.3 percent in favor. The outcome of the referendum represented an embarrassing surprise for

18. The expression "benign neglect", which had encapsulated the attitudes of Washington at the time of the collapse of Bretton Woods (see Chapter 2), was resuscitated twenty years later, mostly by non-American observers.

the Danish political establishment. All the main parties, both those belonging to the government coalition and the opposition, had campaigned in favor of ratification of the Treaty. They had seriously underestimated the effectiveness of the "word-of-mouth" proselytizing in the grass-roots campaign conducted by the heterogeneous and underfunded anti-Maastricht front, which included political organizations as different as the left-wing Socialist People's Party and the right-wing Populist Party.

The Danish "No" boosted the confidence and enthusiasm of the antifederalist groups in Europe, although they continued to constitute minorities in the electorates of all member states. In their view, the Danish results did not stem from a misunderstanding of the Treaty's objectives, but rather from a clear perception of its negative implications. French neo-Gaullists and British Thatcherites notwithstanding, the first official reactions to the Danish shock revealed a widespread tendency to minimize the importance of the event. After all, as a senior German diplomat quoted by the Economist summarized, "24,000 peculiar people" could not be allowed to "stop Europe's momentum".[19] Betting on the "exceptional" character of the Danish results and on the "Europhoric" feelings that still dominated the political landscape south of the Jutland peninsula, French President Mitterand called a referendum on the Maastricht Treaty, to be held in September. In the meantime, renegotiation of the Treaty was promptly ruled out by the EC, while the Danish government began its search for a workable solution to the institutional stalemate.

Yet the confidence of the market in a smooth, fast, and irreversible transition to monetary union had been weakened irreparably. As acknowledged ex post by the EC central banks, "the outcome of the Danish referendum in June was only a catalyst for the subsequent events, which culminated in September 1992 in the most serious crisis of the EMS since its inception".[20]

Doubts about the inevitability of a monetary union that would encompass the majority of the ERM members by the end of the decade may also have been prompted by the slippage of the fiscal performance in much of the system, which began almost as soon as the Maastricht fiscal criteria had been promulgated. Table 3.1[21] shows how the ERM members performed with respect to the deficit criterion (the general government financial deficit should not exceed 3 percent of GDP) and with respect to the debt criterion (the general government's gross financial liabilities should not exceed 60 percent of annual GDP). Among the highly indebted countries, only Ireland showed the kind of budgetary resolve that might entitle it to a flexible interpretation of the fiscal criteria.

19. *The Economist*, June 6–12, 1992, p. 25.
20. Committee of Governors of the Central Banks of the EEC (1993, p. 2).
21. The data are all expressed as percentages of GDP. Source: European Commission and OECD (for Austria, Finland, and Sweden in 1991 and 1992).

Table 3.1. *Performance of ERM members relative to the deficit criterion and the debt criterion*

	DEFICIT / GDP (%)					DEBT / GDP (%)				
	1991	1992	1993	1994	1995	1991	1992	1993	1994	1995
Austria	2.4	2.0	4.1	4.4	5.5	56.6	56.1	63.0	65.2	68.0
Belgium	6.5	6.6	6.6	5.3	4.3	132.6	134.4	141.3	140.1	138.3
Denmark	2.1	2.9	4.5	3.9	2.1	60.9	63.1	66.8	68.7	68.8
Germany	3.3	2.9	3.3	2.5	2.3	42.7	47.3	51.8	54.6	62.5
Finland	1.5	5.8	7.9	5.5	5.0	23.2	42.7	56.2	62.7	69.1
France	2.2	4.0	6.1	6.0	5.0	41.1	45.6	52.9	56.8	59.5
Greece	11.5	12.3	13.2	12.5	11.4	81.7	88.6	117.1	119.8	120.2
Ireland	2.1	2.2	2.3	2.2	2.5	95.3	90.7	92.7	87.9	83.3
Italy	10.2	9.5	9.6	9.0	7.8	103.9	111.4	120.2	122.6	122.1
Luxembourg	1.0	2.5	2.1	2.3	1.4	6.0	7.0	7.0	7.0	8.0
Netherlands	2.8	3.8	3.2	3.0	3.3	76.4	77.1	78.5	79.0	79.4
Portugal	6.5	3.3	7.1	5.7	5.4	62.2	63.2	67.8	70.4	70.8
Spain	4.9	4.2	7.5	6.6	6.2	49.9	53.0	59.4	63.5	66.5
Sweden	1.1	7.5	13.4	10.4	9.2	53.7	69.8	74.6	79.4	84.5
United Kingdom	2.6	6.1	7.9	6.5	4.2	35.5	41.4	47.4	51.6	53.4

3.2   A chronology of the ERM crack-up

3.2.1   *June and July 1992*

Tensions in the foreign exchange market increased in the aftermath of the Danish Referendum, the Italian lira being the most notable target. Italian official foreign reserves had been gradually decreasing since February. In June, the outflow of reserves suddenly became heavy (they shrank from 36,500 to 31,600 million dollars in the month), while lira bond prices fell first in the futures market, then in the cash market.

In July, an unambiguous message was sent by the central banks of the G3 to the world markets: Not even the mildest form of international policy coordination could be achieved under the current circumstances. National monetary priorities dictated the adoption of highly divergent monetary policy stances in Washington, Frankfurt, and Tokyo. Three consecutive adjustments of the official discount rates in the G3 countries took place during that month. On July 2, the US discount rate was reduced from 3.50 to 3.00 percent. This was accompanied by a reduction in the federal funds rate. On July 16, the Bundesbank raised its discount rate from 8.00 percent to the postwar peak of 8.75 percent (although the Lombard rate was kept unchanged).[22] On July 27, the

22. See Figure 3.1.

Japanese discount rate went down from 3.75 to 3.25 percent. The consequent fall in the value of the American currency was temporarily counteracted, but not halted, by central bank purchases of dollars on July 20, reportedly on a large scale.

With short-term interest differentials well above six hundred basis points, portfolio reshuffles from dollar-assets into D-mark-assets enhanced the tensions that had been growing within the ERM since the previous month. Also in July, the outflow of Italian reserves became more intense after a wealth tax on deposits (perhaps perversely aimed at discouraging Italian households and firms from liquidating their holdings of public debt) was coupled with an unhappy announcement that the Italian State would not be financially responsible for the foreign liabilities of the bankrupt state holding company, Ente Partecipazione e Finanziamento Industria Manifatturiera (EFIM).[23] However, on the last day of the month, employers, unions, and the government signed a historic agreement on income policy, disinflation, and labor costs, which reformed the system of industrial relations, abolishing what was left of the *scala mobile*, that is, the automatic indexation of wages and salaries.

3.2.2 August 1992

At a Community level, the crisis reached a first climax at the end of August. On August 25, the US dollar traded at D-mark 1.4, its historical low. The dollar's decline was shared by the British pound sterling, which was quoted on the same day slightly above its ERM floor. No significant recovery took place within the next few days, despite massive intervention in support of the British currency. On August 28, the Italian lira joined sterling at the lower edge of the currency band. Outside the currency markets, new lows were hit by European stock exchanges, Germany's included.

In the view of many European policy makers and observers, the August turmoil was principally as a dollar crisis due to the weakness of the US economy, to the attempt by the Federal Reserve Board to lower long-term bond yields by squeezing short-term rates, and to the lack of interest in and concern for the fate of the dollar shared by the two leading presidential candidates, Bush and Clinton.

Following this line of reasoning, it was believed that no fundamental disequilibrium or significant misalignment was responsible for the current misadventures of lira, peseta, and sterling. A fortiori, there was nothing in the fundamentals to warrant any worry about the French franc. The stability of the ERM had become an article of faith. Needless to say, the desirability, imminence,

---

23. As a result, Italian debt was downgraded by Moody's from AA1 to AA3. Nonetheless, one may wonder on what basis a shaky public holding such as EFIM was allowed to borrow heavily in the international capital market.

or sheer possibility of an ERM realignment (let alone the suspension of membership of any ERM member) were denied repeatedly.[24]

3.2.3   September 1992

In order to boost the credibility of its commitment to defend sterling's position in the ERM, the Bank of England enhanced its capacity for resisting speculative attacks by replenishing its stock of international reserves. It reportedly borrowed ECU 10 billion ($14.5 billion) worth of D-mark from the market on September 3. The Bank of Italy raised the discount rate to 15 percent the day after.

The EC Meeting in Bath The official meeting of EC ministers of finance and central bank governors in Bath on September 5–6, although officially not dealing with ERM-related issues, provided a venue for a chorus of strong complaints against high German interest rates.[25] Reportedly, during the meeting British officials stressed the adverse effects on the level of economic activity, while French officials pointed out the negative political influence on the Referendum to be held two weeks later. Confronted with these complaints, the president of the Bundesbank called for a general realignment in the system as a precondition for an interest rate cut by the Bundesbank, but apparently none of the other participants was willing to entertain this possibility. The resulting stalemate was well reflected in the post-meeting communiqué; this confirmed the general commitment to defend the existing parities but also pointed out that ERM members would "take advantage of any opportunity to reduce interest rates". The communiqué also welcomed the fact that "under present circumstances" the Bundesbank saw no room for further interest rate rises. Nonetheless, the remote possibility of a downward adjustment in German official interest rates was left unmentioned.[26]

In talking to the press, the British chancellor referred to a German "commitment" not to raise interest rates. The use of the term "commitment" did not please the president of the Bundesbank. One day later, Schlesinger stated

24. One of the unavoidable negatives of a "fixed until further notice" exchange rate system like Bretton Woods or the ERM is that it forces officials from time to time into positions where they have to deny the evidence. Unfortunately, this may undermine the credibility of policy commitments in other areas of policy as well.

25. In this paragraph and the following ones, our reconstruction relies on Muehring (1992), Ciampi (1995), and on conversations with Helmut Schlesinger at Princeton University in the fall of 1994.

26. The episode fits the model of ad-hoc cooperation discussed by Padoa-Schioppa: "Ad-hoc cooperation is a method by which partners meet, discuss, and, if they agree, act together. If they do not agree, they will skillfully draft a press communiqué to give the public the impression of a joint commitment to general values and goals, and then return to their respective capitals to conduct ... mutually inconsistent and possibly conflicting policies." (Padoa-Schioppa, 1994, p. 43).

in an interview that the Bundesbank position had in fact not changed since August. According to the reports of the financial press, "Lamont's scuffle with the Bundesbank came at a particularly sensitive time and led money managers, corporate treasurers and others in the currency markets to reevaluate their strategies."[27]

Exchange rate crises in Scandinavia   The dress rehearsal for the ERM crisis was staged in Scandinavia. During the 1980s, the Nordic countries had adopted a system of unilateral target zones vis-à-vis the ECU, not only to import price stability from Germany but also to enhance the chances of their application for full EC membership. Previously, the weakness of the Finnish markka had already led to a devaluation by 12 percent on November 1991. On September 8, the Finnish central bank, out of reserves and unwilling to tolerate a further rise of short-term rates above their current 14 percent level, was forced to float the markka.

The Swedish reaction to the neighbor's crisis went in the opposite direction. Twice in a few hours, the Riksbank raised the marginal lending rate (charged by the central bank for overnight reserves) to 75 percent (at an annual rate). At the same time the Swedish central bank engaged in extensive borrowing from abroad, doubling the stock of official reserves. The speculative wave quickly moved southward and westward. Within the ERM, sterling and the lira approached the floors of their fluctuation zones. The Italian currency pierced its band a few days later, despite heavy official sales of D-marks.

Among the many issues raised by the Scandinavian crisis, two in particular captured the attention of the observers. First, after the collapse of the Finnish peg, the markka had depreciated against the D-mark by almost 13 percent, signalling the presence of a wide gap between official targets and market beliefs. A reasonable case could be made that such a sizable undervaluation of the German currency was unlikely to represent a local aberration, geographically restricted to the Northern periphery of Europe. The governments of the ERM countries could no longer dismiss out of hand the unpleasant possibility that, rather than representing a temporary by-product of the dollar "crash", the speculative tensions reflected the markets' assessment of a fundamental disequilibrium in intra-EC real exchange rates.

Second, if George Soros and his emulators were expecting a realignment within few weeks, and perhaps even just a few days, only a drastic rise in the relevant key interest rates could effectively limit the incentive to borrow weak currencies for speculative purposes, that is, for financing long positions in the D-mark and other currencies perceived as strong. The Swedish case was extremely instructive on this matter. Yet the monetary authorities in most ERM countries

27. Muehring (1992, p. 11).

seemed more likely to keep interest rates in or close to the politically safer one-digit range than to undertake Swedish-style cold turkey strategies, no matter how short-lived. The problem was particularly severe in the United Kingdom, where specific institutional characteristics (90 percent of home mortgages were at floating rather than fixed interest rates, a figure much higher than in the rest of the EC) enhanced the vulnerability of private sector wealth, income, and cash flow to swings in short-term rates. This correspondingly limited the credibility of the commitment of the Bank of England to the defense of sterling.

A proposal for a coordinated realignment By the end of the second week of September, the Bank of Italy and the Bundesbank were forced to acknowledge the unsustainability of the current parity of the lira. Apparently, a few days of strenuous defense of the Italian currency required interventions of 24 billion D-mark in Frankfurt and approximately 60 billion D-mark across Europe. It is striking that, in such a situation, there was no meeting either of the Monetary Committee or of Ministers and central bank governors. Nonetheless, because a devaluation of the lira was considered inevitable,[28] Germany and Italy prepared a proposal that included a 3.5% revaluation of the D-mark against all currencies in the ERM, plus a 3.5% devaluation of the lira (that is, a 7% devaluation of the lira against the D-mark). The Bundesbank would agree to cut interest rates, perhaps up to 100 basis points. Although the precise formula is not known, the magnitude of the interest rate cut was clearly meant to be a function of the number of currencies involved in the realignment (with special reference to the pound and the peseta), as well as of the magnitude of the realignment.

The scheme was ready on Sunday morning and supposedly communicated to officials in the other ERM countries, although British officials claimed that they were never asked to devalue the pound that day. According to other sources, Lamont refused to include the sterling in the realignment, hoping to buy time and benefit from a hoped-for pro-European result of the French referendum the week to follow. A flat refusal came also from the Spanish finance minister, who was on an official visit in Germany.

The realignment of the lira Ultimately, the Italian lira was the only currency to be devalued against the D-mark, by 7%, while the Bundesbank announced a decrease (for the first time in five years) in the key interest rates, apparently

---

28. In his 1978 letter to the Federal Government, Emminger had made clear that the Bundesbank was "starting from the premise that, if need be, the Government would safeguard the Bundesbank [from legal obligations toward other members of the EMS], either by a correction of the exchange rate or, if necessary, by discharging the Bundesbank from its intervention obligations" (quoted in Eichengreen and Wyplosz, 1993, p. 109). According to Kenen (1995), in September 1992 *"the Bundesbank invoked the Emminger letter and asked the German government to negotiate a devaluation of the lira"* (Kenen, 1995, p. 163).

as a quid pro quo for the Italian realignment. The exact magnitude of the cut was known only the day after: On September 14, the Bundesbank lowered the discount rate by 0.50 percent and the Lombard rate by 0.25 percent, down to 9.50 percent.

Puzzled reactions accompanied the announcement of these policy changes. Both changes went in the right direction; both were quantitatively inadequate. An ephemeral appreciation of sterling and, within its new band, of the lira followed. Outside the ERM, the Swedish central bank cut the marginal lending rate from 75 to 20 percent. Less than 24 hours later, the lira reached the bottom of its new band, this time joined by sterling. Market sales of sterling intensified, and any residual hesitation within the private financial sector faded away when the German business newspaper *Handelsblatt* issued a press release which opened as follows: The president of the Bundesbank, Helmut Schlesinger, does not rule out the possibility that, even after the realignment and the cut in German interest rates, one or two currencies could come under pressure before the French referendum.[29]

The loss of reserves for the Bank of England was reported to be around $15 billion, almost half the entire stock. Only slightly less dramatic was the fall of the peseta below its central ERM rate, the within-the-band target level defended by the Bank of Spain.

Black Wednesday   September 16, 1992, has been nicknamed Black Wednesday in England, out of respect for the wounded pride of the British monetary authorities. In the morning the Bank of England raised the minimum lending rate from 10 percent to 12 percent. A few hours later, a new increase to 15 percent was announced but never implemented. Sterling closed below its ERM floor in London. In the evening, the Bank of England announced the "temporary" withdrawal of sterling from the ERM. (A few days later, on September 19, return to the ERM was postponed indefinitely.) Later in the night of Black Wednesday, Italy followed Britain out of the ERM,[30] while the peseta was devalued by 5 percent but stayed within the ERM. Outside the ERM, energetically – and solitarily – leaning against the wind, the Swedish central bank pushed the marginal lending rate toward the spectacular level of 500 percent (at an annual rate).[31]

The day after, all currencies that had been under attack but had survived Black Wednesday were quoted near their ERM floors. The Bank of England

29. Quoted in Muehring (1992, p. 14).
30. Italy rejoined the ERM on November 25, 1996, at a central party at 990 lira to the D-mark.
31. It bears emphasizing that the interest differential (at an annual rate) required to offset an expected 13% depreciation of the currency over a month is about 147 percent, over a week it is about 636 percent, while over a single day it approaches 4,461 percent. Using continuously compounded rates, solve $e^{it} = 1.13$ using $t = 1/12$, $t = 1/52$, and $t = 1/365$ respectively.

validated ex post the expectations of the market by bringing the minimum lending rate back down to 10 percent.[32] The Bank of Ireland instead followed the Swedish recipe; overnight rates were raised to 300 percent (at an annual rate), on September 18.[33]

The French franc comes under attack   The French referendum on the Maastricht Treaty finally was decided in favor of the Treaty on September 20. Yet, as public opinion polls had anticipated already in late August, the victory of the *Oui* was far from overwhelming (only 51.1 percent of those voting were in favor), and, paradoxically, the speculative attacks against the French franc (together with the punt, peseta and escudo[34]) intensified in spite of the pro-Maastricht result. The two countries that had left the ERM did not show any inclination to return to the fold; on September 21, Italy announced that the lira was not bound to rejoin the ERM in the near future, and the day after England cut the minimum lending rate to 9 percent.

On September 23, an unsuccessful attack against the French franc was launched. Through the interventions undertaken to contain the speculative wave, the Bank of France suffered a loss in reserves of about Fr 80 billion[35] and raised the French repo rate up to 13 percent, while the Bundesbank intervened heavily in support of the French franc. Less evident strategies also may have contributed to the survival of the French franc. It was observed, for instance, that throughout the crisis implicit capital controls (leading to positive offshore–onshore interest differentials) and the implicit control of domestic lending rates by the Bank of France (signalled by sizable differentials between money-market and prime rates) helped mitigate the repercussions of the external financial crisis on the rest of the French economy.[36] In other words, it was argued that September '92 witnessed another episode in a long tradition of using "moral suasion", "jaw-boning", and "arm-twisting" as instruments for exercising informal pressure on financial market participants, complementing more market-based instruments of French monetary and credit policy. Formal

32. By cutting interest rates and permitting sterling to depreciate, the UK economy received a boost to internal and external demand that permitted it to recover quite swiftly from the deepest trough in economic activity since the Great Depression of the Thirties. Black Wednesday turned out to be good news for the real economy in the United Kingdom. The analogy with the British decision to go off the gold standard (in 1931), six years after the return (at an overvalued parity) to gold in 1925, is striking.

33. See also Temperton (1993).

34. Greece, the only EC country never to have joined the ERM, also encountered speculative pressures on the drachma in September 1992. The Bank of Greece raised the official lending rate from 30 to 40 percent, intervened heavily in support of the drachma, and tightened capital controls. This last measure was reversed again towards the end of 1992.

35. Since the speculative attack was unsuccessful, most of the reserves lost were back into France by the end of October, as participants in the attack commonly took positions for one month.

36. Marston (1995, pp. 133–135).

exchange controls were explicitly introduced by Spain on September 23 and on the day after by Ireland and Portugal.[37]

Reforms when the roof is caving in   In the following weeks, the quest for a tighter fiscal stance seemed to dominate the political debate in most ERM members affected by the exchange rate crisis.   In particular, Italy (at last) took concrete steps toward an ambitious project of economic reform, which hinged on containment of the budget deficit, privatization of state enterprises, and stabilization of the lira.   The emergency budget for 1993, approved by the cabinet on October 1 and presented to the Parliament three weeks later, involved spending cuts (including a freezing of salaries in the public sector) and tax increases for 1993 amounting to 5.8 percent of GDP.

Meanwhile, the Amato government applied for a special standby loan, worth several billion ECU, from its EC partners. By replenishing the Italian stock of official foreign exchange reserves, depleted by past interventions, the loan was believed to enhance both the likelihood and the credibility of a future re-entry of the lira into the ERM. Tighter fiscal policies were also announced in Portugal and Finland.

3.2.4   Last quarter of 1992

Tensions in the financial markets appeared to ease between October and November. Spanish capital controls were partially lifted on October 5. Key interest rates were adjusted downward: in Germany, the repo rate was trimmed by 15 basis points on October 21; the Italian discount rate was cut by 1 percent on October 23, down to 14 percent; the French repo rate was lowered by 2.5 percent, back to its September level of 10.5 percent.

This pattern was interrupted in the second half of November by a new financial crisis, once again originating in the North. On November 19, the Swedish Riksbank raised the marginal lending rate to 20 percent in yet another attempt to defend the krona against speculative pressures. This time, however, the defense was not pushed to its logical (and extreme) conclusion. Instead, after a few hours, the Swedish central bank decided to float the krona and lower its key rate to 12.5 percent.

The impact on the weaker ERM currencies was immediate. A few days later, on November 22, Spain and Portugal announced a devaluation by 6 percent of

37. This was not in violation of the letter of the Single Market legislation, which retained for member states the right to impose temporary capital controls in order to deal with disorderly exchange markets. It was, however, a further blow to the Maastricht timetable. (See Article 3 of the Protocol on the Convergence Criteria, quoted above). Presumably, the imposition of capital controls can reasonably be interpreted as prima facie evidence of "severe tensions". Spain removed its capital controls again in November 1992, after the second devaluation of the peseta, and Portugal followed suit soon after.

the central parities of the peseta and the escudo. To defend the punt, the third ERM currency under continuous siege, the Bank of Ireland raised its overnight rate to 100 percent (at an annual rate) between November 26 and December 2. On December 10, another Scandinavian currency capitulated: the Norwegian krona was allowed to float, and the Norwegian central bank was free to lower its overnight lending rate by 5 percentage points.

3.2.5   First quarter of 1993

Tension and relaxation kept alternating within the ERM during the first quarter of 1993. On January 4, the French franc was quoted once again near its ERM floor, leading the Bundesbank and the Bank of France to reiterate in a joint statement their willingness to cooperate to defend the French currency. The punt was still under pressure in early January, and its defense required yet another sizable jump in the Irish overnight rate. On January 30, the punt was devalued by 10 percent, despite the high interest rates maintained throughout the month.

Yet these events were perceived as inevitable by-products of the previous crisis, settling shocks rather than symptoms of a new major earthquake in the making. Other events seemed to signal that the financial markets had adjusted to the shocks of the previous months, and that what was left of the ERM was slowly but perceptibly moving toward some sort of workable normality. Plans to link German and French futures exchanges were announced in January. The Italian government dared to issue Eurobonds denominated in D-mark to the tune of 5 billion D-mark, the second-biggest international issue ever. In Denmark, the foreign minister of the new four-party coalition asserted that his priority was to secure a "Yes" vote in the new referendum on Maastricht. It was even possible for the Dutch central bank to reveal in the middle of January that during the crisis it had sold 400 tons of gold, equivalent to a quarter of its gold reserves and the largest official gold sale since the days of the "Gold Pool" under Bretton Woods, without noteworthy reactions on the gold market.[38]

Underlying the relative stillness of these months were widespread expectations of a cut in German interest rates. Such expectations were not unreasonable. An easing of the monetary stance would not appear to be a bad move for a country where industrial production had fallen by 6.7 percent from the previous year (January to January), where domestic engineering orders had declined by 24 percent in a year, and where total output (in the former West Germany) had fallen by 1 percent during the last two quarters of 1992 – while a further 2 percent contraction was anticipated for 1993. Also, monetary growth was slowing, and the inflation rate was expected to fall by at least one percentage point during the

---

38. There is no evidence that the guilder was ever under attack during the period 1992–93. The gold sales may have been a precautionary move to boost foreign exchange reserves.

year. Finally, there were threats of strikes by powerful trade unions and the persistent diplomatic pressures for lower interest rates coming from Washington.

A German interest rate cut eventually materialized on March 18, after the signing of the so-called solidarity pact, an agreement between the Länder and the federal government on how to share the financial burden of the reconstruction in the East. The cut of the German official discount rate by half a percentage point to 7.5 percent helped avert a new currency crisis that could have been triggered by the French general elections of March 28, swept by the neo-Gaullists. Influential elements of the new majority coalition were perceived as less instinctively pro-European than their socialist opponents; they certainly had less political capital invested in the continuation of the "franc fort" policy.

3.2.6 Second quarter of 1993

In April, several key interest rates were lowered, from the symbolic cut of the discount rate in Germany to 7.25 percent to more substantial adjustments of the French intervention and repo rates. Irish key rates, after no fewer than seven cuts in two months, reached a four-year low at 9 percent.

However, these optimistic signals were soon offset by a new outburst of speculative frenzy. On April 27, the peseta was quoted at its lowest level against the D-mark since Spain joined the ERM. The reduction in the German repo rate the day after, down to 7.75 percent, averted another devaluation of the Spanish currency. However, the realignment was simply postponed. The Bank of Spain could not resist protracted attacks, it was said, because the Spanish authorities were short of reserves (including access to credit lines and swaps) that could be used for spot market intervention. Its stock of foreign reserves had fallen to $15–20 billion by the end of April 1993, from a level of more than $50 billion at the end of 1992.

According to widespread rumors (officially denied), the Bank of Spain was pioneering a new strategy for defense of the exchange rate, based on large-scale sales of peseta put options at strike prices as low as 80 pesetas per D-mark. This strike price valued the peseta substantially below both its ERM floor value and the current forward price of the peseta.[39] The presumed logic of the operation was interpreted as follows. By providing market participants with the right to sell pesetas to the Spanish central bank or its agents[40] at some future date, the Spanish authorities were creating the means for the private sector to go long

39. See *The Economist*, May 1 1993, pp. 88–90.
40. The Bank of Spain usually intervenes on the markets through the Spanish association of savings Banks (CECA). In 1993, the CECA started selling large quantities of options, even though it was not normally active in that market. When the markets suspected that these sales were on behalf of the central bank, the option business of other Spanish banks – which had amounted to underlying levels of no more than DM10m–20m a day – were said to have jumped to ten times that amount. The Bank of Spain denied participating in this operation.

in the D-mark without immediate spot sales of pesetas. Actually, to the extent that market participants hedged their put options, they would have been likely to buy pesetas in the spot market.

Also, by selling options in vast amounts (up to Dm 1 billion daily) – the argument went – the Spanish central bank was providing the financial sector with a clear signal about its determination to defend the exchange rate parity and avoid a large capital loss. In fact, if the peseta were to crash and if its spot price in terms of D-marks were to fall below the strike price at the moment the options could be exercised, the central bank would be faced with the obligation to come up with large quantities of now expensive D-marks.[41]

Such turned out to be the case. Unorthodox strategies notwithstanding, the Bank of Spain was unable to resist the speculative selling waves against the peseta. On May 13, after a new series of heavy attacks against the peseta, the central bank abandoned the defense of the ERM band and asked for a new realignment, the third since the beginning of the crisis. The twin devaluation by 6.5 percent of the Portuguese escudo followed rapidly.

Good news for the ERM came from Denmark on May 18. In the second national referendum, the supporters of the Maastricht Treaty obtained a sound victory (gaining the support of 56.8 percent of those voting). This in turn removed the main obstacle to the process of ratification of the Treaty in Britain.

In the weeks following the Danish *Ja*, the stability of the ERM was hastily (and prematurely) interpreted as a return to the golden days of the late 1980s. The spectacular fall of French interest rates reached its climax on June 21, when the intervention rate was lowered to 7.00 percent, below its German counterpart (the German discount rate stood at 7.25 percent) for the first time in 26 years. Analogous albeit less heroic cuts by other European central banks led to substantial convergence of short-term European rates, despite the sizable gaps still existing for long-term yields.

The performance of French interest rates unleashed a wave of national pride in France and caused previously unheard questions to be raised throughout the EC. Was the D-mark still a suitable cornerstone for the ERM under present circumstances? What prevented the French franc from joining the German currency as a co-anchor of a revamped ERM? Did not economic fundamentals show that the time had come for a devaluation of the D-mark against the French currency? A peak (or nadir) of rhetoric was reached by commentators drawing parallels between the role of the United States in the collapse of Bretton Woods and the role of Germany within the ERM: Bretton Woods had collapsed when

41. There is a historical precedent. During the crisis leading up to the sterling devaluation of 1967, the UK government adopted the strategy of purchasing sterling in the forward market. After the devaluation, the British monetary authorities incurred a large capital loss through their commitments to provide foreign exchange at a price they (wrongly) believed would be equal to or less than the price that would prevail in the spot market at the date of maturity of the forward contracts.

Europe and Japan had refused to import American inflation; the ERM was bound to break up in the near future, whenever France decided to stop importing inflation from Germany.[42]

3.2.7   The August 1993 epilog

Such illusions and flights of fancy were short-lived. No later than mid July, the ERM was once again under pressure, following the now familiar pattern. The French franc was quoted slightly above its ERM floor, and for the first time after six weeks, French money market rates were again above their German counterparts. Tensions had built up in Denmark as well, forcing its central bank to raise a key interest rate. With the Bundesbank refusing to adjust its rates in the meeting of its Council on July 15 – the last before summer vacation – the point of no return was reached for the ERM.

A decision to raise the Danish discount rate even further did nothing to discourage the speculators. On July 30, almost all ERM currencies were quoted at the bottom of their bands against the D-mark, the only exceptions being the guilder and the punt. After an emergency weekend meeting in Brussels, a thorough revamping of the ERM was announced on August 1. Most of the surviving "hard" ERM was replaced by a much weaker scheme for exchange rate targeting, almost indistinguishable from a free float. The size of the bands was widened from 4.5 percent to 30 percent (15 percent on either side of the unaltered central parities). The sole exception was the exchange rate between D-mark and guilder, whose target zone remained unchanged. On August 3 and 4, the Bundesbank announced some minor cuts in German interest rates, thus appearing to confirm the opinion of *The Economist*, that the Bundesbank had been "inscrutable to the end".

3.2.8   Wider band, greater flexibility?

When the widening of the band was announced, financial markets seemed to act on expectations of aggressive cuts in interest rates by France and other low inflation countries that suffered from high unemployment rates and high cyclical deficits.[43] Virtually all currencies but the Dutch guilder depreciated within their wider bands. Before the end of 1993, the maximum depreciation from the central rate was as high as 6.95% for the Belgian franc, 8.93% for the

42. According to Jacques Mélitz, "toward the end of May, the French authorities embarked on an unsustainable course of aggressively pushing down their short-term interest rates without any genuine intention of abandoning the policy of the franc fort. They persistently tested the market's willingness to hold francs at equal and lower interest rates than those on marks. By implication, they were also pressuring the Bundesbank to reduce its own interest rates more quickly." (Mélitz, 1994, p. 61)

43. Quoting IMF publications, Kenen (1995) points out that expectations of rate cuts were held even in official quarters.

Danish krona, 5.7% for the French franc, 4.37% for the Irish pound, 4.94% for the Portuguese escudo, and 5.77% for the Spanish peseta.

Nonetheless, it was apparent that "markets ... misjudged the policy preferences of authorities in the countries involved" (Commission of the European Communities, 1994, p. 96). Domestic authorities looked at wider bands as a safeguard against speculation rather than using the additional room for domestic monetary expansion. As a result, by the end of 1993, most currencies were close to or even above their central rate. Yet, while de-facto moving their currencies back to the previous narrow bands, central bankers were not showing any interest in a de-jure restoration of the old system.

CHAPTER 4

Financial markets and ERM credibility

4.1   Capital market liberalization and "convergence plays"

The goal of this chapter is to complement the narrative of the 1992–93 events by focusing on the behavior of international financial markets. The recent literature has devoted considerable efforts to analyzing determinants and dynamics of ERM credibility as perceived by market participants and reflected in movements in asset prices as well as in the composition of financial portfolios. Section 4.1 presents a few relevant stylized facts characterizing European capital flows. Section 4.2 reviews the most common measures of ERM credibility. After discussing the performance of those measures, Section 4.3 addresses to what extent financial markets were able to anticipate the 1992–93 crises.

In the policy and academic debate, the coexistence of exchange rate stability and free capital mobility in Europe has long been regarded as problematic, if not impossible. In the late 1980s, many analysts shared a deep skepticism regarding the medium-term stability of the ERM. The process of liberalization, as traced in the European Council Directives 86/566 and 88/361, was expected to increase the vulnerability of weak currency countries to rapid capital outflows, thus raising the probability of a crisis.[1]

The emphasis on the disruptive potential of capital mobility is the straightforward corollary of the consensus view that attributed a key role to capital controls (most prominent in France and Italy) in maintaining exchange rate stability in Europe during the 1980s. The rationale for restricting capital mobility is often presented in terms of a simple application of a standard open-economy model à la Mundell-Fleming. Capital controls allow a country to maintain some degree of monetary autonomy, in spite of a commitment to exchange rate stability, by decoupling fluctuations in domestic interest rates from changes in world rates and/or expectations of currency depreciation. To the extent that monetary independence is desirable, and the constraint of Padoa-Schioppa's (1985) trio (or quartet) of inconsistent policies is binding,[2] capital mobility should be limited.

---

1. Among the contributions focusing on the implications of capital liberalization for the ERM, see Artis (1988), Basevi (1988), Wyplosz (1988), Begg et al. (1991).
2. The principle (derived within the Mundell-Fleming framework) states that fixed exchange rates, independent monetary policies, and free capital mobility are mutually inconsistent. A variant of the principle introduces free trade in the proposition.

Against this background, Begg and Wyplosz (1993) observe nevertheless that granting independence to national monetary authorities does not seem to have been the key function of capital controls in the context of the ERM. Instead, they were used rather effectively to dampen speculative pressures, thus keeping the frequency of realignments low:

> capital controls, always leaky over the long run, work during a crisis because they put a cap on the amount of assets that can be transferred per unit of time. They provide a breathing space to organize a realignment without ever abandoning the fixed exchange rate regime.[3]

In the same spirit, Giavazzi and Giovannini (1989) argue that capital controls helped avoid or delay realignments during periods of crisis in the system, most notably during episodes of dollar weakness, thus facilitating the process of inflation convergence.[4] The acknowledgment of the benefits from capital controls in terms of exchange rate stability, however, need not imply a positive assessment of their social desirability. Capital restrictions also distort financial decision making and therefore affect the efficiency of financial markets. Bini-Smaghi and Micossi (1990), for instance, provide evidence purporting to show that, in the experience of the ERM, microeconomic efficiency losses may have more than offset macroeconomic benefits. In addition, the threat of capital flight can be an effective deterrent to unsustainable or otherwise undesirable macroeconomic policies. By neutralizing this threat, capital controls can delay necessary policy corrections.

To many observers in the early 1990s – when most countries in the ERM had removed controls and barriers to the free circulation of capital – it came as a surprise that despite fuller and freer capital mobility, nominal exchange rates remained stable within the narrow zones of fluctuation established following the 1987 realignment. Anticipating large destabilizing capital flows, many had predicted a higher volatility of domestic interest rates. Such increase in volatility did not materialize; if anything, the volatility of onshore interest rates fell.

By and large, the empirical evidence seemed to support the alternative thesis, according to which capital liberalization was bound to stabilize the ERM, by reducing the perceived probability of realignments.[5] By the time of the Bath meeting (first week of September 1992), European capital controls were history, and the option of realignment was regarded as politically unmentionable.[6] Ironically, in the following weeks two currencies left the ERM and other currencies

---

3. Begg and Wyplosz (1993, p. 31).
4. "If high-inflation countries had been forced to realign as soon as higher-than-average inflation (combined with the rigidity of the nominal exchange rate) started hurting competitiveness, then the system would have been indistinguishable from a crawling peg: all discipline gains would have vanished." (Giavazzi and Giovannini, 1989, p. 197)
5. See for example Bodnar (1991), and Gros and Thygesen (1992).
6. See Chapter 9 below.

were devalued, while strict (albeit temporary) capital controls were reintroduced by several weak-currency countries.

The liberalization of the European financial markets led to substantial cross-border capital flows into higher-yielding ERM currencies. In the five years preceding the crisis, the capital account surplus of Italy moved from 11,721 to 26,583 billion liras, and the capital account surplus of Spain doubled from 1,418 to 3,229 billion pesetas.[7] Underlying these large portfolio reshuffles were two different sets of financial strategies. First, investors exploited new opportunities for cash-flow stabilization through international diversification and global risk-sharing. Second, international investors attempted to exploit intra-ERM interest differentials, betting on the stability of the exchange rate parities. Such strategies were referred to as "convergence plays."

Goldstein et al. (1993) argue that in the "hard ERM" many international investors and corporations were taking large open (speculative) positions, predicated on the assumption of a smooth progression towards increasing exchange rate stability. The argument can be summarized as follows. To hedge against fluctuations of the returns (in dollars) on long positions in high-yielding currencies, such as the lira, corporate investors and portfolio managers sold D-marks forward against the dollar, expecting to be able to sell liras and purchase the necessary D-marks on maturity, at a future spot price below the one implied by uncovered interest parity. That is, they sought to profit from a stability of the lira/D-mark parity that was greater than that implied by the current interest differentials.

An interesting piece of information can be derived from the Italian balance of payments in the first half of 1992, as discussed by Tabellini (1994). Over this period, there were widespread concerns about the fragility of the lira/ECU parity. Nonetheless, while domestic residents were responsible for a net capital outflow amounting to 30 trillion liras, banks and foreign institutional investors contributed to a large overall net inflow. Capital outflows of course intensified in the summer and turned into a full-blown speculative attack in the weeks preceding the crisis.

Why did we observe two-way capital flows: domestic resident investing in foreign currency–denominated assets, and institutional investors and financial institutions investing in lira-denominated assets? Tabellini (1994) argues that one feature of the new monetary regimes in the hard EMS helps shed light on this issue. As the market understood that the commitment to stable exchange rates was taken seriously by governments and central banks, realignments were expected to take place only in exceptional circumstances and when confronted with a very large speculative attack. As an attack required coordination among market participants, large financial companies felt that they would have an

7. Goldstein et al. (1993, Table 4, p. 9).

informational advantage enabling them to cover their position in time before a devaluation. Noninstitutional investors felt much less secure of being able to "jump ship" at the very last moment. They therefore started to sell Italian government bonds early on in the year.

4.2   Defining and measuring ERM credibility

Most assessments of ERM credibility rely on the analysis of interest differentials,[8] based on the following procedure introduced and popularized in a series of articles by Lars Svensson. Assuming that exchange rate risk premia are negligible,[9] the standard uncovered interest parity (UIP) condition states that interest differentials on similar assets with the same maturity must be equal to the expected rate of currency depreciation over the period

$$i_{t,M} - i^*_{t,M} = \frac{E_t s_{t+M} - s_t}{M} \tag{4.1}$$

where $i_{t,M}$ is the domestic interest rate at time t on an asset maturing at $t + M$, i^*_{t+M} is the corresponding rate on an asset denominated in the currency of the foreign country (say Germany), E_t is the expectation operator, and s_j is the logarithm of the spot exchange rate at time j. The exchange rate is defined in terms of local currency per unit of foreign currency. The average credibility of the government commitment to defend the existing parity can be assessed by verifying whether realized interest differentials are consistent with the maximum and minimum levels of the exchange rate allowed within the currency band. In other words, the currency band is on average credible between t and $t + M$ if

$$\frac{s^l - s}{M} < i_{t,M} - i^*_{t,M} < \frac{s^u - s}{M} \tag{4.2}$$

where s^l and s^u are respectively the floor and the ceiling of the currently defended currency band.[10] Similar measures of credibility can be derived from data on forward and futures markets.

Note that raw interest differentials measure the total expected rate of depreciation. This rate is the product of the expected jump in the exchange rate and the probability the market assigns to that jump. For instance, an expected depreciation of 5% may correspond to a 50% probability of a 10% realignment, as well as to a 10% probability of a 50% realignment.

8. See the survey in Marston (1995, ch. 5). On the credibility of the single ERM currencies, see Molho (1992) (Italy); Girardin and Marimoutou, 1992 (France); Geadah, Saavalainen, and Svensson (1992) (Denmark and other Nordic non-ERM countries); Masson (1995) (United Kingdom); Kremers (1990) (Ireland).
9. A discussion of the size of currency risk premia in the presence of a less than fully credible target zone is provided by Svensson (1992), who argues that real and nominal risk premia from devaluations are relatively small proportions of the interest rate differential.
10. See Svensson (1991).

Conceptually, we can distinguish between the expected rate of realignment of the central parity of the band and the expected rate of exchange rate appreciation or depreciation within the existing currency band. Let s^c denote the central parity and x the deviation of the current exchange rate from the central parity, that is, $x \equiv s - s^c$. Assuming that UIP holds, the interest differential can then be related to the expected changes in both variables as follows:

$$i_{t,M} - i^*_{t,M} = \frac{E_t \Delta s^c_{t+M}}{M} + \frac{E_t \Delta x_{t+M}}{M}. \tag{4.3}$$

Note that neither the expected change in the central parity $E_t \Delta s^c_{t+M}$ nor the expected change in the deviation from the central parity (the expected rate of depreciation within the band) $E_t \Delta x_{t+M}$ is directly observable, whereas the interest differential is. If one had a way of recovering an estimate of the expected rate of depreciation within the band from the data, one could subtract this estimate from the observed interest differential to obtain an estimate of the expected change in the central parity.

This procedure is known as the drift-adjustment of interest differentials (see Bertola and Svensson, 1993). The estimation of the expected rate of depreciation within the band – based on the standard model of target zones due to Krugman (1990), often "adjusted" to account for mean-reversion in exchange rate behavior – in principle requires (1) the solution of the exchange rate as a (nonlinear) function of the fundamentals, and (2) the prediction of the future values of the fundamentals over the relevant time horizon. In practice, various theoretical and econometric shortcuts are applied in order to come up with numerical estimates of the expected rate of depreciation within the band.

An alternative source of information on devaluation expectations is provided by the summary measures of exchange rate forecasts compiled by firms such as Consensus Economics of London or Money Market Services. Typically, these firms collect forecasts by financial institutions, multinational firms, and commercial forecasters at regular intervals. For instance, Consensus Economics has conducted a monthly survey since October 1989, asking participants to provide by fax three-month and one-year forecasts for several spot exchange rates expressed in terms of the US dollar. The means and standard deviations of the forecasts for each currency are published monthly.

The class of tests considered above assesses whether financial markets anticipate that future exchange rates will on average fall inside the band. A different class of tests, based on currency option contracts, can provide additional information on the probability distribution that financial markets use to form expectations of future exchange rates (see for example Dumas, Jennergren, and Näslund, 1993).

Using currency option prices, Campa and Chang (1996) estimate the "intensities of devaluation" (defined as the product of all possible realizations of the exchange rate outside the band multiplied by their probabilities) and build arbitrage-based tests that address the following question: Do financial markets attach any positive probability to the event that future exchange rates fall outside the band within a given time span? In other words, rather than testing credibility on average, they test the much stricter hypothesis of absolute (100%) credibility of the exchange rate band.

To illustrate the difference between these two procedures, consider the (admittedly unrealistic) case in which agents assign the same probability to either a revaluation or a devaluation of the central parity beyond the limits of the band. This situation is consistent with average credibility of the target zone; as the interest rate differential averages out deviations from the central parity on both sides, a Svensson-type test should not record any credibility problem. In principle, however, put and call option prices should reflect the expectations of exchange rate movements in either direction: Full credibility should be rejected by the arbitrage test based on option prices.

The tests develop from two restrictions that a perfect credibility of exchange rate imposes on currency option pricing. We will illustrate these restrictions by means of a simple example. Let the D-mark be the foreign currency and the lira the domestic currency, and consider a European-style call option on the D-mark with strike price K and maturity at $t + M$. Perfect credibility implies that the price of the call option per D-mark, $Call_{K,M}$, cannot exceed the present discounted value of the maximum profit compatible with the defense of the exchange rate band for the lira:

$$Call_{K,M} \leq \frac{S^u - K}{1 + i_{t,M}} \equiv U_{K,M}^{MAX} \tag{4.4}$$

where uppercase S denotes exchange rates in levels, as opposed to logs, and S^u is the upper edge of the currency band for the lira. $U_{K,M}^{MAX}$ is the maximum price for a D-mark call option within a credible lira band. Note that when $K = S^u$, it must be the case that $U_{S^u,M}^{MAX} = 0$.

The restriction above provides a first test of perfect credibility. This is illustrated in Figure 4.1, which shows the behavior of option prices (on the y-axis) as a function of strike exchange rates (on the x-axis) in a fully credible target zone. From (4.4), we know that a D-mark call option with $K = S^u$ should be worthless: $Call_{S^u,M} = U_{S^u,M}^{MAX} = 0$. From this point, we can draw the straight line $S^u D$ with slope $-(1 + i_{t,M})^{-1}$. The first option-based test of perfect credibility, Eq. (4.4), only restricts option prices to lie below the line $S^u D$, that is, not to fall in region II of the graph.

A second restriction follows from the property that the call option price is a convex decreasing function of the strike price. Intuitively, an increase by one lira in the strike exchange rate decreases the price of the D-mark call option by the full present discounted value of one lira, conditional on the option

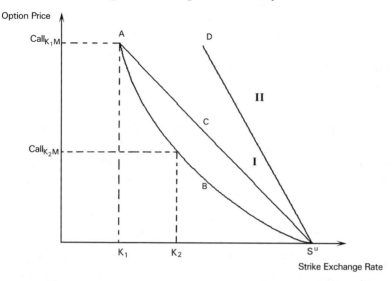

Figure 4.1. Tests of exchange rate credibility based on option prices.

finishing in-the-money, or by zero, conditional on the option finishing out-of-the-money.

Suppose that we can observe the prices of at least two D-mark call option contracts with the same maturity M but with different strike exchange rates K_1 and K_2, where $K_1 < K_2$. Consider the straight line joining the price of the first contract $Call_{K_1,M}$ with $Call_{S^u,M} = U_{S^u,M}^{MAX} = 0$, drawn in Figure 4.1 as the line $S^u CA$. Conditional on the exchange rate band being credible, (weak) convexity of the pricing function clearly requires that the price of the other option (with the higher strike price), $Call_{K_2,M}$, not lie above this line. In fact, starting from the point $U_{S^u,M}^{MAX} = 0$, for $K < S^u$, option prices draw some convex function in the space (the curve $S^u BA$ in Figure 4.1). While the degree of convexity depends on some (unknown) probability distribution of future exchange rates, linearity of this function is clearly the limiting case. If this is not the case, the price of the D-mark call option with strike price S^u, $Call_{S^u,M}$, cannot be zero; we can reject 100% credibility of the upper band threshold S^u. The second (strong) test is therefore:

$$Call_{K_2,M} \leq \frac{Call_{K_1,M}}{S^u - K_1}(S^u - K_2), \quad K_1 < K_2. \tag{4.5}$$

Implementing such a test requires data on two otherwise identical options with different strike prices. When only one data point is available, the same procedure could still be applied by estimating the price of a second call option as follows. Consider a contract with strike price equal to the lower threshold of the band, with price $Call_{S^l,M}$. Under the maintained assumption that S^l is perfectly credible, this option will be exercised with probability one. In this case, the expected payoff of such an option is equal to the difference between the expected future exchange rate, $E_t S_{t+M}$, and the strike exchange rate S^l.

The price $Call_{S^l,M} = (E_t S_{t+M} - S^l)/(1+i_{t,M})$ can then be calculated by using the forward rate, denoted F_{t+M}, as an estimate of the expected future exchange rate $E_t S_{t+M}$. Option prices consistent with full credibility of the band now trace a convex function joining the two endpoints, $(F_{t+M} - S^l)/(1 + i_{t,M})$ and 0. As before, under full credibility, option prices can never lie above the straight line between these two endpoints. Such restriction provides us with a more flexible version of the second test of credibility:

$$Call_{K,M} \leq \frac{\left(F_{t+M} - S^l\right)}{(1 + i_{t,M})} \frac{(S^u - K)}{(S^u - S^l)} \equiv U_{K,M}^{MIN}. \tag{4.6}$$

By comparing $U_{K,M}^{MAX}$ with $U_{K,M}^{MIN}$, the second test is clearly stricter than the first one. Any observation falling between the $S^u CA$ line identified by (4.5) or (4.6) and the line $S^u D$ identified by (4.4) – that is, region I in the graph – would not reject 100% credibility according to the first test, but it would reject it according to the second test.

4.3   Exchange rate expectations before the crisis

4.3.1   Statistical analysis of credibility

In the literature, the different measures of ERM credibility have been related to sets of more or less plausible determinants of private sector expectations using statistical or econometric techniques. Among the variables included in the analysis as predictors of future exchange rates, we typically find money, output, inflation, unemployment, international reserves, trade balances, real exchange rates, measures of fiscal deficits, and dummies to account for structural breaks (realignments) and for country- or period-specific institutional features. In some cases, the time interval since the last realignment is included among the explanatory factors as a proxy for government reputation.

Using several econometric specifications of credibility models, Rose and Svensson (1994) conclude that there are few significant channels of macroeconomic influence on realignment expectations, with the potential exception of inflation differentials.[11] In Chen and Giovannini (1994), both the deviation of the exchange rate from the central parity and the time interval since the last realignment are significant factors increasing credibility. The first variable is

11. For an earlier related analysis see Collins (1988).

evidence for mean-reversion within the band,[12] and the second variable is offered as a proxy for the central bank's reputation as a defender of the parity – the absence of realignments improves the central bank's reputation over time, because this absence is viewed as evidence of the (unobservable) underlying objectives and motivation of the monetary authority.

Mean-reversion within the band is a well-documented phenomenon (see Svensson, 1993, among others). The empirical assessment of reputation effects is the subject of an ongoing debate. The question is whether a decision by the government not to realign the parity this period, despite the occurrence of an unfavorable shock to the economy, reduces or increases the likelihood of a future realignment.

Drazen and Masson (1994), for example, point out that the government, on the one hand, by choosing not to realign this period, reveals itself as tougher on inflation than had been expected previously. This is the reputation channel and *ceteris paribus* it makes a future realignment less likely. On the other hand, when adverse shocks have persistent negative effects, the absence of a realignment this period could make a future realignment more likely if the current failure of the government to realign weakens its ability to withstand pressures for future realignment, say through a cumulative worsening of competitiveness or unemployment.[13] Even if the government has acquired a strong reputation as inflation fighter, the cumulative effects of tough policies in the past may make the exchange rate regime increasingly fragile over time. This is the case, for example, if there is hysteresis in unemployment.

4.3.2   Credibility is mostly joint in the ERM

What do we know about the performance of the ERM credibility measures presented in the previous section? An interesting stylized fact established by the empirical analysis of credibility is that bilateral interest differentials vis-à-vis Germany tend to be very strongly correlated across EU member countries. In Figures 4.2, 4.3, and 4.4 we plot three-month interest differentials against the D-mark for each ERM currency and other non-ERM currencies – including the US dollar for the sake of comparison – during the periods 1979–1983, 1984–1987, and 1988–1991 respectively[14]; vertical spikes corresponds to realignment dates. The figures show that for many countries expectations of devaluations were recurrently high through the EMS sample period (on a few occasions we can detect expectations of a D-mark devaluation). Note that there are instances

---

12. Rose and Svensson (1994) document the same empirical regularities in estimating their drift-adjusted measures of realignment expectations.
13. See also Chapter 5 below.
14. We use daily three-month Euromarket bid-rates, quoted at 10 a.m. Swiss time. Source: BIS.

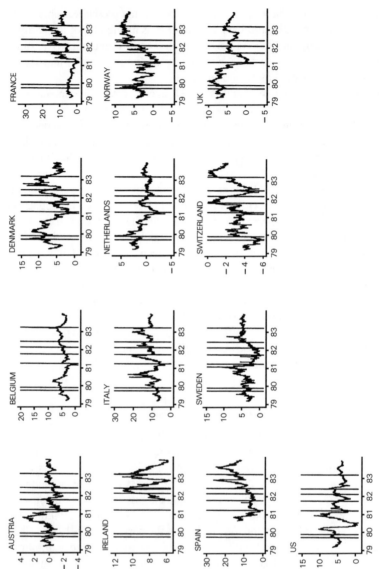

Figure 4.2. 3-month interest differentials against Germany, 1979–83.

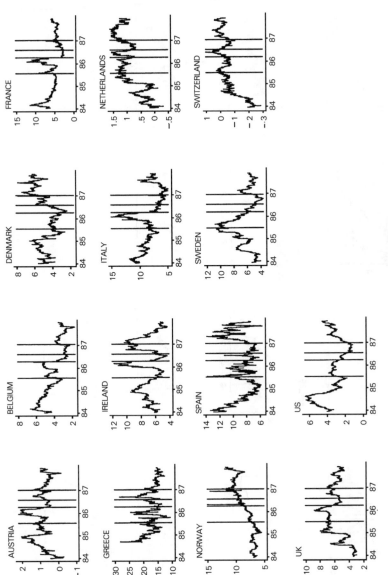

Figure 4.3. 3-month interest differentials against Germany, 1984–87.

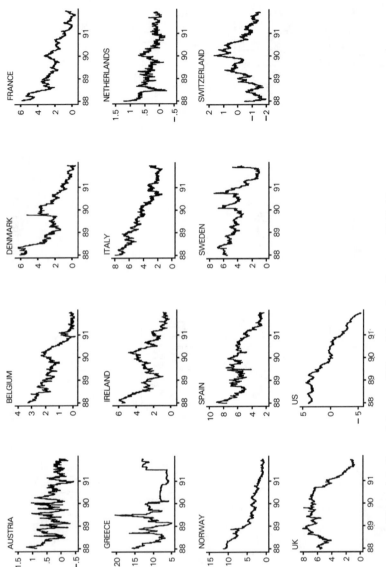

Figure 4.4. 3-month interest differentials against Germany, 1988–91.

when a realignment came as a surprise to financial markets, and other instances where firm expectations of a devaluation were not validated ex post by the policy makers.

Although ERM credibility is highly variable over time, many movements of the interest differentials appear to be common in sign and to a lesser extent in magnitude across currencies. This is prima facie evidence of a systemic common component driving EMS-wide expectations. Also, there is a clear downward trend (i.e., increasing credibility) since 1987.

Rose and Svensson (1994) provide both simple measures of contemporaneous correlations – all positive and highly statistically significant[15] – and principal component or factor analysis estimates applied to their drift-adjusted measures of credibility. As many movements in this measure can be explained with a single factor, they conclude that a large component of ERM credibility is in fact joint to the system. The systemic or common nature of devaluation expectations across currencies is an important empirical feature of the EMS, and one that has to be taken seriously in any thorough theoretical and empirical analysis of the events of the period.[16]

4.3.3   To what extent did private market anticipate the crisis?

The picture we have painted in the previous section refers to the whole EMS sample period from 1979 to 1992. We now turn to the analysis of the ERM credibility in the subsample from January 1992 to the crisis in September 1992.

Figure 4.5 provides a set of graphs plotting the interest rate differentials on three-month Eurocurrency deposits. Vertical spikes correspond to the Monday following the first Danish referendum and to Black Wednesday. Three features stand out. First, for all countries other than Portugal, there is evidence of stable or improving credibility before the first Danish referendum, followed by a slight worsening of credibility after the referendum. In the case of Italy, it is easy to spot the effect of the special tax on deposits, announced on July 6 and soon followed by the international financial difficulties of the State-owned enterprise EFIM. The July crisis, however, seems to be more than offset by the agreement on labor costs reached at the end of that month.

By late August, there is evidence that the financial markets were expecting a generalized revaluation of the D-mark. Interest differentials were high in Italy, Spain, and Portugal, and positive but low in the United Kingdom, Ireland, and Denmark. French differentials were lower than 1%. Rose and Svensson

---

15. The lowest correlation coefficient is equal to 0.6.
16. In this respect, De Grauwe (1994) addresses the empirical assessment of credibility by taking cross-country averages of interest differentials vis-à-vis Germany as well as of macroeconomic variables. He forcefully argues that, in addition to inflation differentials, unemployment is indeed an important determinant of credibility.

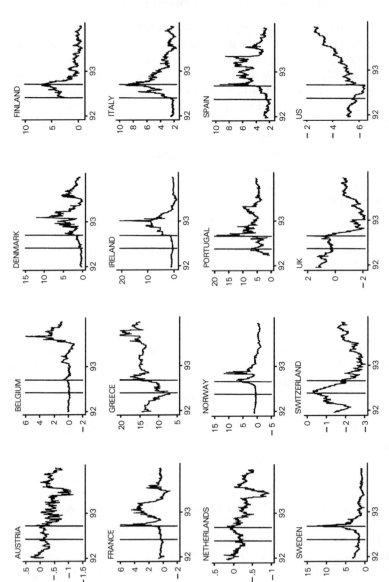

Figure 4.5. 3-month interest differentials against Germany, 1992–93.

(1994) report that the behavior of their one-month common (in)credibility factor rose on the 25th of August, the date when the first polls regarding the French referendum on Maastricht were released, but also the date of a historic low of the dollar against the D-mark. The increase in the value of the common factor was modest but persistent through the Italian devaluation on September 14, up to Black Wednesday. Nonetheless, compared to previous realignment episodes, its level was not unusually high.

A similar but more accurate picture can be derived from the Campa and Chang (1996) measures of "realignment intensity" and from tests for absolute credibility based on currency option prices. Using data on three- and six-month option prices, the tests are unable to reject 100% credibility of the pound–mark exchange rate band before early August 1992, that is, up to a few weeks before the withdrawal of this currency from the ERM. Yet, at the time, the realignment intensity for the sterling pound remained in the neighborhood of 3 to 4% over a six-month horizon. This implies that only a 25% probability would have been attributed to the actual 16% depreciation that the pound suffered in the subsequent six months.

In the case of the French franc, full credibility is rejected between late August through mid October 1992, as well as between late November 1992 and early April 1993. Nonetheless, the realignment intensity never reached 2%. As regards the lira–mark exchange rate band, applying (4.4) to six-month option data shows that the band lacked credibility as early as November 1991; however, three-month option data reject full credibility only in early June 1992. It is somehow surprising to learn that the lira did not exceed a realignment intensity of 2.5% prior to its exit from the system.

Average exchange rate forecasts are even more conservative. Figure 4.6 plots the average forecasts for the lira, the French franc, and the pound against the D-mark.[17] The mean forecast shows no expectations of devaluation for either the lira or the pound. Kenen, Mercurio, and Pesenti (1996) observe that for the ERM currencies before September 1992, the cross-sectional variance of forecasts against the dollar (an indicator of heterogeneity of beliefs in the currency market) could have been substantially independent of the forecast variance for the D-mark vis-à-vis the dollar only to the extent that forecasters were predicting a realignment within the EMS. When this hypothesis is tested, they find that the coefficient of variation of the forecasts for the D-mark is a strongly significant regressor for the coefficient of variation of the ERM currencies (especially lira and French franc), providing further evidence against the anticipation of a large-scale crisis.

---

17. These intra-ERM average forecasts are obtained by taking the ratios between average forecasts against the dollar. Source: Consensus Economics.

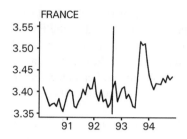
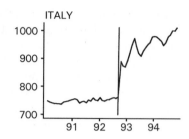

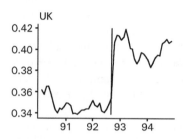

Figure 4.6. 3-month exchange rate forecasts against the D-mark, 1990–94.

4.3.4   *Summing up the evidence*

We conclude this section on ERM credibility by restating the three main conclusions. Regarding the whole EMS sample period, first, most movements in
credibility are common across ERM members. In determining the strength and
viability of the exchange rate regime, domestic factors therefore interact with
some common shock(s) at the union-wide level.

Second, perhaps unsurprisingly, there is little or no evidence of correlation
between measures of credibility and current and lagged values of macroeconomic variables. The only exception is that inflation differentials tend to predict
interest differentials.

Third, focusing the analysis on 1992, ERM credibility increases on average in
the first five months of the year and decreases slightly following the Danish referendum. It also seems to be affected by the behavior of the US effective exchange
rate, with a depreciation of the dollar being associated with a strengthening of
the D-mark within the ERM. By late August, the available evidence suggests
that financial markets were expecting a generalized revaluation of the D-mark,
by a magnitude that was variable across countries (Italy, Spain, and Portugal
show the highest interest differentials), modest overall, and significantly smaller
than the magnitudes of the depreciations that were actually realized. In this
sense, the events of mid-September included an important element of surprise.

CHAPTER 5

Modelling currency crises

5.1   Exchange rate crises and speculative attacks

In the aftermath of the 1992–93 events, there has been a revival of academic interest in analyzing and modelling the timing and determinants of currency crises and speculative attacks on fixed exchange rate regimes. Many recent contributions offer valuable elements for an interpretation of the logic of the ERM crisis. Informed by the historical reconstruction presented in the previous chapters, we now provide a synthetic survey of the current literature. This also lays the groundwork for our own theoretical construction in Chapters 6, 7, and 8.

5.1.1   Exogenous and endogenous policies

There exist two approaches to modelling exchange rate crises. The first approach, pioneered by Krugman (1979),[1] focuses on the timing and the mechanics of a speculative attack when national authorities pursue policies that are inconsistent with the indefinite defense of the exchange rate parity.[2] The second approach looks at optimizing policymakers who are assumed to have good reasons to peg the currency – for example, because a peg is seen as a commitment technology for reducing the undesirable consequences of an inflationary bias – but not at any price.[3] They may, therefore, find it optimal to abandon the exchange rate parity under certain circumstances. Throughout this chapter, we will label the two modelling strategies as, respectively, the "exogenous-policy" and the "endogenous-policy" approach.[4]

In Krugman's model, domestic credit expansion persistently exceeds the growth of money demand at a fixed exchange rate. When coupled with an exogenous lower bound on international reserves (and the assumption that even a solvent government cannot borrow infinite amounts of reserves), a "natural" collapse would finish off the fixed exchange rate regime even if speculative

---

1. See also, among others, Salant and Henderson (1978) and Flood and Garber (1983, 1984).
2. Surveys of models of exchange rate crises especially focused on the Krugman approach are provided by Agénor, Flood, and Bandhari (1992); Blackburn and Sola (1993); and Garber and Svensson (1995).
3. See for example Flood, Bhandari, and Horne (1989); Obstfeld (1991, 1994); DeKock and Grilli (1993); and Ozkan and Sutherland (1994a,b).
4. For a comparative analysis of the two approaches, see Cavallari and Corsetti (1996).

attacks were not feasible. Adding perfect international capital mobility, a weak no-arbitrage condition and interest-sensitive money demand provides a simple framework to describe the dynamics of a collapse brought about by a rational speculative attack.[5]

The exact timing of an exchange rate crisis, however, may not be determinate if, as suggested by Obstfeld (1986), policies are inconsistent with a pegged exchange rate only conditional on a successful speculative attack having occurred. Consider markets in which agents are atomistic (have small net worth, are credit-constrained, and do not collude), so that no single speculator can drive international reserves to their minimum threshold level by herself. Then, no one will attack the currency unless she expects that a sufficient number of other agents will do so at the same time.[6] In this case, the timing – and indeed the occurrence – of a speculative attack becomes indeterminate, since it depends on strategic uncertainty regarding the coordination of the private sector on one particular regime of expectations. In every period during which the fixed exchange rate regime has not yet collapsed, two instantaneous equilibria are possible, one characterized by a run on international reserves leading to an exchange rate crisis and collapse of the parity, and another one in which no attack occurs and the peg survives.

According to the endogenous-policy approach, the exchange rate "crisis" is the implementation of a contingent rule that combines two monetary policy regimes. In the first regime, domestic credit is consistent with the defense of the announced parity; in the second, monetary policy optimally responds to fundamentals. Each period, the policy maker considers the costs and benefits of maintaining the peg for another period and rationally decides whether or not to abandon the parity (to exercise her escape clause). In contrast to the exogenous-policy approach, an exchange crisis is associated with the availability of reserves – or, more generally, with the feasibility of the peg that is being tested by the international financial markets – only to the extent that such factors affect the costs and benefits of alternative monetary policies.

Since the commitment to defend the announced parity is only imperfectly credible, the expectations game between the private and the public sector may once again generate multiple instantaneous equilibria. Typically, as we discuss in Chapter 7, there will exist one equilibrium in which private agents coordinate their expectations on low nominal wages and nominal interest rates, while (at

5. If for any reason, even a reason totally unrelated to fundamentals of the economy (say, because of a rational speculative bubble or because of the presence of noise-traders and bandwagon effects), the international financial markets believe that the current nominal parity is not appropriate, a regime of unrestricted capital mobility becomes the perfect stage for a central bank solo on financial suicide. The Krugman model stresses the destabilizing effects of constraints on the ability of the central bank to borrow reserves. These effects are stronger when these limits are known by the private sector.

6. See the discussion in Grilli (1986).

least) one other equilibrium is characterized by high nominal wages and interest rates. The chances that the currently pegged exchange rate parity is maintained during the period are high in the first equilibrium and low in the second one. Theory has little to say about the mechanism that coordinates the private sector's expectations, so a speculative wave undermining the viability of the peg can be envisaged as a sudden (exogenous) switch from one regime of expectations to the other. Therefore, the occurrence and the exact timing of an exchange rate crisis is indeterminate in the second approach, too.

5.1.2   The role of official reserves

In Krugman (1979), an exchange rate crisis coincides with a speculative attack on the international reserves of the Central bank. The discrete jump in reserves that is necessary to rule out arbitrage opportunities in the exchange market is determined by a timely drop in the demand for money in anticipation of a positive rate of currency depreciation after the crisis. Thus, for a speculative attack to occur, money demand must be interest sensitive. However, if exchange rate crises are seen as rational responses to the "excessive" welfare costs of defending a peg, it is certainly possible that such crises may occur in the absence of a speculative attack on international reserves, that is, regardless of the interest sensitivity of the demand for money. Reserve losses preceding a crisis also are certainly possible (and likely) in the framework of Obstfeld (1994), appropriately amended so as to include a monetary dimension.[7] But reserve losses per se would not (or need not) play any causal role in determining the timing of the abandonment of the peg and the magnitude of the subsequent change in the exchange rate.

Note that if there were no borrowing constraints on foreign reserves, an unconditional defense of a fixed exchange rate would always be feasible technically. After all, the exchange rate is the price of one currency in terms of another, so in principle the price of any weak currency could be sustained by sharply reducing its quantity either through repeated sale of borrowed foreign reserves or the contraction of domestic credit. What is relevant for the stability of the exchange rate here is not the technical feasibility of such a tough course of action, but rather its perceived costs.[8]

7. See Cavallari and Corsetti (1996).
8. As Maurice Obstfeld and Ken Rogoff (1995) write,

> A central banker absolutely determined to maintain its exchange rate has the technical ability to do so.... By reducing the domestic high-powered money supply sufficiently – something that is normally entirely within a central bank's power – it can prevent its currency from depreciating.... That defense of a currency is technically possible does not mean it is easy or painless. Sharp reductions in the monetary base can lead to dramatic interest rate increases which, if sustained, can have devastating effects on the economy. These effects occur, of course, because of nominal rigidities.... It is because the authorities care about the side-effects of drastic monetary tightening that speculators can prevail.

In reality, of course, there are limits to the amount of international reserves that even the most virtuous government committed to the defense of the exchange rate parity can borrow. This is most easily seen by considering the case where additional international reserves are bought with funds obtained through "domestic credit contraction" rather than being borrowed directly, that is, by issuing additional government debt. If the government can borrow only by issuing interest-bearing claims (bonds) denominated in its own currency, the counterparty to this deal exposes herself to exchange rate (devaluation) risk. Unless the commitment of the borrowing government to defend the parity at all cost is fully credible, the potential purchaser of the government debt will become increasingly reluctant to part with international reserves, recognizing that the attractiveness of a devaluation to the borrowing government increases with the amount of domestic currency debt that is outstanding.

This problem would be avoided if the government wishing to acquire additional international reserves were to issue foreign currency–denominated bonds. If outright repudiation is ruled out, this would remove the borrowing constraint as long as the interest rate on international reserves is at least as high as the interest rate on the debt issued to finance their acquisition. If the interest rate on reserves is lower than the interest rate on the domestic debt, the government's solvency constraint would be adversely affected by an acquisition of reserves financed by borrowing. In this case there would be an upper bound on the amount of reserves that can be acquired. A foreign exchange crisis, with the government running out of reserves and being forced to abandon the peg, would again be a possibility. Note that in this case, a foreign exchange crisis would always be a fiscal or solvency crisis, rather than just an international liquidity crisis.[9]

If there are limits on the amount of international reserves that can be borrowed or acquired in other ways, one could envisage a unifying model in which the exchange rate peg is abandoned for one of two reasons. Either reserves have not yet run out and the government optimally chooses to abandon the peg (the voluntary collapse), or reserves have run out and the government is forced to abandon the peg (the involuntary collapse). If additional reserves can always be acquired but only at increasing marginal cost, the distinction between the voluntary and the involuntary collapse would vanish. The government would decide whether or not to stick to the peg by balancing the sunk cost of abandoning the peg against both its short-run price and employment objectives and the additional cost of securing the reserves required to maintain the peg. With a reserve-constrained government, the international financial markets clearly can play a much more active role in bringing down a fixed exchange rate regime than is allowed for in the models of the endogenous policy approach described above.

9. See Buiter (1986, 1987, 1989).

Table 5.1. *Classification scheme for existing literature on exchange rate crises.*

	Type of approach	
	Exogenous policy	Endogenous policy
Policy objectives		
Output stabilization	Willman, 1988	Obstfeld, 1994, model 3.2 This book, Chapter 7
Fiscal stabilization	Krugman, 1979 Flood and Garber, 1984	Obstfeld, 1994, model 3.1 DeKock and Grilli, 1993
Spillovers		
Unilateral peg model	All of the above	All of the above
Systemic model	Gerlach and Smets, 1994	This book, Chapter 8

5.1.3   A classification scheme

These considerations can be used to build a classification scheme that helps us to relate our contribution to the existing literature on exchange rate crises. Such a scheme has three dimensions. The first dimension refers to what broad approach the contribution is following, that is, whether policy rules are derived from policy preferences or simply posited by assumption. The second dimension is on what policy objectives the model is focusing (fiscal stabilization, output stabilization, etc.). The first and second dimensions together characterize the ongoing expectations game between the domestic policy maker and the private sector. The third dimension consists of the specification of the ongoing international policy game. In most models of exchange rate crises, the international setting is taken as given. As shown in this book, a relevant alternative focuses on Center–Periphery structural spillovers and on strategic interactions among the national authorities in the exchange rate system.

Table 5.1 presents our classification scheme in a compact way, providing for each cell a few examples of contributions fitting the particular characteristics under consideration. Note that the scheme does not include uniqueness versus multiplicity of equilibria as a classification category. Examples of models with multiple instantaneous equilibria are indeed possible for each cell in the scheme.

We have discussed the first (exogenous–endogenous) dimension at length in the previous section. Regarding the second dimension (policy objectives), although the literature presents a variety of model specifications, it is possible to classify most contributions depending on whether they focus on "output and inflation stabilization" or on "public debt stabilization". Willman (1988) and Obstfeld (1994, Section 3.2) provide examples of the first approach. The well-known model of Krugman (1979) can be interpreted as belonging to the second group, insofar as the excessive rate of domestic credit creation is attributed to the need to finance persistent government budget deficits. The "output and inflation stabilization" approach will be thoroughly discussed in Chapters 6 through 8 below. Nonetheless, it is worth stressing that the main results could also be derived by specifying a debt-stabilization game. We elaborate on this below.

Models of exchange rate crises and debt stabilization typically draw on the theory of tax smoothing developed by Barro (1979) and extended to include an (unanticipated) inflation tax by Mankiw (1987). The basic version of this model is as follows. Given both a positive stock of outstanding nominally denominated interest-bearing public debt and an exogenous path of public spending on goods and services, the public sector can raise revenue through conventional distortionary taxation or through an unexpected burst of inflation. The unanticipated inflation tax acts as a capital levy on the stock of nominally denominated interest-bearing debt[10] and is therefore nondistortionary.[11] The social loss is assumed to be decreasing in the unanticipated rate of inflation and increasing in both the conventional distortionary tax rate, which can be interpreted as the (average marginal) income tax rate, and the realized rate of inflation.[12]

As is well known, the tax smoothing principle states that a permanent increase in spending (or even a temporary increase in spending, to the extent that it affects the periodized permanent spending flow) should be met by a permanent increase in all tax rates by a magnitude that is inversely related to the marginal social disutility from their use. A problem with using the unanticipated inflation tax is that, while unanticipated or surprise inflation extracts fiscal revenue from the holders of the government's nominally denominated interest-bearing debt, social welfare is assumed to be reduced by the realized rate of inflation. With rational expectations, and in the absence of a commitment technology that allows the public sector to target price stability in a credible way, the time-consistent expected inflation rate is high enough to prevent policy makers from yielding to the temptation to resort to a surprise monetization of the public debt. Without credible precommitment, discretionary fiscal and monetary policy generates the social inefficiency familiar from the literature on the time inconsistency of optimal policies.

To the extent that it is credible, a peg of the currency increases social welfare through its effect on the expected rate of inflation. Nonetheless, in a stochastic

---

10. Unanticipated inflation of course also imposes (like anticipated inflation) a capital levy on noninterest-bearing money balances.

11. The government actually also appropriates resources through seigniorage which is approximately equal to the anticipated inflation tax on its non-interest-bearing monetary liabilities, but this is played down or ignored in the models just mentioned. The optimal use of the anticipated inflation tax is discussed in Chapter 10.

12. It would also be increasing in the anticipated rate of inflation if the distortionary effect of anticipated inflation on the demand for money were properly allowed for.

environment, there could be circumstances in which a low level of inflation may turn out to be suboptimal. Specifically, exchange rate crises occur when particular contingencies make the social cost of raising explicit tax rates higher than the social cost of reverting to time-consistent inflation, net of the social benefits from raising current revenue through a surprise burst of inflation. Variations on this model underlie the contributions of Obstfeld (1994, model 3.1) and DeKock and Grilli (1993), among others.

The third dimension of our classification scheme consists of the set of hypotheses about the characterization of the international economy as a system. The vast majority of models focus on a "unilateral peg" policy pursued by a small open economy. A few contributions use a two-country model with a Center and a representative Periphery country and analyze strategic interaction between the two central banks. An exception is Gerlach and Smets (1994), which extends the analysis of Flood and Garber (1984) to show that a speculative attack against one currency may accelerate the "warranted" collapse of a second parity because of international spillover effects on competitiveness. Yet they do not allow for strategic interactions among policy makers. In the model we introduce in Chapter 6, we argue that explicit recognition of both structural international spillovers and international strategic interactions (that is, the "systemic" aspects of the exchange rate regime) is essential for understanding the collapse of an exchange rate system like the ERM.

5.2   Fundamental models of the ERM crisis

Motivated by our classification scheme, we briefly review in this section a few representative models of the 1992–93 financial crisis that emphasize the role of macroeconomic fundamentals. We discuss three models, each focussed on a specific fundamental factor: the German reunification shock (an external shock to the other ERM countries), the high unemployment and lost competitiveness attributed to five years of disinflation policies in some of the Periphery countries, and contagion (or "domino") effects due to international policy spillovers. Because these contributions have shed light on different important sources of exchange rate tension leading to the crisis, we will return to them in Chapter 7. There we will reinterpret each model within our analytical framework and address issues that have not been adequately analyzed by the literature. Chapter 7 will also include a discussion of multiple equilibria and self-fulfilling speculative attacks.

5.2.1   The role of shocks in the Center

The role of the post-unification German policy mix, held responsible for exporting a regime of high interest rates throughout Europe, is the main factor determining the probability of an exchange rate crisis in the model of Ozkan and Sutherland (1994b), a unilateral-peg, output-stabilization, endogenous-policy model according to our taxonomy. These authors abstract from domestic sources of imbalances in the period preceding the crisis; there are neither excessive deficits nor domestic credit expansion inconsistent with the indefinite survival of the peg. In their model, prices are fixed in both the short and the long run, regardless of the behavior of the exchange rate; output is demand determined, while aggregate demand is a negative function of both the interest rate[13] and the exchange rate.[14]

The source of uncertainty in the domestic economy is external, since it depends on shocks hitting the foreign interest rate. Exchange rate crises occur because the recessionary implications of a high foreign interest rate can be offset through a devaluation that increases output by boosting international competitiveness. Consider a series of permanent shocks to the foreign interest rate that lower domestic aggregate demand and employment via their effect on the whole spectrum of domestic interest rates. As emphasized in the literature on irreversible investment,[15] a simple static rule (such as "resort to a devaluation when the current welfare cost of adhering to the peg exceeds the current social value of remaining in the ERM forever; keep the peg otherwise") may not be optimal because it does not explicitly allow for the possibility (the option) of making a switch between exchange rate regimes in the future. Once this possibility is properly taken into account, the optimal rule depends on the probability that the foreign interest rate will revert to a lower level in a sufficiently short period of time.

Depending on this probability, it may be optimal to postpone the switch to a free float. Uncertainty therefore makes for "hysteresis" in policy making. With rational expectations, however, private agents will incorporate such a policy rule in their information sets and build expectations of a regime shift into interest rate differentials. The behavior of private agents trying rationally to anticipate the timing of a collapse will tend bring the collapse forward in time, running counter to the effects of hysteresis in policy making.

5.2.2   Shock persistence and the cumulative costs of a peg

The role of costs that policy makers have incurred in the past in order to build up the credibility of their disinflation policy is explored by Drazen and Masson (1994), who assume that shocks to unemployment are persistent over time.

---

13. Specifically, the argument in the demand function is a weighted average of nominal interest rates at different maturities. Through such a specification, the authors are able to relate the term structure of interest rate, derived under the expectation hypothesis, to the level of the aggregate demand.

14. With inflation expectations fixed, nominal and real interest rates are the same. With domestic and foreign price levels fixed, the nominal exchange rate equals the real exchange rate.

15. For a textbook reference see Dixit and Pindyck (1994).

Consider a social welfare function that is decreasing in both inflation and unemployment. Add asymmetric information about the true attitude of the policy makers towards inflation (its "type"). If a negative shock to unemployment hits the economy in the current period, a government that maintains the peg – in the face of high and rising unemployment – signals to the private sector its determination to pursue its pre-announced policy, and thus enhances its credibility (i.e., the perception by the private sector of the likelihood that its type is of the "truly-tough-on-inflation" variety). Even if the private sector revises its inflation expectations downward (increasing the stability of the peg in the future),[16] the current increase in unemployment will imply, *ceteris paribus*, higher future unemployment – because of shock persistence – and therefore a higher probability of a future devaluation for a government of any type.[17] While the credibility of the policy makers benefits from its record of being tough, the credibility of the policy may decrease over time because of the consequences for future unemployment of tough policies implemented in the past.

This model focuses nicely on the crucial issue of the cumulative costs of disinflation policies in relatively simple terms. Governments that build up their credibility by sticking to an exchange rate peg over a prolonged period, in the face of adverse economic shocks, may see the "bill" for their past tough policy choices increasing faster than their reputation. If this is the case, a peg may become more and more fragile over time, and an exchange rate crisis (or a realignment) is bound to happen even if the commitment of the policy makers is relatively firm.[18]

5.2.3 Contagion effects

The third issue concerns contagion effects during the crisis. Gerlach and Smets (1994) extend the Flood and Garber (1984) model to the case of three countries (two small Periphery countries and a Center), tracing the effects on the competitiveness of Periphery country j of a devaluation by Periphery country i. Both countries have a lower limit on the stock of international reserves, below which

16. Market participants update their expectations in a Bayesian way.
17. The magnitude of the devaluation is taken as exogenous in the model, rather than being optimally determined.
18. The kind of persistence in the level of unemployment considered by Drazen and Masson is suggestive of hysteresis, in that current unemployment is a function of its own lagged realization and of the current inflation surprise. According to the natural rate hypothesis, we should interpret the rate of unemployment corresponding to the absense of surprise inflation as the current natural rate of unemployment. Such a specification raises an interesting issue regarding the relationship between government targets and the structure of the economy. Should the target rate of unemployment follow the evolution of the natural rate? Note that when the target is kept constant (as assumed by the paper under consideration), the inflationary bias (that is proportional to the distance of the natural from the targeted level of unemployment) varies over time as a function of the past history of the game.

the peg is abandoned. The rate of domestic credit expansion in country i (say, Finland) is higher than in country j (say, Sweden). This implies that country i will be the first to experience a speculative attack. The question addressed in the paper is whether a collapse of country i's currency can precipitate a crisis in country j.

The contagion (or domino) effects of a crisis stem from two channels. First, real money demand is defined in terms of the nominal money stock deflated by the CPI. A devaluation of the Finnish currency reduces the Swedish CPI (through the Finnish import component) and thus reduces the nominal demand for money in Sweden. With domestic credit predetermined, international reserves will fall. Second, since money wages are sticky, Sweden experiences a loss in competitiveness that further reduces money demand through its effect on the level of economic activity. A falling money demand brings about reserve losses that speed up the collapse of the Swedish parity.

While we believe that this contribution goes in the right direction, the analytical framework chosen by Gerlach and Smets prevents the authors from exploring the role of the international policy game among national authorities. Exchange rate crises turn out to be mechanically linked to domestic imbalances (excessive domestic credit creation), while international spillovers affect only the exact timing of the collapse. In fact, in discussing the practical relevance of their model, the authors mainly emphasize exchange rate crises that better fit their paradigm, such as those in the Nordic countries.

We share with these authors the belief that it is *not* appropriate to address the crisis of a system of exchange rates with the analytical framework of a single small open economy pegging its exchange rate against some large economy (or of a two-country model) and focusing exclusively on domestic credibility issues and imbalances. We differ from their approach in that we visualize a system of fixed exchange rates mostly as a mechanism for international policy coordination. This leads us to explicitly model the objective functions of the domestic policy makers, and to explore the role of international spillovers of domestic policies within the framework of an ongoing international policy game.

A Center–Periphery model

6.1   Introduction

The goal of the next four chapters is to offer a systematic approach to the theory of currency crises in a multicountry setup. Chapter 6 introduces our analytical framework. Focusing on the strategic interactions between the private and public sectors in a representative country, as well as the mechanism of expectations formation, Chapter 7 presents the key results of the unilateral peg literature as special cases of our model. Chapter 8, instead, devotes particular attention to the role played by international policy spillovers in the demise of a fixed exchange rate system and explores in detail the systemic dimensions of the monetary policy game. Finally, Chapter 9 focuses on the implications of the systemic view for our reconstruction of the 1992–93 ERM events.

Following the recent literature, the modelling strategy we adopt here considers an exchange rate crisis primarily as the rational policy response to excessive welfare costs of defending a peg. As a result, our construction excludes a number of analytical elements that play a key role in the traditional theory of balance of payments crises (Krugman, 1979; Flood and Garber, 1983, 1984). For instance, in our model money demand is not assumed to be interest sensitive, whereas this assumption is a crucial building block in the exogenous-policy literature. By the same token, our model does not explicitly consider the role of international reserves, either as a constraint or as an objective.

The general characteristics of the international monetary policy game considered in these chapters will be familiar to most readers. In fact, to maintain both theoretical focus and algebraic tractability, we have chosen to follow – to the extent possible – the structure and conventions of a typical "textbook" model.[1] By presenting our results against a well-known background, we attempt to make immediately evident to the reader the links with (and the departures from) the existing literature.

In our framework, the economy consists of $N + 1$ countries, the first N of which represent the Periphery of the system, while the last is the Center. All countries in the system are structurally symmetric as regards size, technology,

---

1. The standard references are Hamada (1976), Cooper (1985), Buiter and Marston (1985), and in particular Canzoneri and Henderson (1991). Recent developments are surveyed in Currie and Levine (1993), Ghosh and Masson (1994), and Persson and Tabellini (1995).

and consumption preferences. However, there exist crucial macroeconomic and institutional dissimilarities between Center and Periphery. Our theoretical construction hinges on the impact of demand shocks, originating in the Center, on the performance and the policies of the Periphery countries. The emphasis on IS shocks in the Center country as the only source of (exogenous) uncertainty is motivated by the stylized facts preceding the collapse of the ERM, in particular the demand boom associated with German unification as reviewed in Chapter 3. Nonetheless, our setup could easily be extended to encompass currency substitution shocks or supply-side productivity disturbances.

In describing the model, all variables other than interest rates are in natural logarithms. All Center variables are starred, and the Periphery countries are indexed with a subscript i, for $i = 1, 2, ..., N$. Unless otherwise explicitly stated, throughout these chapters Greek letters (both lowercase and uppercase) refer to constant, positive parameters.

6.2   The Center country

Output supply in the Center, denoted by y^*, is a deterministic function of employment, n^*, subject to decreasing returns to scale:

$$y_t^* = (1 - \alpha)n_t^* \quad 0 < \alpha < 1. \tag{6.1}$$

Labor is supplied inelastically, and profit-maximizing competitive firms equate the marginal product of labor to the real wage. The money wage in the Center is denoted w^*, and p^* is the Center's GDP deflator:[2]

$$w_t^* - p_t^* = -\alpha n_t^*. \tag{6.2}$$

The real exchange rate and the consumer price index of the Center are defined as follows. Let $s_{i,t}$ be the nominal spot exchange rate of the ith Periphery country (expressed as the ith country's currency per unit of Center currency), and let s_t be the nominal effective exchange rate of the Periphery vis-à-vis the Center, that is,

$$s_t \equiv \frac{1}{N} \sum_{i=1}^{N} s_{i,t}. \tag{6.3}$$

Given the assumption of symmetry, in (6.3) the effective nominal exchange rate is simply the arithmetic average of the nominal exchange rates in the Periphery.[3] Similarly, let $p_{i,t}$ be the GDP deflator of the ith Periphery country

---

2. Strictly speaking, efficiency in the labor market requires $\widehat{w}_t^* - p_t^* = \ln(1 - \alpha) - \alpha n_t^*$, where $\widehat{w}_t^*$ is defined as the logarithm of the nominal wage. For notational simplicity, in what follows we define $w_t^* \equiv \widehat{w}_t^* - \ln(1 - \alpha)$.

3. The generalization to a weighted average, to account for asymmetries in country size among the Periphery countries, would leave our qualitative results unchanged.

(in local currency). The real exchange rate of the Periphery country i vis-à-vis the Center is defined as

$$z_{i,t} = s_{i,t} - p_{i,t} + p_t^*. \tag{6.4}$$

The effective real exchange rate of the Periphery vis-à-vis the Center, z, is then given by

$$z_t \equiv \frac{1}{N} \sum_{i=1}^{N} z_{i,t}. \tag{6.5}$$

It is convenient to define $\tilde{p}_t$ as the effective price level of the Periphery as a whole, measured in the Center's currency:

$$\tilde{p}_t \equiv \frac{1}{N} \sum_{i=1}^{N} (p_{i,t} - s_{i,t}). \tag{6.6}$$

Assuming a constant share of imports in consumption, β (which applies to each of the Periphery countries as well as to the Center), the Center's CPI is defined as follows

$$q_t^* \equiv (1 - \beta) p_t^* + \beta \tilde{p}_t = p_t^* - \beta z_t \quad 0 < \beta < \frac{1}{2}. \tag{6.7}$$

We restrict the propensity to import β to be less than one-half, which is equivalent to assuming home bias in consumption in our model. As will become clear later, this assumption rules out the possibility that real interest differentials and real expected depreciation between Center and Periphery move in opposite directions.

Real aggregate demand in the Center depends on external competitiveness (as indexed by the effective real exchange rate of the Periphery vis-à-vis the Center z), the Center's real interest rate r^*, and an aggregate demand shock λ^*:

$$y_t^* = \lambda_t^* - \delta z_t - v r_t^*. \tag{6.8}$$

The real interest rate in the Center is its nominal interest rate i^* minus the expected proportional rate of change in its consumer price index, q^*:

$$r_t^* \equiv i_t^* - E_t q_{t+1}^* + q_t^* \tag{6.9}$$

where E_t denotes the expectation operator conditional on information available in period t.

Assuming a constant-velocity money demand function, equilibrium in the money market requires

$$m_t^* = p_t^* + y_t^* = w_t^* + n_t^* \tag{6.10}$$

where m^* denotes the Center's nominal money stock. At the end of period $t - 1$, that is, before the Center's shock λ_t is realized and the Center's m_t^* is determined and observed, wage setters choose the money wage prevailing in period t. Their objective function is to minimize the forecast deviation of employment from the full employment level (here normalized to zero). Therefore, they solve

$$\min_{w_t^*} E_{t-1} \frac{1}{2}\left(n_t^*\right)^2 \tag{6.11}$$

subject to (6.10). Since $n_t^* = m_t^* - w_t^*$, this implies that nominal wages are equal to the expected money supply, and employment (or output) is a function only of the Center's own monetary innovations:

$$w_t^* = E_{t-1} m_t^* \tag{6.12}$$

$$n_t^* = m_t^* - E_{t-1} m_t^*. \tag{6.13}$$

6.3   The Periphery countries

Periphery countries have the same technology as the Center. Thus, using self-explanatory notation, the supply-side equations characterizing the Periphery are given as

$$y_{i,t} = (1 - \alpha)n_{i,t} \tag{6.14}$$

$$w_{i,t} - p_{i,t} = -\alpha n_{i,t}. \tag{6.15}$$

The first key dissimilarities between Center and Periphery appear in the aggregate demand equation:

$$y_{i,t} = \lambda + \delta z_{i,t} - \nu r_{i,t}. \tag{6.16}$$

While the behavioral parameters δ, ν, and β are identical in both the Center and the Periphery, the parameter λ in (6.16) is constant. (Recall that, in the demand equation of the Center country (6.8), λ^* is a random variable.) In other words, in our analysis we abstract from country-specific and time-specific IS shocks hitting the Periphery countries. The only source of exogenous uncertainty is a perturbation of aggregate demand in the Center, which affects all Periphery countries simultaneously and symmetrically.

Also, in (6.16) we assume that Periphery countries import (export) goods and services exclusively from (to) the Center country, that is, that intra-Periphery trade is negligible.[4] This is the reason why only the bilateral real exchange rate of country i relative to the Center, z_i, enters into the demand equation for the ith country output.

At a first sight, this assumption may appear excessively unrealistic. Needless to say, concerns with competitive gaps within the Periphery have been frequently raised by national policy makers and by both import-competing and exporting sectors in Europe since the inception of the ERM, affecting the determination of Community-wide exchange rate policies. However, while the

4. However, as shown below, no such restriction is imposed on trade in financial claims.

mechanics of our computation of the equilibrium would be different, and considerably more complex in analytical terms, a model that included intra-Periphery trade would not add anything substantial to our understanding of the systemic origins and consequences of a currency crisis. In fact, the results we would obtain in a more elaborate setup would not significantly alter the conclusions reached within our framework. For instance, one of the properties of our model is that a devaluation in a given Periphery country shifts global demand towards the country's products and causes a real appreciation in all other Periphery countries. But this is precisely the same qualitative result we could obtain very easily in a model that focused directly on intra-Periphery competitiveness. Thus, the assumption simply allows us to omit algebra-intensive but inessential considerations without also impairing the theoretical adequacy of our construction as a model of intra-ERM economic relations.

The remaining structural equations describing a Periphery country are straightforward. The real interest rates in the ith country is

$$r_{i,t} = i_{i,t} - E_t q_{i,t+1} + q_{i,t} \tag{6.17}$$

while the CPI is given by

$$q_{i,t} = p_{i,t} + \beta z_{i,t}. \tag{6.18}$$

By analogy with the Center, real money balances, money wages, and employment in the Periphery are determined as follows:

$$m_{i,t} - p_{i,t} = y_{i,t} \tag{6.19}$$

$$w_{i,t} = E_{t-1} m_{i,t} \tag{6.20}$$

$$n_{i,t} = m_{i,t} - E_{t-1} m_{i,t}. \tag{6.21}$$

We finally assume that assets denominated in different currencies are perfect substitutes in private agents' portfolios, so the uncovered (nominal) interest parity condition holds:

$$i_{i,t} = i_t^* + E_t s_{i,t+1} - s_{i,t}. \tag{6.22}$$

Note that, given (6.22), with perfect capital mobility the uncovered interest parity condition must hold for any pair of currencies in the system. In other words, our model encompasses free trade in financial claims both between Center and Periphery and among the Periphery countries themselves, even though there is no intra-Periphery trade in goods and services.

6.4   The objective function of the Center

The preferences of the policy authority of the Center country i are described by equations (6.23)–(6.26):

$$L_t^* \equiv E_t \sum_{\tau=0}^{\infty} k^{*\tau} \ell_{t+\tau}^* \qquad 0 < k^* < 1 \tag{6.23}$$

$$\ell_t^* \equiv \frac{1}{2}\left[\left(n_t^* - \bar{n}^*\right)^2 + \sigma\left(q_t^* - \bar{q}_t^*\right)^2\right] \tag{6.24}$$

$$\bar{n}^* = 0 \tag{6.25}$$

$$\bar{q}_t^* = 0. \tag{6.26}$$

Policy makers minimize the mathematical expectation of a time-additive loss function (6.23) defined over the infinite future. The authorities' discount factor is denoted k^*. The single-period loss function ℓ_t^* (6.24) is quadratic in the deviation of actual employment and CPI from their current target levels, $\bar{n}^*$ and $\bar{q}_t^*$ respectively.

Three features of the Center's policy preferences are worth emphasizing. First, as shown in (6.25), the Center country's target level of employment, $\bar{n}^*$, equals the "full-information", natural rate of employment (zero).[5] This implies that no systematic inflationary bias (of the kind considered in Kydland and Prescott, 1977, and Barro and Gordon, 1983a,b) affects the Center economy in a time-consistent equilibrium.[6] Second, as shown in (6.26), there is no CPI target drift: $\bar{q}_t^*$ is constant and normalized to zero, so that exchange rate or monetary changes do not lead to a "re-basing" of the price level target. In other words, the Center provides a (potential) nominal yardstick for the system as a whole by targeting the level, rather than the rate of growth, of the CPI. Third, the Center does not have an explicit exchange rate target (or welfare losses associated with failing to meet an exchange rate target).

A straightforward implication of our setup is that, in general, the Center is not insulated from exchange rate movements and price changes in the Periphery. In fact, (6.7) makes clear that stable consumer prices in the Center require a stable real exchange rate against the Periphery. Thus, in (6.24) and in most of our analysis, the most appropriate choice of the Center's targeted price index is the CPI q^* – which allows for a direct influence of Periphery prices and nominal exchange rates on the Center's national welfare – rather than the GDP deflator, p^*. However, in Chapter 7, we will find it analytically convenient to deviate temporarily from this specification and to assume instead that the domestic deflator p^* (instead of q^*) enters the Center's social welfare function. In such a scenario, the Center is fully insulated from internal and external shocks (that is, from the Periphery's reaction to the Center's demand shock). In fact, the Center is able to achieve a national first best, with both full employment and price stability, simply by following the Friedman-style monetary rule $m_t^* = 0$.[7] Although restrictive, this simplification will be particularly helpful in the analysis of multiple self-fulfilling equilibria in the Periphery

5. In the absence of exogenous shocks, $m_t^* = E_{t-1}m_t^*$ implies $n_t^* = 0$ in (6.13).
6. See below, par. 6.4.2.
7. The implications of this specification are explored in detail in Buiter, Corsetti, and Pesenti (1997).

countries. As intra-Periphery or Periphery-to-Center spillovers are not central to our reworking of the unilateral peg model, the cost of the simplification is small. In Chapter 8, when such spillovers take center stage, we revert to the use of the CPI as the price level target.

6.5   The objective function of the Periphery

6.5.1   Employment targets and inflationary bias in the Periphery

Consider now the objective function for a representative Periphery country authority:

$$L_{i,t} \equiv E_t \sum_{\tau=0}^{\infty} k_i^\tau \ell_{i,t+\tau} \quad 0 < k_i < 1 \tag{6.27}$$

$$\ell_{i,t} \equiv \frac{1}{2} \left[(n_{i,t} - \bar{n}_i)^2 + \sigma (q_{i,t} - \bar{q}_{i,t})^2 \right] + c_i I_{i,t} \quad \bar{n}_i > 0; \quad c_i > 0 \tag{6.28}$$

$$I_{i,t} = \begin{cases} 0 & \text{if } s_{i,t} = \bar{s}_{i,t} \\ 1 & \text{otherwise} \end{cases}. \tag{6.29}$$

Equation (6.27) is the analog of (6.23) above. The right side of (6.28) is the sum of two components, the first one (in brackets) similar to (6.24), the second one specific to the Periphery countries. Ignoring for now this second component, note that in the Periphery the target level of employment, $\bar{n}_i$, exceeds the rational-expectations equilibrium or "natural" level, which in this model is equal to zero. Following the standard conventions it is assumed that, because of exogenous (and unremovable) distortions in the Periphery labor market, the full-employment output level is socially suboptimal.

The well-known theoretical implication of such a conflict between public preferences and equilibrium constraints is that an equilibrium with full monetary discretion does not support the first-best allocation, and the economy of the Periphery is affected by an inflationary bias à la Kydland-Prescott/Barro-Gordon: Monetary discretion will have only inflationary repercussions in the economy, with no systematic effects on real wages, employment, and the level of economic activity.

6.5.2   The advantages of "tying one's hands"

The theoretical roots of the view of the ERM as a means to provide a nominal anchor to a domestic policy maker without anti-inflationary credibility are to be found in the debate accompanying the early rational expectations revolution in macroeconomics. From this debate we know that in a world with forward-looking expectations and exogenous uncertainty, first-best rules have two features. First, they require a credible commitment; second, they are always contingent rules, that is, optimal reactions to the random shocks that hit the economy.[8] For instance, the first-best contingent rule for a Periphery country facing shocks to investment, consumption, or export demand would be to let its currency float against the Center and "lean against the wind," say, by implementing (temporary) expansionary policies in response to unexpected cyclical downturns.

If in the eyes of market participants such a contingent managed float were aimed at stabilizing output around its full information equilibrium value (or natural rate level), there would be no adverse effect on inflationary expectations from any exchange rate and money stock variations engineered by the policy authority. Market participants would have no reason to fear that the application of an optimal contingent rule would add to the underlying inflationary pressures, say, by generating a sustained increase in the rate of monetary growth. If, however, the relevant policy target is a level of unemployment below the natural rate, expansionary monetary policies that represent the optimal response to adverse circumstances may be bundled with inflationary policies that systematically attempt to lower unemployment below its full-information equilibrium value. The public sector may be unable to commit to a first-best contingent policy in a credible way. To the extent that market participants become aware of the inflationary bias in policy making, inflation expectations will remain high.

A credible commitment to a fully optimal contingent rule is hardly feasible. Adherence by the policy makers to the rule must be readily verifiable, so that the degree of policy flexibility is effectively limited by the information available to the private sector.[9] Adding elements of bounded rationality (limited information-gathering and processing capacity) to this picture reinforces the argument in favor of simple, unconditional (noncontingent, fixed or "open-loop"[10]) rules, which are easier to monitor than contingent rules. Other things being equal, a commitment by policy makers to unconditional rules, such as a fixed nominal exchange rate parity, appears more credible than a commitment to any contingent rule.

8. See for example the discussion in Buiter (1981), and Minford (1995).
9. If there is asymmetric information between the policy maker and the private sector, about either the state of the economy or the objectives of the policy maker, the private sector faces a "signal extraction" problem: it has to decide whether a particular monetary policy action represents the faithful application of the pre-announced contingent rule, or an opportunistic attempt to exploit a short-term employment-inflation trade-off that would be a violation of the optimal contingent rule.
10. An open-loop policy is a specified sequence of policy settings, whose time path is independent of the future evolution of the economy. In contrast, a closed-loop policy is a feedback rule that links policy actions to events, developments, and shocks in the evolution of the economy.

In the light of these considerations, a peg represents a second-best strategy by a policy maker to reduce the inflationary bias by giving up discretion in monetary policy, and to impose price stability on itself by "tying one's hands". A fixed exchange rate facilitates domestic disinflation and helps strengthen the reputation of the domestic policy maker by "importing credibility" from the price-stabilizing Center.[11]

6.5.3   Realignment costs and commitment technology

A fixed exchange rate policy would obviously be time-inconsistent if the target unemployment rate is below the natural rate, unless reneging on the commitment to defend the announced parity entailed a loss of utility for the policy maker: the higher the opportunity cost of switching to a float, the higher *ceteris paribus* the reliability of the peg. In (6.29), this "commitment technology" is formalized as follows. The positive constant c_i denotes the exogenously given welfare cost of abandoning the peg. Country i's policy makers suffer a welfare loss equal to c_i when the current exchange rate deviates (no matter by how much) from the announced exchange rate parity, indexed by $\bar{s}_{i,t}$. Only if the exchange rate target is maintained, will the sunk welfare loss be zero.

These costs are best understood as a proxy for the wide array of nonquantifiable political interests underlying the defense of a given exchange rate target, ranging from national chauvinism tout court to fears of professional loss of prestige, reputation, and influence. They may also reflect a widespread belief that exchange rate stability is a public good in its own right, quite apart from its (possible) anti-inflationary implications.

From a different albeit complementary vantage point, the notions that the capacity to precommit is valuable and that credible commitments can be achieved even in the absence of third party enforcement have been formalized in repeated or dynamic noncooperative game theory. An assessment of these issues, even a partial one, would require a prolonged detour from the main objective of our book. It is sufficient to recall here that the (infinite) repetition of situations involving strategic interactions among players and/or considerations related to gains and losses of reputation (in a world with uncertainty and asymmetric information) may make it possible to avoid the dilemma of the time inconsistency of optimal plans. The devaluation "costs" faced by the policy makers would then reflect the anticipated future losses associated with the reaction of the market, both in terms of persistent inflationary expectations and lower credibility. It would be possible to appeal to this literature to justify – or reinterpret – the assumption that there is a sunk cost to a country of abandoning its exchange rate peg. In the context of our model, the ad-hoc cost of reneging on a fixed

---

11. Among the best introductions to the theoretical underpinnings of the "discipline view" are Giavazzi and Pagano (1988), and Giavazzi and Giovannini (1989, ch. 5).

exchange rate commitment permits the great analytical simplification of finessing the explicit treatment of a repeated game.[12] We will touch upon these issues again briefly in Chapter 7.

To sum up, in our model market participants take the existence of a commitment technology as a datum: The higher the common-knowledge lump-sum costs c_i that the policy authority will "pay" if it reneges on its announced target, then the higher the degree of commitment by the policy authority to the defense of the peg. An extremely high value of c_i implies that, regardless of internal and external circumstances, the policy authority will subordinate its other objectives to the defense of the current exchange rate. A negligible value signals that governments will always let the currency float or, equivalently, set it at the value most conducive to the achievement of its other objectives. Intermediate values can be rationalized in terms of escape clauses that allow for the possibility of realignments in the presence of specific contingencies, that is, realignments that depend on the size of the shock hitting the domestic economy.[13]

As considered at length in Chapter 1, the notion that the ERM had any effectiveness at all as a reputation-building device nowadays encounters increasing skepticism. In what follows, it is by no means our intention to espouse or rehabilitate the normative implications of this thesis. In fact, it is worth emphasizing that the motivation underlying the decision to peg is irrelevant for our analysis. Our results would go through unchanged if the Periphery countries decided to adopt a fixed exchange rate regime for any exogenous reason – for instance, because of political considerations related to the process of market liberalization and economic integration.

Yet, the intellectual histories of the ERM (such as Begg and Wyplosz, 1993) have repeatedly pointed out that, from the mid 1980s until the 1992–93 currency crises, the anti-inflationary discipline of fixed rates provided the most common – albeit not necessarily the most convincing – economic argument in favor of the ERM.[14] Overlooking the sources of strategic interaction between

---

12. Our model does not explicitly consider the endogenous building up and loss of reputation and credibility of monetary policy. From the definition of the variable $I_{i,t}$ given in (6.29), it is apparent that the past sequence of policy actions does not affect the ongoing game between the private and the public sector. In the recent literature there are a few attempts to derive endogenously costs and benefits of a devaluation within a game-theoretical structure (see for instance De Kock and Grilli, 1993). Most contributions take the alternative route of a parametric specification, without attempting to model the underlying game structure explicitly.

13. In a series of articles, Maurice Obstfeld (1991, 1994, and 1995) has pointed out that, since escape clauses of the kind considered in this chapter raise the possibility of multiple equilibria in the disinflation game between the private and public sectors, their existence may have destabilizing effects for the fixed exchange rate regime. This subject will be analyzed extensively in the next chapter.

14. As Begg and Wyplosz (1993, p. 23) write, "despite inconclusive formal evidence, most students of the EMS have accepted the German dominance hypothesis. The frequency of this conclusion seems to arise from the usual view that if you don't see what you believe, then buy adequate glasses."

Center and Periphery, and thus the potential scope for monetary cooperation
and coordination, the discipline view emphasized the role of the ERM as a
reputation-building device for inflation-prone European countries, and the role
of the exchange rate peg against the D-mark as a viable and effective nominal
anchor.

Therefore, we have kept the discipline approach, inherited from the pre-crisis
literature, as the conceptual framework wherein to cast our theoretical analysis
and reconstruction of the 1992–93 events. To avoid misleading interpretations,
however, we reiterate that accepting the consensus view as a positive analytical
tool need not imply the acceptance of its normative implications.

6.5.4   Exchange rate and price targets in the Periphery

Over time, the Periphery country's CPI target level $\bar{q}_{i,t}$ and the nominal exchange rate target $\bar{s}_{i,t}$ may evolve, but not independently from each other. It
should be kept in mind that, for a given value of the Center's GDP deflator
p_t^* (or the Center's CPI, q_t^*), fixing $\bar{q}_{i,t}$ and $\bar{s}_{i,t}$ is equivalent to targeting some
level of the real exchange rate. In Chapter 7, we will briefly touch upon the
implications of the choice of an "incorrect", misaligned exchange rate target.
However, in much of what follows we shall focus on the case where there is
no inescapable conflict between the objectives for the internal and the external
value of the currency. The price level target therefore will be assumed to evolve
consistently with the exchange rate target, as specified in (6.30) and (6.31):

$$\bar{q}_{i,t} = \bar{s}_{i,t} + \bar{q}_t^* \tag{6.30}$$

$$\bar{s}_{i,t} = s_{i,t-1}. \tag{6.31}$$

The interpretation is straightforward. Periphery countries want to import
price level stability from the Center. They do this by pursuing a domestic price
level target $\bar{q}_{i,t}$ that equals the Center's price level target $\bar{q}_t^*$ at the target rate of
exchange $\bar{s}_{i,t}$. The exchange rate target of a Periphery country is the exchange
rate inherited from the previous period, independent of whether a realignment
has occurred or not. Both targets are part of the private sector's information set at
the time when wage contracts are determined.[15] The set of assumptions spelled
out in this and the previous section guarantee that, despite the multiperiod nature
of our model, the effects of a devaluation only last for one period.

6.6   The semireduced form of the model

In this section, we present a semireduced form of our model, expressing all
endogenous variables as functions exclusively of exogenous, predetermined,
or control variables. We introduce here the crucial distinction between system-
wide and country-specific (or domestic) shocks to fundamentals. It is important

15. In other words, $\bar{s}_{i,t}$ and $\bar{q}_{i,t}$ are both known at time $t - 1$.

to observe that, while all results in what follows are expressed in state space (that is, as functions of the size of the relevant shocks), it would be straightforward to reinterpret them in terms of time series, once we specified the dynamic process followed by λ_t^*.[16]

6.6.1   The system-wide perspective

First, consider the bilateral real interest rate differential between the ith country and the Center country:

$$r_{i,t} = r_t^* - \beta(E_t z_{t+1} - z_t) + (1 - \beta)(E_t z_{i,t+1} - z_{i,t}). \tag{6.32}$$

By summing over the N Periphery countries, the average interest rate differential between the Periphery and the Center will be

$$\frac{\sum_i r_{i,t}}{N} = r_t^* + (1 - 2\beta)(E_t z_{t+1} - z_t). \tag{6.33}$$

Note that the real interest rate differential and the expected rate of depreciation of the real exchange rate between Center and Periphery move in the same direction if and only if $\beta < 1/2$, that is, if there is home bias in consumption. We maintain this assumption throughout.

A few intermediate steps are helpful to characterize the reduced form equation for the Center's effective real exchange rate. First, using both the previous expression together with the aggregate demand functions (6.8) and (6.16) and the resource constraint of the economy as a whole,

$$\frac{\sum_i y_{i,t}}{N} - y_t^* = (1 - \alpha)\left(\frac{\sum_i n_{i,t}}{N} - n_t^*\right) \tag{6.34}$$

we obtain a first-order stochastic difference equation in z_t:

$$z_t = \gamma E_t z_{t+1} + \phi\left(\frac{\sum_i n_{i,t}}{N} - n_t^*\right) - \left(\frac{\gamma}{v(1 - 2\beta)}\right)(\lambda - \lambda_t^*) \tag{6.35}$$

where

$$\gamma \equiv \frac{v(1 - 2\beta)}{2\delta + v(1 - 2\beta)} < 1 \qquad \phi \equiv \frac{1 - \alpha}{2\delta + v(1 - 2\beta)}. \tag{6.36}$$

As the effective real exchange rate z_t is a forward-looking variable, we impose a no-bubble condition, thus ruling out "explosive" divergence between the behavior of the real exchange rate and the behavior of its fundamentals. Solving (6.35) with such a boundary condition yields

$$z_t = \phi\left(\frac{\sum_i n_{i,t}}{N} - n_t^*\right) + \epsilon_t \tag{6.37}$$

---

16. For instance, our analysis of the "timing" of a realignment in Chapter 8 – formulated in state space – could be re-cast in dynamic terms.

where ϵ_t is defined as

$$\epsilon_t \equiv \frac{\gamma}{\upsilon(1-2\beta)} \sum_{\tau=0}^{\infty} \gamma^\tau E_t(\lambda^*_{t+\tau} - \lambda). \qquad (6.38)$$

In (6.37), the effective real exchange rate depends both on the difference between the current monetary innovations (i.e., the employment levels) in the Periphery and in the Center and, through the forward-looking variable ϵ_t, on real shocks in the Center. Thus, the Center's real exchange rate appreciates either when the Periphery adopts a looser monetary stance than the Center, or when the Center experiences a demand boom.

The stochastic variable ϵ_t indexes the exogenous shock to the fundamentals of our international economy. It bears emphasizing that the current realization of ϵ_t is the innovation to the present discounted value of current and expected future demand disturbances over the infinite horizon. In other words, the real exchange rate today is affected not only by the magnitude of the observed current demand shocks (λ^*_t), but also by whether or not these shocks are believed to persist over time, by whether structural breaks in the distribution of the shocks are expected to occur in the future, and by the characteristics of the "learning" process followed by market participants – in sum, by how private agents use currently available information to forecast future scenarios, revising and adapting their beliefs. In the following chapter, we will explore in more detail the implications of these considerations for our reconstruction of the ERM events.

6.6.2   The country-specific perspective

Next, it is straightforward (albeit algebraically tedious) to show that the bilateral real exchange rate of Periphery country i vis-à-vis the Center is

$$z_{i,t} = \xi(1-\theta)\, n_{i,t} + \epsilon_t - \xi\theta \sum_{j\neq i} n_{j,t} - \phi n^*_t \qquad (6.39)$$

where the parameters θ and ξ are defined as

$$\theta \equiv \left(\frac{\delta - \upsilon\beta}{2\delta + \upsilon(1-2\beta)}\right)\frac{1}{N}, \qquad \xi \equiv \frac{1-\alpha}{\delta + \upsilon(1-\beta)} = \frac{\phi}{1-N\theta} > 0. \qquad (6.40)$$

Note that the sign of θ is ambiguous. This parameter will play a key role in the model of policy coordination introduced in Chapter 8, where we discuss in detail its economic interpretation.

The bilateral real exchange rate in (6.39) depends on both the domestic monetary stance (through the term $\xi(1-\theta)\,n_{i,t}$) and a combination of external factors, indexed in what follows by $\upsilon_{i,t}$, where

$$\upsilon_{i,t} \equiv \epsilon_t - \left(\xi\theta \sum_{j\neq i} n_{j,t} + \phi n^*_t\right). \qquad (6.41)$$

From the vantage point of the ith Periphery country, the term $v_{i,t}$ represents the relevant macroeconomic disturbance hitting the domestic economy. In (6.41), the shock includes two components. The first component, indexed by ϵ_t, affects all Periphery countries symmetrically, since it depends on current and future anticipated disturbances to the aggregate demand of the Center country. The second component of the country-specific shock (in brackets) depends on the monetary innovations (i.e., the employment levels) of not only the Center but also all other countries in the Periphery. Summarizing, while the comprehensive shock $v_{i,t}$ is always country-specific – hence indexed by the i subscript – it reflects the behavior of all the other countries in the system.

For any Periphery country, the key macroeconomic variables can be expressed in semi-reduced form as functions of $v_{i,t}$. For instance, using (6.16) and (6.39), the real interest rate in country i becomes

$$r_{i,t} = v^{-1}\{\lambda + [\delta\xi(1 - \theta) - (1 - \alpha)]n_{i,t} + \delta v_{i,t}\}. \tag{6.42}$$

Inspection of (6.42) brings out an important feature of our model: For given monetary policies in the rest of the system, n_t^* and $\sum_{j\neq i} n_{j,t}$, the spillovers from a positive demand shock in the Center result in an increase of the real interest rate in country i. In other words, positive demand shocks in the Center country directly translate into negative demand shocks in the Periphery through their effect on the real interest rate.

For future reference, it is useful to write the semi-reduced form equations for the CPI as

$$q_{i,t} = [\alpha + \beta\xi(1 - \theta)]n_{i,t} + w_{i,t} + \beta v_{i,t} \tag{6.43}$$

and for the bilateral nominal exchange rate vis-à-vis the Center as

$$s_{i,t} = [\alpha + \xi(1 - \theta)]n_{i,t} + w_{i,t} - \left(w_t^* + \alpha n_t^*\right) + v_{i,t}. \tag{6.44}$$

The intuitions underlying these equations are simple. Other things equal, a depreciation of its nominal exchange rate raises both employment and the CPI in country i. Conversely, for a given exchange rate, the level of domestic nominal wages affects employment and consumer prices asymmetrically: a high expected money stock, *ceteris paribus*, is associated with low employment and high prices. Employment and output in the Periphery increase with a monetary expansion or a wage surge in the Center, since both events raise the Center prices (recall that $p_t^* = w_t^* + \alpha n_t^*$), boosting the demand for the Periphery countries' exports.

6.6.3   *Shocks to fundamentals and policy spillovers*

Consider now the impact of the Center demand shock on the economies of the Periphery. *Ceteris paribus*, Equation (6.37) shows that an increase in demand for the Center's output requires a real effective appreciation of the Center's currency against the Periphery. The monetary authority in the Center country could counteract these pressures by allowing domestic prices to rise. In this case, the demand boom in the Center would be absorbed internally and would not have significant negative consequences in the Periphery; heuristically, the changes in ϵ_t and n_t^* would offset each other in (6.41), leaving $v_{i,t}$ unaffected everywhere in the Periphery.[17]

If the Center is unwilling to tolerate the inflationary consequences of the internal demand boom, the shock is transmitted to the Periphery. Focusing on a single Periphery country, and assuming for now that the stance of monetary policy in the other Periphery countries does not change, the mechanism of transmission is straightforward. As the demand boom raises interest rates in the Center by more than in the Periphery (6.32), capital flows from the Periphery to the Center. If the monetary authorities in the Periphery country do not react to the fall in the demand for domestic currency, the equilibrium exchange rate depreciates in both nominal and real terms against the Center, and the CPI level in the Periphery country increases. To avoid the weakening of the domestic currency and defend the exchange rate target, the monetary authorities of the Periphery country must accommodate the external shock by decreasing the domestic money supply. In this case, the defense of the peg, as shown by (6.44), has a recessionary impact on the domestic economy of the Periphery country.

In a multicountry setup, however, the policy scenario is considerably more complex. In fact, (6.41) makes clear that from the vantage point of each individual Periphery country, the impact of the shock originating in the Center depends not only on the policy response of the Center itself, but also on the monetary behavior of the rest of the Periphery. If θ is positive (see below), the role played by a monetary expansion in the rest of the Periphery is analogous to the role played by a monetary expansion in the Center. By bringing the effective terms of trade of the Center closer to its equilibrium level, an expansion anywhere in the Periphery represents a "shock absorber" for the rest of the system.[18] This argument lies at the core of our analysis of the structural and strategic systemic links among Periphery countries. We will consider its implications in detail in Chapter 8.

17. It can be easily checked that, although the real exchange rate remains constant, there are pressures toward a generalized nominal appreciation of the Periphery currencies against the Center.
18. Of course, when we move from the partial-equilibrium approach considered so far to general-equilibrium considerations, it should be clear that the policy stance of every country in the system is jointly determined as a function of the exogenous shock to fundamentals ϵ_t.

CHAPTER 7

Unilateral pegs and escape clauses: The role of domestic credibility

7.1   Exchange rate crises as equilibrium outcomes

The first step in our analysis of the international equilibrium is the determination of the optimal monetary policy of a representative Periphery country. At any point in time, the problem faced by country i's policy makers can be thought of as a nested choice. First, they will determine whether to maintain or abandon the peg, knowing that reneging on the commitment to peg the currency brings about a reduction of utility by some fixed amount c_i. Second, contingent on the peg having been abandoned, the size of the monetary expansion (or contraction) will be chosen. Given the positive relation between a country's money supply and its exchange rate (6.44), this translates into the determination of the optimal size of the realignment.

At the time when such decisions are taken, the monetary authority of the Periphery country i takes into account the following variables: the demand shock in the Center, ϵ_t; the stance of monetary policy in the rest of the system, that is, m_t^* and $m_{j,t}$ for all Periphery countries $j \neq i$; the wage rate set in the domestic labor market, w_t; and the Center's wage level, w_t^*. As a first step, we consider the problem from a partial-equilibrium perspective, taking these variables as parameters. Later in this chapter we derive the rational expectation equilibrium level(s) of the wage rate. Abstracting from international policy linkages (i.e., maintaining the assumption that m_t^* and $m_{j,t}$ are given), we analyze the possible equilibrium configurations of the game between the public and private sectors in any Periphery country. Chapter 8 shifts the focus of the analysis from domestic credibility to the international policy game. In that chapter, for given wages we will consider the implications of modelling a multicountry exchange rate regime as a general-equilibrium monetary game.

7.1.1   The choice of an optimal monetary policy

The optimal policy rule for country i combines two different monetary regimes. In one regime, the money stock is consistent with the survival of the peg; in the other, the peg is abandoned, and the money supply responds optimally to fundamentals. In general, the identification of an optimal monetary policy is rather difficult when the objective functional of the policy maker is defined over an infinite horizon. Nonetheless, two features of our model allow a considerable simplification of the analysis.

First, the time-consistent solutions we are considering are restricted to memoryless strategies: current and anticipated future policy actions are not affected by the past history of the game (that is, the actual sequences of past policy actions). Second, there is no intertemporal carryover, either through wage setting or through asset accumulation. The only dynamics in our model stem from forward-looking expectations (through the wage setting process and the uncovered interest parity relationships) and two structural lags: the assumption that the money wage is set one period in advance, and the behavior of the target nominal exchange rate of the Periphery countries. Neither the lag in money wage setting nor the lag in the determination of the target nominal exchange rate results in a proper, predetermined, state variable entering the reduced form of the model and affecting its solution(s). Because of these characteristics, in our setup the optimal policy is derived by taking into account the single-period loss function $\ell_{i,t}$ only.[1]

Consider first the monetary policy adopted when the peg is defended.[2] It is determined by taking (6.44) and substituting the current exchange rate target $\bar{s}_{i,t}$ for the left-hand side variable $s_{i,t}$. Rearranging, we obtain

$$n_{i,t}^{FX} = m_{i,t}^{FX} - w_{i,t} = \frac{\bar{s}_{i,t} - w_{it} + w_t^* + \alpha n_t^* - v_{i,t}}{\alpha + \xi(1 - \theta)} \qquad (7.1)$$

where the superscripts FX mean "conditional on defending the peg".

Consider then the optimal monetary policy conditional on the peg having been abandoned. Once the current exchange rate parity is no longer a (binding) target or constraint, the policy maker will minimize the loss function $L_{i,t}$ by choosing $m_{i,t}$ such that:

$$\frac{\partial \ell_{i,t}}{\partial m_{i,t}} = n_{i,t}^{FL} - \bar{n}_i + \sigma[\alpha + \beta\xi(1 - \theta)]\left(q_{i,t}^{FL} - \bar{q}_{i,t}\right) = 0 \qquad (7.2)$$

where the superscripts FL mean "conditional on abandoning the peg". Solving

---

1. The introduction of a state variable in the model would not modify the essential features of the solution. As an example, Obstfeld (1994) considers a tax smoothing model where the loss function of the policy makers includes inflation and distortionary tax rates. Since inflation produces seigniorage, policy makers solve an optimal tax structure problem subject to the public sector intertemporal budget constraint. They pursue a unilateral peg in order to reduce the level of the interest rate, paying a lump-sum exogenous cost in case they devalue. The private sector sets the interest rate one period in advance. The public sector then chooses the monetary policy regime after observing the realization of a shock to the primary deficit. See also Velasco (1996).
2. As a reminder, while in our model the policy instruments are the stocks of domestic money, we often find it notationally convenient to express our results in terms of monetary innovations $(m_{i,t} - E_{t-1}m_{i,t})$ which, in our setup, translate one-to-one into employment levels $n_{i,t}$.

the above expression for the country's monetary policy yields

$$n_{i,t}^{FL} = m_{i,t}^{FL} - w_{i,t} = \frac{\bar{n}_i - \Lambda[w_{i,t} - \bar{q}_{i,t} + \beta v_{i,t}]}{A[\alpha + \xi(1 - \theta)]} \tag{7.3}$$

where A and Λ are defined as follows:

$$A \equiv \frac{1 + \sigma[\alpha + \beta\xi(1 - \theta)]^2}{\alpha + \xi(1 - \theta)}, \qquad \Lambda \equiv \sigma[\alpha + \beta\xi(1 - \theta)]. \tag{7.4}$$

The policy maker will opt for abandoning the peg if and only if the loss under a peg is larger than the loss associated with a devaluation, including the lump-sum welfare cost c_i:

$$\frac{1}{2}\left\{\left[\left(n_{i,t}^{FX} - \bar{n}_i\right)^2 + \sigma\left(q_{i,t}^{FX} - \bar{q}_{i,t}\right)^2\right] - \left[\left(n_{i,t}^{FL} - \bar{n}_i\right)^2 \right.\right.$$
$$\left.\left. + \sigma\left(q_{i,t}^{FL} - \bar{q}_{i,t}\right)^2\right]\right\} \geq c_i. \tag{7.5}$$

7.1.2   The shadow devaluation rate

There is a simple yet informative way of characterizing the optimal switching rule between the two regimes. We define the *shadow devaluation rate* (henceforth the SDR) as the difference between the (optimally chosen) value of the exchange rate if the peg were abandoned and the target exchange rate. In what follows, the SDR will be denoted $\Delta\tilde{s}_{i,t}$, so that the prevailing exchange rate conditional on the abandonment of the peg will be $s_{i,t}^{FL} = \bar{s}_{i,t} + \Delta\tilde{s}_{i,t}$. By definition, the SDR is the rate of exchange rate depreciation that at the margin equates the social benefits of higher employment with the costs of higher inflation.

We can obtain an expression for the SDR by using n^{FL} in (7.3) together with the reduced form for the nominal exchange rate (6.44):

$$\Delta\tilde{s}_{i,t} = \frac{\bar{n}_i}{A} + \frac{A - \beta\Lambda}{A}v_{i,t} + w_{i,t} - \bar{s}_{i,t} - p_t^* + \frac{\Lambda}{A}(\bar{q}_{i,t} - w_{i,t}) \tag{7.6}$$

where $p_t^* = w_t^* + \alpha n_t^*$. The SDR is a linear, increasing function of the country-specific shock, $v_{i,t}$, the wage rate w_t as well as of the employment and price level targets. It is a negative function of the Center price level and trivially, of the exchange rate target.

The meaning of the expression above is best understood by rewriting the SDR as a function of the differential of employment in the two alternative regimes $n_{i,t}^{FX} - n_{i,t}^{FL}$, that is, the loss of employment due to the defense of the existing parity. Alternatively, the SDR can be written as a function of the price level gap $q_{i,t}^{FX} - q_{i,t}^{FL}$, that is, the inflation benefit from maintaining the peg:

$$\Delta\tilde{s}_{i,t} = [\alpha + \xi(1 - \theta)]\left(n_{i,t}^{FL} - n_{i,t}^{FX}\right)$$
$$= \left[\frac{\alpha + \xi(1 - \theta)}{\alpha + \beta\xi(1 - \theta)}\right]\left(q_{i,t}^{FL} - q_{i,t}^{FX}\right). \tag{7.7}$$

In either case, the SDR provides a measure of the welfare opportunity cost of maintaining the peg.

It can be shown that the optimal choice of exchange rate regime (7.5) involves only the evaluation of the employment gap and the price level gap. Therefore, substituting equation (7.7) into (7.5), the authorities will abandon the peg if and only if condition (7.8) holds:

$$|\Delta \tilde{s}_{i,t}| \geq \sqrt{\frac{2c_i[\alpha + \xi(1 - \theta)]}{A}} \equiv \tilde{c}_i. \qquad (7.8)$$

Interpreting this expression, there exists a threshold value of the shadow devaluation rate that triggers an optimal devaluation (or revaluation). The threshold value $\tilde{c}_i$, defined by the right-hand side of the above inequality, translates the welfare cost of abandoning the peg into the metric of the SDR. Using (7.8), the exchange rate behavior of the ith Periphery country implied by its optimal monetary policy can now be completely characterized as follows:

$$\begin{aligned} s_{i,t} &= \bar{s}_{i,t} & \text{if } |\Delta \tilde{s}_{i,t}| < \tilde{c}_i, \\ s_{i,t} &= \bar{s}_{i,t} + \Delta \tilde{s}_{i,t} & \text{if } |\Delta \tilde{s}_{i,t}| \geq \tilde{c}_i. \end{aligned} \qquad (7.9)$$

Note that $\tilde{c}_i$ is constant and defined symmetrically for both positive and negative rates of devaluation. In principle, the escape clause specified in our analysis does not preclude the possibility of a revaluation of the central parity rather than a devaluation. However, to simplify our analysis, in the rest of this chapter we will consider realizations of the shock for which the only relevant alternative for country i's policy makers is between a peg and a devaluation against the Center. In other words, we restrict the support of the shock to be such that a revaluation by country i is never optimal, ruling out by construction any shocks to fundamentals that would correspond to large negative values of the shadow depreciation rate (so that $\Delta \tilde{s}_{i,t} \geq -\tilde{c}_i$).[3] The extension to the general case is simply a corollary of the analysis to follow.[4]

Expressions (7.9) can be illustrated with a simple picture that captures the key features of our model. Consider Figure 7.1. On the x-axis we put the support of the shock. On the y-axis we have the shadow and the actual devaluation rates (both conditional on private agents' expectations), as well as the adjusted welfare cost of a devaluation $\tilde{c}_i$. The zero on the y-axis corresponds to the existing parity.

The level of the shock $\bar{v}_{i,t}$ at which the shadow depreciation rate crosses the cost line divides the support of the shock in two regions. The policy makers will find it optimal to defend the exchange rate if the shock falls in the region to the

---

3. It bears emphasizing that for any finite support of the distribution of the fundamentals, there always exists an employment target $\bar{n}_i$ high enough to ensure that a revaluation will never be optimal.

4. Occasionally, we will report the general results in footnote.

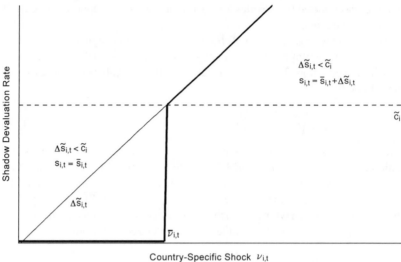

Figure 7.1. The shadow devaluation rate.

left. They will optimally abandon the peg in the region to the right. By construction, the optimal devaluation rate conditional on abandoning the peg coincides with the shadow rate. Thus, the actual devaluation rate will be zero in the region to the left of the threshold, and equal to the SDR in the region to the right.

How does this result relate to the existing literature on currency crises and speculative attacks? It is perhaps surprising that, analytically and conceptually, the SDR provides a unifying framework for different classes of models that at first sight appear theoretically unrelated. In the context of exogenous policy speculative attack models, according to the taxonomy of Chapter 5, Flood and Garber (1984) showed that the private sector will launch a speculative attack, depleting reserves and forcing an abandonment of the fixed parity, as soon as the path of the shadow floating exchange rate crosses the fixed parity from below. In our setup, the government optimally chooses to abandon the fixed parity as soon as the shadow floating exchange rate exceeds the fixed rate by a margin sufficient to cover the sunk devaluation cost. The fixed cost of abandonment means that the shadow floating exchange rate can differ from the parity by some margin without triggering any realignment.[5]

7.2   Imperfect commitment and expectations formation

We can now focus on the domestic policy game between national monetary authorities and the private sector. In this section, we close our model by

---

5. For a discussion, see Cavallari and Corsetti (1996).

determining the domestic nominal wage rate, based on rational expectations of future domestic monetary policies. Since policy makers do not "tie their own hands" and do not commit themselves to the defense of the exchange rate target under all possible contingencies, market participants at time $t-1$ will forecast $m_{i,t}$ by combining expectations concerning two scenarios, the first one consistent with the defense of the fixed exchange rate (for $\Delta \tilde{s}_{i,t} < \tilde{c}_i$), the second one with policy discretion (for $\Delta \tilde{s}_{i,t} \geq \tilde{c}_i$).

7.2.1 Devaluation thresholds and the probability of a crisis

It follows from our previous analysis that the probability of a realignment is equal to the probability that the shadow devaluation rate, as a function of the country-specific shock, is equal or above the devaluation threshold. Thus, we define the probability of a realignment as $\pi_{i,t} \equiv \Pr\{\Delta \tilde{s}_{i,t} \geq \tilde{c}_i\}$. Wage setters' forecasts will be obtained by taking the expectations of $m_{i,t}^{FX}$ and $m_{i,t}^{FL}$ conditional on, respectively, the defense of the peg and a devaluation, and combining them according to their respective probabilities:

$$E_{t-1}m_{i,t} = (1 - \pi_{i,t})E_{t-1}\left[m_{i,t}^{FX} \mid \Delta \tilde{s}_{i,t} < \tilde{c}_i\right]$$
$$+ \pi_{i,t}E_{t-1}\left[m_{i,t}^{FL} \mid \Delta \tilde{s}_{i,t} \geq \tilde{c}_i\right]. \tag{7.10}$$

The previous expression can be simplified as follows. Recalling (7.7) we observe that

$$\frac{\Delta \tilde{s}_{i,t}}{\alpha + \xi(1-\theta)} = n_{i,t}^{FL} - n_{i,t}^{FX} = m_{i,t}^{FL} - m_{i,t}^{FX}. \tag{7.11}$$

Substituting (7.11) into (7.10) and rearranging, we obtain

$$w_{i,t} = E_{t-1}m_{i,t}$$
$$= E_{t-1}m_{i,t}^{FL} - \left(\frac{1 - \pi_{i,t}}{\alpha + \xi(1-\theta)}\right)E_{t-1}[\Delta s_{i,t} \mid \Delta \tilde{s}_{i,t} < \tilde{c}_i]. \tag{7.12}$$

According to (7.12), wages are set by taking the expected money supply under flexible exchange rates and "adjusting" it downward to account for the contingencies in which the peg will survive, for a given distribution of the shadow devaluation rate.

The derivation of an analytical expression for (7.12) is by no means straightforward. Both the realignment probability $\pi_{i,t}$ and the conditional expectation of the SDR depend on market participants' knowledge (at time $t-1$) of the future distribution of the demand shock, as well as on all monetary policies in the rest of the system. In general, we cannot express $\Delta \tilde{s}$ and m^{FL} as functions of a unique index of both demand and policy variables (ϵ_t, n_t^*, and $n_{j,t}$ for $j \neq i$). To see this, consider (7.3) and (7.6). Note that, while the Center demand shock and foreign monetary policies affect $n_{i,t}^{FL}$ only through $v_{i,t}$, they affect $\Delta \tilde{s}_{i,t}$ (and therefore $n_{i,t}^{FX}$) through both $v_{i,t}$ and the Center's price deflator p_t^*.

Obviously, the analysis of wage expectations formation would be easier if p_t^* were constant over time. It is instructive to see under what conditions this would actually be the case. In Chapter 6, we observed that a constant $m_t^* = 0$ (so that $p_t^* = 0$) would be pursued by an optimizing policy maker if the GDP deflator, p^*, rather than the CPI, q^*, entered its objective function (6.24). Thus, one can achieve a considerable gain in tractability at the price of a simple change in the specification of the policy maker's preferences in the Center country. It is straightforward to show that, under the new specification, both w_t^* and n_t^* would all be optimally set equal to zero. Note that this particular specification captures the (implicitly) maintained view of the behavior of the Center country that characterizes most of the unilateral peg literature, when the unilateral peg is pursued by a small open economy. In the same spirit, we develop our analysis in the rest of this chapter by positing

$$p_t^* = 0 \qquad \text{for all } t \tag{7.13}$$

as a maintained assumption. We will return to our original specification in Chapter 8.

We know from (7.6) that the SDR is a linear, increasing function of the demand shock $v_{i,t}$. By using the devaluation threshold $\bar{v}_{i,t}$ in (7.10), when $p_t^* = 0$, wages can be rewritten as follows:

$$w_{i,t} = E_{t-1} m_{i,t} = (1 - \pi_{i,t}) A \left(\frac{\bar{s}_{i,t} - [E v_{i,t} \mid v_{i,t} < \bar{v}_{i,t}]}{(1 - \pi_{i,t}) A + \pi_{i,t} \Lambda} \right)$$
$$+ \pi_{i,t} \left(\frac{\bar{n}_i + \Lambda(\bar{q}_{i,t} - \beta[E v_{i,t} \mid v_{i,t} \geq \bar{v}_{i,t}])}{(1 - \pi_{i,t}) A + \pi_{i,t} \Lambda} \right). \tag{7.14}$$

To determine the rational expectation of the wage rate, we need to evaluate the equilibrium level of the devaluation threshold $\bar{v}_{i,t}$. This can be done by substituting expression (7.14) in the definition of the shadow devaluation rate (7.6). In terms of the realignment rule (7.8), country i will devalue its currency if the following condition holds:

$$\left(\frac{A - \beta \Lambda}{A} \right) v_{i,t} + \left[\frac{\bar{n}_i + \Lambda(\bar{q}_{i,t} - \bar{s}_{i,t})}{(1 - \pi_{i,t}) A + \pi_{i,t} \Lambda} \right] - \left(\frac{A - \Lambda}{A} \right)$$
$$\times \left[\frac{(1 - \pi_{i,t}) A [E v_{i,t} \mid v_{i,t} < \bar{v}_{i,t}] + \pi_{i,t} \Lambda \beta [E v_{i,t} \mid v_{i,t} \geq \bar{v}_{i,t}]}{(1 - \pi_{i,t}) A + \pi_{i,t} \Lambda} \right] \geq \tilde{c}_i. \tag{7.15}$$

We determine the equilibrium interior value(s) of the devaluation threshold by taking expression (7.15) to hold with equality, and solving for $v_{i,t} = \bar{v}_{i,t}$.

Without further assumptions on the distribution of the shock to fundamentals $v_{i,t}$, very little can be said about the properties of the devaluation threshold $\bar{v}_{i,t}$.

An important point is that, in general, expression (7.15) will be nonlinear, so that its root need not be unique. This feature is what raises the possibility of multiple instantaneous equilibria.

7.2.2 An example

As in Obstfeld (1994), we choose to illustrate the latter point by means of a parametric example. Take the case of $v_{i,t}$ being uniformly distributed over a symmetric domain $[-\mu_{i,t}, +\mu_{i,t}]$. The expressions for the probability of abandoning the peg $\pi_{i,t}$ and the conditional means of the shock are as follows:

$$\pi_{i,t} = \int_{\bar{v}_{i,t}}^{\mu_{i,t}} \frac{dx}{2\mu_{i,t}} = \frac{\mu_{i,t} - \bar{v}_{i,t}}{2\mu_{i,t}} \tag{7.16}$$

$$E(v_{i,t} \mid v_{i,t} < \bar{v}_{i,t}) = \int_{-\mu_{i,t}}^{\bar{v}_{i,t}} \frac{x\,dx}{\bar{v}_{i,t} + \mu_{i,t}} = \frac{\bar{v}_{i,t} - \mu_{i,t}}{2} \tag{7.17}$$

$$E(v_{i,t} \mid v_{i,t} \geq \bar{v}_{i,t}) = \int_{\bar{v}_{i,t}}^{\mu_{i,t}} \frac{x\,dx}{\mu_{i,t} - \bar{v}_{i,t}} = \frac{\mu_{i,t} + \bar{v}_{i,t}}{2}. \tag{7.18}$$

Interpreting expression (7.16), large values of the devaluation threshold $\bar{v}_{i,t}$ (e.g., close to the upper boundary of the shock $\mu_{i,t}$) are associated with a high probability of survival of the peg, and low values (e.g., close to $-\mu_{i,t}$) imply a greater likelihood of a collapse. Upon substitution, the realignment rule (7.15) – taken to hold with equality – becomes:

$$\frac{2\mu_{i,t} A[\bar{n}_i + \Lambda(\bar{q}_{i,t} - \bar{s}_{i,t})] + \frac{1}{2}(A - \beta\Lambda)\left[A(\bar{v}_{i,t} + \mu_{i,t})^2 - \Lambda(\bar{v}_{i,t} - \mu_{i,t})^2\right]}{A[A(\bar{v}_{i,t} + \mu_{i,t}) - \Lambda(\bar{v}_{i,t} - \mu_{i,t})]} = \tilde{c}_i.$$

$$\tag{7.19}$$

The previous expression is a quadratic equation in $\bar{v}_{i,t}$. If an interior solution exists, it has either one root or two roots; moreover, we have to consider the possibility of corner solutions.

Various possible outcomes are illustrated in Figure 7.2. We plot both the devaluation cost $\tilde{c}_i$ (expressed in the metric of the SDR) and the SDR evaluated at the devaluation threshold $\bar{v}_{i,t}$ (as defined by the left-hand side of (7.19)) against the set of all possible threshold values $\bar{v}_{i,t}$; this set obviously consists of the support of the shock $[-\mu_{i,t}, \mu_{i,t}]$. The exogenous devaluation cost is represented by a line that is parallel to the x-axis. In the graph, we include three levels of $\tilde{c}_i$, labelled $\tilde{c}_1, \tilde{c}_2, \tilde{c}_3$. The shadow devaluation rate is nonlinear in the interval $-\mu_{i,t} \geq \bar{v}_{i,t} \geq \mu_{i,t}$ and becomes a straight vertical line above the upper boundary and below the lower boundary.

The equilibrium devaluation thresholds are identified by the intersection of the curve with the devaluation cost $\tilde{c}_i$. When the devaluation cost is very high or very low ($\tilde{c}_1$ or $\tilde{c}_3$), there are no interior solutions; when the devaluation cost

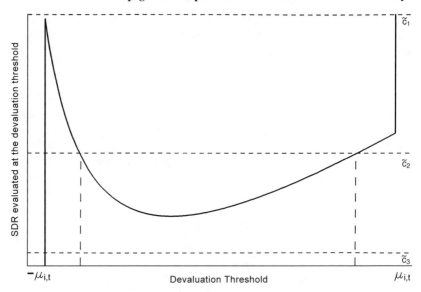

Figure 7.2. Determining the devaluation thresholds.

lies in the intermediate range (e.g., $\tilde{c}_2$) there are two points of intersection that identify two equilibrium thresholds. As considered above, the threshold "to the right" is associated with a low probability of a crisis, the threshold to the left with a high probability. It is straightforward to show that private agents' expectations of the future money stock (and thus of future wage rates) associated with the low threshold are higher than expectations (and wages) associated with the high threshold. We will return to this point in Section 7.3.1.

Figure 7.3 provides a graphical synthesis of our analysis so far. In the top graph we reproduce Figure 7.2, corresponding to an intermediate level of $\tilde{c}_i$, such that there are two crossing points, identifying two possible equilibrium levels for the devaluation threshold. Before the wage contracts are signed (at time $t - 1$), we have two possible levels of wages and therefore two possible levels of the shadow devaluation rate, depending on which instantaneous equilibrium market participants coordinate their expectations. This is shown in the graph at the bottom of the figure, where we include two SDR lines consistent with rational expectations. Needless to say, once the wage contracts are signed (at time t), there will be only one shadow devaluation locus relevant for the analysis.

7.2.3   A note on misaligned exchange targets

We can now illustrate a simple corollary of our model related to the choice of an "incorrect," misaligned exchange rate target by the government. Note that

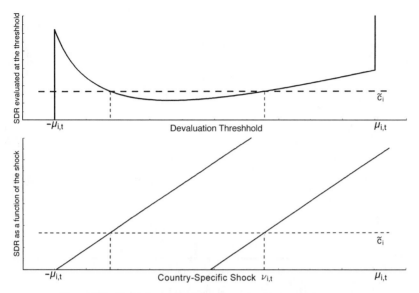

Figure 7.3. Multiple equilibria under rational expectations.

the first term in the numerator of (7.19) includes the difference between the two nominal variables targeted by the domestic authority, $\bar{q}_{i,t} - \bar{s}_{i,t}$. Clearly, the choice of $\bar{q}_{i,t} - \bar{s}_{i,t}$ affects the probability of an exchange rate crisis through its impact on the devaluation threshold. In fact, if the price level in the Center is stable over time, any target for $\bar{q}_{i,t} - \bar{s}_{i,t}$ translates into a real exchange rate target.

Figure 7.4 considers the effects of the choice of an overvalued exchange rate target, that is, $\bar{s}_{i,t} < \bar{q}_{i,t}$. The shadow devaluation rate under the benchmark case[6] $\bar{q}_{i,t} = \bar{s}_{i,t}$ is represented by the solid line. If the policy maker in the Periphery country targets $\bar{s}_{i,t} < \bar{q}_{i,t}$, the SDR shifts upward (the dotted line), lowering the high (or good) equilibrium threshold to the right.[7] This means that the probability of a crisis increases if the private sector coordinates on the high threshold equilibrium. In our reconstruction of the crisis in Chapter 3, we have pointed out that the adoption of politically ambitious but economically debatable exchange rate targets may have contributed to the snowballing of events leading up to Black Wednesday. The role of this kind of miscalculations, however, should not be overemphasized in a balanced assessment of the crisis. To highlight the effects of other, (in our view) more crucial issues,

6. Strictly speaking, $\bar{q}_{i,t} = \bar{s}_{i,t} + \bar{q}_t^*$, but since the Center's price level target is constant and normalized to zero, this reduces to $\bar{q}_{i,t} = \bar{s}_{i,t}$.
7. Note that the adoption of an overvalued real exchange rate target paradoxically increases the low (or bad) equilibrium threshold to the left.

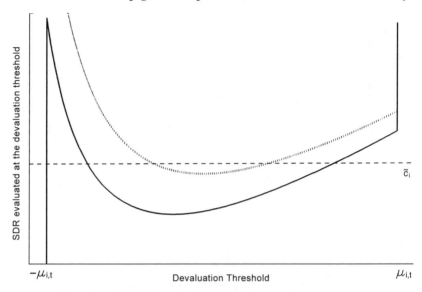

Figure 7.4. The effects of misaligned exchange rate targets.

we assume $\bar{q}_{i,t} = \bar{s}_{i,t}$ throughout the remainder of the analysis and do not explore further the implications of this particular manifestation of policy makers' irrationality.

7.3   Multiple equilibria, self-fulfilling expectations, and the ERM crisis

Summarizing the analysis up to this point, exchange rate "crises" occur in our model if and only if the policy makers find it suboptimal to keep the currency pegged. For a given distribution of exogenous shocks to fundamentals, and for given social preferences, the model endogenously determines the probability of survival of the announced exchange rate parity. A currency crisis is always triggered by a realization of the shock high enough to raise the benefit from a devaluation above its costs. Under rational expectations, the threshold between shocks that can trigger a devaluation and shocks that cannot depends on the commitment technology (indexed by the cost of abandoning the peg, c_i), as well as on the coordination of the private sector on a particular equilibrium. Heuristically, and referring to Figure 7.3, a sudden jump of the country-specific shock from the left to the right of a constant devaluation threshold represents a fundamentals-driven crisis. Conversely, a sudden downward jump of the devaluation threshold from the "good" to the "bad" equilibrium, for given fundamentals, represents a self-fulfilling crisis.

As reviewed in Chapter 4, one of the most striking pieces of empirical evidence regarding the ERM crisis in September 1992 is that interest rate differentials had been low and/or falling up to a few weeks before the onset of the speculative wave of attacks against most European currencies. In the summer, the credibility of the current parity grid had worsened somewhat, but only to a very limited extent. Other indicators, based on option prices or surveys of exchange rate forecasts, confirm these findings. Moreover, wage moderation was the norm when labor contracts were up for renewal in 1992. In other words, no available indicator suggests that labor and financial markets anticipated and predicted correctly the impact of the imminent financial turmoil.

According to several observers, this empirical evidence supports the hypothesis that the crisis was caused by self-fulfilling speculative attacks, responding to a sudden (and unpredictable) change in market participants' beliefs about the stability of the system, rather than to a change in the state of economic fundamentals.[8] The popularity of the idea of self-fulfilling speculative attacks must be largely attributed to its ability to explain the large, generalized forecast errors without postulating widespread irrationality or financial market inefficiencies.

To illustrate the theoretical underpinning of this interpretation, we can use the graphical apparatus introduced above. Consider Figure 7.2, and assume first a devaluation cost as low as $\tilde{c}_3$. It is apparent that in this case, rational agents will not believe the government's announcement of no devaluation. In fact, for any nominal wage derived on the assumption that the current peg will be maintained with a strictly positive probability, the policy maker's temptation to devalue would be too strong, no matter how mild the observed external shock. In other words, wage setters' conjectures would not be validated ex post by the behavior of the monetary authority. Rational expectations are formed by positing $\bar{v}_{i,t} = -\mu_{i,t}$, that is, $\pi_{i,t} = 1$. Conversely, for a cost of a devaluation that is sufficiently high (such as in $\tilde{c}_1$), the announcement of a fixed exchange rate regime is perfectly credible. The highest cost line crosses the welfare loss differential at the upper boundary of the shock support, and the solution of the model requires $\bar{v}_{i,t} = \mu_{i,t}$ ($\pi_{i,t} = 0$).

The relevant results for our discussion are associated with intermediate values of the devaluation cost, where the cost line crosses the shadow depreciation locus twice, identifying two possible interior equilibrium thresholds. Suppose that the economy somehow coordinates on a high threshold equilibrium (on the right). If a devaluation is perceived as a low-probability event, workers settle for a low nominal wage level and employment is, *ceteris paribus,* high. Only a very adverse realization of the shock (a large value of $v_{i,t}$) will force the monetary authorities to abandon the defence of the exchange rate target in

---

8. See for instance the discussion in Eichengreen and Wyplosz (1993).

order to maintain employment stability. The fact that the system will indeed be safe against devaluation except in the case of very high values of $v_{i,t}$ validates, ex post, the wage setters' initial conjecture.

Suppose instead that market participants coordinate on the bad (low $\bar{v}_{i,t}$) interior equilibrium, so that unions perceive a high probability of a devaluation. Because the nominal wage rate (which reflects the higher probability of a future devaluation) is now relatively high, the monetary authorities will be forced to use a devaluation to restore competitiveness in the international markets in response to even mild shocks. Only if the conditions turn out to be extremely favorable will policy makers prefer to keep the exchange rate fixed.[9]

It is worth emphasizing the self-fulfilling nature of expectations in both equilibria. If nominal wages happen to be set at a low level, the monetary authorities will be helped by favorable internal conditions in their commitment to defend the parity. Exchange rate stability (as well as the associated restrictive monetary policy) will confirm, ex post, the correctness of wage setters' expectations. By the same token, if nominal wages are set at a high level, the optimal response to external shocks is likely to be a devaluation. The monetary expansion associated with a devaluation validates, ex post, the inflationary expectations of market participants that generated the original high wage. Policy decisions depend on past market expectations embodied in the current wage; market expectations reflect anticipated future policy decisions. Due to this circularity, expectations in a sense depend on expectations themselves, and the coordination of the public on either set of beliefs is completely arbitrary and unpredictable, although not irrational.

It is sometimes argued that self-fulfilling speculative attacks are a simple corollary of the above analysis. An exchange rate crisis may occur because of a self-fulfilling shift in market expectations, with no apparent change in fundamentals. In this case, indicators such as wage inflation or interest rate differentials, observed before the crisis and therefore based on the good equilibrium outcomes, would not provide any indication that a crisis was anticipated and imminent.[10]

A problem with the logical foundations of this view of the crisis is that, although it demonstrates the possibility of the existence of multiple instantaneous equilibria, the theory is silent on the mechanisms underlying the (sudden

9. Note that even though the outcomes in the good and bad equilibrium are rather different, the deviation of the equilibrium exchange rate from the defended parity that triggers a devaluation is exactly the same (as shown by (7.8)).
10. Even a supporter of the "fundamental" interpretations of the ERM crisis such as Krugman (1996) admits that "the only argument that one might make on behalf of a self-fulfilling crisis story would be one that relies heavily on the absence of early warning signs in the financial markets." However, "at the very least, one must consider the alternative hypothesis of some myopia on the part of investors."

shift in the) private sector's coordination on a particular expectation regime. The analysis of a speculative attack as a self-fulfilling prophecy requires a leap from the theoretical identification of the existence of multiple equilibria to the characterization of an economic process (in "real time") that the model per se has nothing to say about. Theory is not (yet) able to provide useful pointers on how alternative equilibria are selected when multiplicity occurs: modelling expectations coordinating mechanisms requires further theoretical structures and/or ad-hoc assumptions.

Indeed, in most contributions in the literature, the coordination of private sector expectations depends on exogenous, subjective uncertainty; that is, the model is augmented with an arbitrary probability distribution defined over all possible equilibrium outcomes. Responding to some exogenous "switch", both wages and nominal interest rates are suddenly higher than they would have been had the private sector coordinated on a good equilibrium. The models considered have the property that, provided fundamentals are weak enough, there is in each period a positive probability that a "self-fulfilling" speculative attack will occur.

One might appeal to the foregoing analysis to observe that financial instability induced by the presence of multiple instantaneous equilibria is clearly a point against escape clauses in a peg, and perhaps a point against a peg tout court.[11] However, the welfare implications of these results are by no means straightforward. Consider the social loss function evaluated ex ante (i.e., before the shock is observed) but conditional on a particular set of expectations (i.e., for given wages). With multiple equilibria, the expected loss in the future can take different values. It can be shown that the expected loss associated with the bad equilibria (low threshold) is always larger than the expected loss associated with good equilibria (high threshold): The loss under a fixed rule, such as an inflexible peg, will typically be at some level between these two.

Consider now the unconditional expected loss function, evaluated before wage setters coordinate on a particular equilibrium. To the extent that the coordination mechanisms are specified in terms of exogenous uncertainty, the expected loss in the presence of an escape clause is an average of welfare levels in all equilibria, with weights given by the same "sunspot" probabilities that coordinate the assignment of market participants to the various regimes.[12] For these reasons, the welfare ranking of the exchange rate regimes is effectively indeterminate. For exactly the same structural parameters and social preferences, depending on the exogenous sunspot probability distribution, it is possible that a pure float is preferred to a peg with an escape clause even though an inflexible

11. See the discussion in Obstfeld (1991).
12. On sunspot equilibria see for example the discussion in Woodford (1990).

peg dominates the float; for a different probability distribution, the peg with escape clause could dominate any other policy scheme.[13]

Ultimately, as Obstfeld (1994) and Obstfeld and Rogoff (1995b) suggest, the contribution of such a black-box approach to our understanding of the logic of a currency crisis hinges primarily on its ability to rationalize the sudden "jump" in expectations that brings about a speculative attack. With reference to the ERM events, for instance, it could be argued that what appears prima facie as an arbitrary and irrational switch in currency traders' beliefs should be interpreted as the shift from one rational expectation equilibrium to another. Nonetheless, if taken too literally (i.e., self-fulfilling prophecies were the cause of the crisis), this extreme view would offer but a superficial phenomenological explanation of the 1992 currency crises, and of the persistent financial instability that followed.

7.4   Open issues in the "self-fulfilling" vs. "fundamental" debate

It has been argued that despite the conceptual weaknesses inherent in the multiple equilibria story reviewed in the previous section, the interpretation of the ERM events based on self-fulfilling prophecies should be given credit because alternative "fundamental" explanations do not perform very well empirically. In other words, the self-fulfilling view is claimed to be more successful in fitting the stylized facts of the ERM crisis relative to other theories.

Of course, supporters of the self-fulfilling view do not ignore the role of fundamental imbalances in the unfolding of a currency crisis. After all, the interplay between expectations and policy actions analyzed in the previous section does not necessarily generate a multiplicity of equilibria. A necessary condition for multiple equilibria to exist is the presence of a "credibility problem." If the country committed to a peg has sufficiently strong fundamentals, there will be a unique rational expectation equilibrium; this is the case in Figure 7.2, when the devaluation cost is as high as $\tilde{c}_1$ and the commitment to the defense

---

13. As a corollary consider what would happen if we specified a money demand equation that is interest sensitive. A shift from the good to the bad equilibrium would now be associated with a sudden contraction of money demand (because the nominal interest rate rises in response to the increase in the expected rate of depreciation of the currency), possibly implying reserve depletion. Such speculative waves would increase the probability of devaluation during the period; nonetheless, they would be neither sufficient nor necessary for the exchange rate parity to be abandoned. Underlying a devaluation remains the rational decision made by the policy makers, who, for given private sector expectations, would efficiently assess the state of the economy after the realization of the current shock to fundamentals. In spite of the appearances, a sudden reshuffle of private portfolios would be the effect, and not the cause of such a regime shift. Of course, it may be possible or even plausible that for some specification of both the structure of the economy and the preferences of the policy makers, the level of reserves may directly or indirectly affect the perceived costs of a defense of the peg.

of the peg is reliable in the face of the maximum potential size of the macroeconomic shock. Under a different parameter configuration, reflecting "weak" fundamentals, there will be multiple rational expectation equilibria; this is the case considered in Figure 7.2 when the devaluation cost is $\tilde{c}_2$.

The point of the self-fulfilling view is that the observed fundamental imbalances in Europe were not large enough to curtail the credibility of the "hard ERM" parities and trigger the persistent wave of large-scale speculative attacks between 1992 and 1993. The fundamentals typically referred to in the literature include various measures of employment, economic activity, relative prices, and fiscal deficits. The behavior of key macroeconomic variables is analyzed by using a variety of tests, generally carried out with reference to standard small open economy, unilateral peg models. Supporters of the self-fulfilling view stress two stylized facts emerging from the analysis: (1) there is no clear evidence of widespread deterioration of current macroeconomic indicators preceding the crisis (the worsening competitiveness and fiscal outlook in Italy are generally recognized as an exception to this general picture), and (2) fundamentals do not seem to differ before and after the crisis. Based on this evidence, Eichengreen, Rose, and Wyplosz (1994, p. 29) conclude:

> It does not appear ... that the policy imbalances to which first-generation models direct attention are obviously associated with the incidence of speculative attacks on ERM currencies. This absence of significant differences in the ERM subsample is consistent with the predictions of second-generation models emphasizing multiple equilibria and self-fulfilling attacks. The high capital mobility and abundant international liquidity of the relatively recent ERM period, which make self-fulfilling attacks relatively easy to launch, may explain this contrast.

Other economists have taken issue with this reading of the empirical evidence. Regarding point (1) above, for instance, it has been argued that there is enough evidence of a deterioration of fundamentals before the crisis, corroborating traditional explanations. As Krugman (1996) writes "it is hard to see on what basis one would use the ERM crackup as evidence for self-fulfilling crises. Fundamentals relevant to the willingness of governments to continue pegging their currencies had clearly worsened, and showed every sign of continuing to worsen."

Regarding point (2) one could argue that, on logical grounds, the fact that fundamentals do not differ before and after a currency crisis is evidence against an interpretation based on self-fulfilling expectations. This is because, as first pointed out by Flood and Garber (1984) and Obstfeld (1986), the existence of multiple equilibria is based on the policy maker's validation ex post of the initial private sector conjectures. To the extent that variables related to monetary and interest rate policies are included in the empirical measures of fundamentals, a structural break in the latter should indeed be detected after a successful self-fulfilling attack.

In principle, one could save the story by conceding that it only requires expectations of a change in the policy regime at some date in the future, and that these expectations are for some reason not reflected in any of the observable variables that have become available subsequent to the crisis. The same observable fundamentals therefore failed both to predict the regime shift before it occurred and to reflect the regime shift after it had occurred. It is hard to tell a reasonable story rationalizing both predictive failures.

Also, introducing in the analysis the possibility of future regime shifts in models with forward-looking private agents makes the resolution of the "self-fulfilling vs. fundamentals" issue virtually impossible on empirical grounds. In fact, expectations shifts triggered by self-fulfilling prophecies and expectations shifts reflecting anticipated future changes in fundamentals are to a very large extent observationally equivalent.

In our opinion, a correct approach to the debate "self-fulfilling vs. fundamentals" requires first and foremost a theoretical and analytical framework that is able to account for all fundamental imbalances, and to blend them together in a coherent view of the crisis. As shown in Chapters 3 and 4, the evidence on the behavior of fundamentals in the months preceding the crisis supports the view that the system was subject to unequivocal strain; this view is reinforced if the set of traditional macroeconomic fundamentals is extended to encompass less "standard" variables, such as a widespread weakening of political consensus regarding the virtues of the hard ERM and the Maastricht project.

However, the identification of different sources of strain (loss of competitiveness, fall in political consensus, excess demand in Germany after reunification) tells us very little about the timing and intensity of the currency crises since September 1992. There is no direct way to reconcile the magnitude of domestic imbalances and the size of devaluations. In many cases, actual devaluations appear to be disproportionate relative to the tensions experienced earlier in the system.

Moreover, as correctly pointed out by supporters of the self-fulfilling view, the fundamental interpretations of the crisis have so far failed to bring to light the logic and the mechanism underlying the sudden and generalized outbursts of financial distress in the system. Also, they have not paid enough attention to the fact that there seem to be few empirical signs of a structural break in monetary policy after the crisis.

In this book, we will show that it is possible to provide a more articulate interpretation of the ERM events that fits the existing evidence without postulating arbitrary shifts in self-fulfilling expectations. The focus of our attention is not on the intrinsic instability of financial markets when governments attempt to peg their currencies. Rather, we trace the root of the ERM currency crisis to the instability of the policy agreements that support a regime of fixed exchange rates.

The rest of Chapter 7 and all of Chapters 8 and 9 are devoted to the task of building a fundamental explanation of the crisis encompassing both domestic and systemic elements. We present a comprehensive interpretation of the crisis, in which we identify the key factor triggering the eruption of the 1992–93 events with the perception of a policy regime switch, from coordination to noncoordination, as signaled by the modalities of the first realignment since the inception of the hard ERM. We also explain why the very factors underlying the transformation of economic tensions into economic crises can also account for the absence of a structural break in ERM fundamentals; specifically, we show that restoring equilibrium in a noncooperative system is associated with the absence of a generalized monetary "loosening," and with the persistence of a regime of relatively high real interest rates.

The first step in our reconstruction focuses on a brief discussion of the role played by domestic political and economic factors in contributing to the emergence of tensions in the ERM. We start by revisiting a few popular interpretations of the ERM crisis within the analytical framework of our model.

7.5   Revisiting theories based on domestic fundamentals

7.5.1   *Perceived changes in the commitment to exchange rate stability*

The focus of our first interpretation of the emergence of tensions as the result of domestic developments is on the policy makers' commitment to exchange rate stability. It has been argued that the results of the first Danish referendum, and later public opinion polls in France, led policy makers to reassess the political payoff from supporting the Maastricht agenda and an inflexible defense of the ERM parities. In the other words, they brought about a fall in the perceived political cost of resorting to a devaluation to correct domestic imbalances.

Consider the impact of a reduction in the sunk costs of devaluation (say, from $\tilde{c}_1$ to $\tilde{c}_2$) on the equilibrium threshold in Figure 7.2. A reduction in $\tilde{c}_i$ lowers the threshold for a devaluation, thus increasing the probability of a crisis if the private sector coordinates on the good equilibrium. The result is intuitively appealing. For any given distribution of the external shock, a lower political cost of maintaining a fixed exchange rate implies a weaker commitment to the defense of the current parity. Market expectations are therefore revised, bringing about a further increase in the probability of a realignment.

While the consequences of a reduction in the costs of devaluation can be analyzed conveniently within our theoretical framework, our model does not address its causes. In principle, changes in devaluation costs should be modeled endogenously in a full-fledged political economy model. The interplay of economic and political factors should be made explicit in terms of acceptable primitives.

The literature provides a few examples of such theoretical exercises, in which $\tilde{c}_i$ is evaluated as the present discounted value of future welfare losses associated with a particular policy scenario. Froot and Rogoff (1991) point out the destabilizing endgame effects of the Maastricht timetable for EMU, insofar as deadlines raise the temptation to resort to a final realignment (by lowering $\tilde{c}_i$) before locking in the exchange rate irrevocably at a fixed Euro conversion rate. Currie (1992), among others, carries out welfare analysis comparing EMU to alternative exchange rate arrangements.

For the purpose of illustrating the main issues, we will make a simple attempt to square the policy makers' perceived cost of abandoning the peg with their policy goals. Consider a simple two-period model in which the abandonment of the current ERM parity jeopardizes a country's chance of joining EMU in the second period. In this case, $\tilde{c}_i$ represents the differential between expected welfare (estimated according to a loss function such as (6.28)) under EMU and under an alternative exchange rate regime.

There are at least two open questions in evaluating expected welfare in terms of the social welfare function (6.28). First, what will the monetary policy of the newly formed monetary union be? Second, what is the relevant alternative to participating in the union?

The issue of identifying the expected monetary stance of the European central bank following EMU can be addressed using the approach in Alesina and Grilli (1993). These authors focus on how different national preferences over inflation and unemployment will affect the European Central Bank's inflationary bias. Assuming that the ECB's attitude towards inflation will reflect domestic biases (say, the ECB's σ in equation (6.28) will be some weighted average of national σs), then, the union-wide inflationary bias will be higher than the one prevailing in the most disciplined countries and lower than that prevailing in the least disciplined countries.

Regarding the second issue, exclusion from EMU does not rule out the possibility, or even the desirability, of a peg against the common currency. In principle, governments of excluded countries can always announce and implement a peg against the new European currency. A different alternative is to resort to a (managed) float.

A key result of comparative welfare analysis within the framework of a disinflation game is that even the sign of the net gain from EMU over alternative regimes (thus, the sign of $\tilde{c}_i$) is ambiguous (Currie, 1992). It is quite possible that a flexible unilateral peg is preferred over an irrevocably fixed exchange rate regime. Unless the perceived gains from monetary union are microeconomic efficiency gains and/or are based on non-economic considerations, there is no a priori reason to expect that giving up exchange rate flexibility raises the economic well-being of a nation.

The existence of multiple instantaneous equilibria brings about further complexities and ambiguities in comparing welfare levels between a peg and EMU. By construction, the perceived reward from maintaining the unilateral peg will be increasing in the exogenous (sunspot) probability of the private sector coordinating on a good equilibrium in the future. The possibility of self-fulfilling speculative attacks – that is to say, financial instability – may radically change the assessment of the welfare implications of different exchange rate arrangements, depending on the probabilities attached to the private sector coordinating on alternative equilibria. A monetary union (i.e., irrevocably fixed exchange rates) typically dominates bad equilibria under a flexible peg, but may also be dominated by some good ones, when the case for flexibility is strong enough. Decision making under these conditions is difficult, for it depends on the (unobservable) likelihood of the private sector coordinating on alternative equilibria.[14]

In the end, there is little doubt that the first Danish referendum contributed to the upsurge of exchange rate tension in the ERM during the summer of 1992. Nonetheless, interpreting the ERM events exclusively in terms of perceived changes in policy makers' commitment to exchange rate stability is likely to flounder between the Scylla of the trite and obvious and the Charybdis of arbitrary postulates, intricate scenarios, and ambiguous theoretical conclusions. While such prospects need not discourage the truly intrepid from further research in the area, it certainly encourages the pursuit of alternative interpretations.

7.5.2   Learning and beliefs updating

Explanations of the ERM crisis based on fundamentals have singled out the fiscal deficits and the investment boom associated with the German reunification process, as well as the tightening of German monetary policy to contain inflationary pressures. However, in assessing the role of the German reunification shock in the currency crisis, most observers have been puzzled by the long delay between the May 1990 reunification and the EMS 1992–93 events. If indeed the German shock (and its macroeconomic implications) was the root cause of the ERM collapse, forward-looking currency markets should have been able to anticipate the coming turmoil, and the stability of the parity grid should have been undermined well before the fall of 1992.

This puzzle should be examined in the light of a model where shocks to fundamentals have forward-looking components. Our model emphasizes that the country-specific shock ($v_{i,t}$) includes a forward-looking variable (ϵ_t), defined as the present value of current and future demand disturbances λ_t^* (broadly

14. In this respect, it is important to stress that even monetary unions are by no means irreversible. The presence of escape clauses, quantitatively but perhaps not qualitatively different from the ones analyzed so far, cannot be ruled out a priori, especially when political decision-making is largely carried out at national level.

interpreted to include the German fiscal stance following unification). Such a specification makes clear that the sign and intensity of current shocks to λ_t^* may be only weakly related to movements in forward-looking macro variables like ϵ_t. More weight should be given to the stability of the distribution of the shocks, their persistence over time, and indeed to the learning problems associated with shocks that are to a large extent unprecedented. We provide two simple examples explaining these points.

The perceived persistence of the shocks Consider the impact on country i of a positive innovation to λ_t^* in the Center. Maintaining the assumption $p_t^* = n_t^* = 0$, a positive shock λ_t^* increases country i's real interest rate, reducing aggregate demand and employment and generating pressures towards a depreciation of its currency vis-à-vis the Center.

Suppose that, for a constant λ, the relative demand disturbance is generated by the following process

$$\lambda_t^* - \lambda = \rho\left(\lambda_{t-1}^* - \lambda\right) + \eta_t \quad 0 < \rho < 1 \tag{7.20}$$

where the innovation η_t is *i.i.d.* with zero mean. The higher the coefficient of serial correlation ρ, the more persistent the relative demand disturbance. Thus, evaluating (6.38) under our assumption, it follows that an instantaneous demand shock in the Center of size λ_t^* translates into a shock to fundamentals ϵ_t equal to

$$\epsilon_t = \frac{\gamma}{\nu(1 - 2\beta)}\left(\frac{\lambda_t^* - \lambda}{1 - \gamma\rho}\right). \tag{7.21}$$

The shock ϵ_t is proportional to the current demand disturbance λ_t^*, and its size (in absolute value) is clearly increasing in the degree of serial correlation ρ.

Arguably, to the extent that the unprecedented nature of the demand shock in the Center made it difficult to evaluate the parameters of its structural form, forecasters' estimates of the degree of persistence were likely to be subject to revisions over time.[15] A sudden quantitative reassessment of ρ in market participants' expectations translates into a discrete jump of the present value of demand shocks ϵ_t and of the entire structure of country-specific shocks. This jump increases exchange rate tensions in the system.[16] In conclusion, the unanticipated shock to fundamentals may be the result of updating beliefs about

15. This would fit the Keynesian belief that the determination of exchange rates and other asset prices is the result of a "conventional valuation," that is, the "outcome of the mass psychology of a large number of ignorant individuals, liable to change violently as the result of a sudden fluctuation of opinion" (Keynes, 1936, p. 154).

16. It could even be large enough (that is, from a level below the devaluation threshold $\bar{v}_{i,t}$ to a value above it) to trigger a currency crisis. Needless to say, a revision in the estimate of ρ is associated with the updating of beliefs regarding the entire distribution of ϵ_t. In other words, both $v_{i,t}$ and $\bar{v}_{i,t}$ might jump per effect of a change in the estimated ρ.

the value of ρ, without any apparent deterioration in current variables in the Center country.[17]

Signal extraction and forecast errors   In our second example, we assume that the shock has permanent and transitory components that private agents are not able to disentangle from each other. In this case, it is well known that rational forecasts will be characterized by a typical adaptive pattern and "learning" behavior. As the magnitude and duration of the West-to-East fiscal transfers associated with German unification was only revealed gradually, the full implications of the shock for the stability of the exchange rate could only emerge over time.

Once again, a specific example, based on a standard signal extraction problem, may help clarify the issue under consideration. Assume that the relative demand shock is generated by the following process:

$$(\lambda_t^* - \lambda) = \vartheta_t + \mu_t \tag{7.22}$$

$$\vartheta_{t+1} = \rho\vartheta_t + \eta_{t+1} \tag{7.23}$$

for $t \geq 0$. Different from the earlier example, the parameter ρ is now assumed to be known. The random variables μ and η are orthogonal to each other and satisfy:

$$E\mu_t = 0, \quad E\mu_t^2 = \sigma_\mu^2, \quad E\mu_t\mu_{t-j} = 0 \tag{7.24}$$

$$E\eta_t = 0, \quad E\eta_t^2 = \sigma_\eta^2, \quad E\eta_t\eta_{t-j} = 0. \tag{7.25}$$

Market participants observe a relative demand shock, but they are not able to assess correctly the weight of its permanent as opposed to its transitory component, although they know σ_μ^2 and σ_η^2 and the entire past history of $(\lambda_t^* - \lambda)$. Under these assumptions, macroeconomic fundamentals converge asymptotically to the following distributed lag of the realized demand disturbances:[18]

$$\epsilon_t = \frac{\gamma}{v(1 - 2\beta)} \frac{1}{1 - \gamma\rho} \frac{\kappa}{\rho} \sum_{\tau=0}^{\infty} (\rho - \kappa)^\tau \left(\lambda_{t-\tau}^* - \lambda\right) \tag{7.26}$$

where

$$\kappa = \frac{\rho\Sigma}{\Sigma + \sigma_\mu^2} \tag{7.27}$$

17. These considerations illustrate once again the formidable identification problems in assessing fundamental explanations of the crisis as opposed to interpretations based on self-fulfilling speculative attacks. Suppose we observe a sudden increase in the real interest rate in the Center, given an unchanged fiscal policy (say, $\lambda_t^* = \lambda_{t-1}^*$). Is this a symptom of a shift from one instantaneous equilibrium to another, or rather it is caused by a rational revision of the estimated degree of shock persistence? Problems of observational equivalence make the comparison between the two models inevitably difficult.

18. The standard textbook reference is Sargent (1987, p. 230).

and Σ is the stationary solution to the following equation:

$$\Sigma_{t+1} = (\rho - \kappa_t)^2 \Sigma_t + \sigma_\eta^2 + \kappa_t^2 \sigma_\mu^2. \tag{7.28}$$

As $\rho - \kappa < 1$, a large and persistent variation in the relative demand shock starting at, say, time t_0 will translate into a relatively mild variation in the (discounted) fundamental ϵ_t. Only gradually will ϵ_t reflect the full impact of the shock: ϵ_t will initially undershoot its steady state level and will grow over time as forecasters slowly adapt their expectations. According to this view, the period spanned by the German unification announcement and the symptoms of its disruptive effects on the ERM parities need not be short, in particular if forecasters' priors assign a large weight to the variance of temporary shocks σ_μ^2 relative to σ_η^2.

Fiscal and monetary mix Learning and beliefs updating about the magnitude of the demand shock associated with the reunification of Germany help explain the delay between this event and the buildup of disruptive tensions in the ERM. In 1990 and 1991, there was considerable uncertainty about the magnitude and duration of the West-to-East fiscal transfers.

However, as stressed in Chapter 3, most of the exchange rate tension was generated by the monetary stance of the Bundesbank in reaction to the fiscal expansion accompanying the reunification. A regime of high and persistent interest rates in Europe therefore emerged only gradually over time, as the uncompromising attitude of the Bundesbank – insofar as interest rate policy was concerned – was revealed rather gradually and emerged fully only at the dawn of the crisis (see the pattern of German interest rates in Figures 3.1 and 3.2). As late as the week before the crisis, at the Bath meeting on September 5–6, 1992, an interest rate cut was still considered a feasible policy option by many ERM policy makers.

The relevant question is whether and to what extent the revelation and perception of the intransigence of the German authorities translated into a reassessment of the likelihood of a persistence of the high interest rate regime in Europe. The question is addressed in Chapters 8 and 9.

7.5.3   *Inherent weakness of disinflation policies*

The third fundamental explanation points to an inherent weakness of any price/output stabilization policy based on pegging the exchange rate. If either inflation has inertia or the new exchange rate regime is not perfectly credible, the policy initially results in an appreciation of the real exchange rate. Worsening competitiveness affects the trade balance, production, and employment. To correct such imbalances without devaluing the nominal exchange rate, a country must push its domestic rate of CPI inflation below that of the Center country and offset the initial real appreciation. To the extent that prices and wages adjust only sluggishly, the costs of the required deflation are high, undermining the credibility of the commitment to maintain the exchange rate parity.

A model with one-period wage contracts like ours can only offer a partial account of these effects, based on the consequences of imperfect credibility for the output and competitiveness of a country in the short run. The issue should be addressed within models that encompass multiperiod wage contracts, or that permit the costs of disinflation policies to last for more than one period. In the model of Drazen and Masson (1994) discussed earlier, for instance, a tough stance in defense of the exchange rate parity increases the "natural" rate of unemployment over time. In this example, the presence of a state variable – the "memory" of past unemployment rates – captures the cumulative cost of defending the peg. A currency crisis can occur despite stable or even improving current fundamentals.

The hypothesis that the ERM crisis reflected gaps in cost competitiveness across countries, stemming from the cumulative effects of inflation differentials over time, has been supported by a several economists.[19] Empirically, such an interpretation applies reasonably well to a number of countries, including Italy and Spain. It is controversial, however, when used to explain why speculative attacks hit the currency of countries, such as France, where the signs of deteriorating external competitiveness – conventionally measured by real exchange rates based on relative CPIs or unit labor costs – were ambiguous. The British case is also puzzling as changes in cost competitiveness were relatively slight over the entire period from 1987 to 1995. One could argue that in both cases the incipient loss of competitiveness was suppressed through a high and rising unemployment rate, which created doubts about the political sustainability of the exchange rate policy. According to this interpretation, both France and the United Kingdom suppressed an incipient loss of competitiveness with rising unemployment.

If misalignments across countries were at the root of the ERM crises, one would expect that the size of individual countries' nominal depreciations since September 1992 would match, on average, the size of the cumulative competitiveness gaps that opened up during the hard ERM years. In general, however, empirical evidence does not support the presence of a direct link between cumulative cost competitiveness changes and changes in nominal exchange rates. According to a study of the European Commission,

> In some cases, [changes in nominal exchange rates] have offset the cost-competitiveness gains or losses recorded over the period from 1987 to 1992. In others, they have led to net gains or losses in cost competitiveness compared with the trends over that period. In those countries whose competitiveness had deteriorated sharply between 1987 and 1992, the nominal changes which

19. See for instance Feldstein (1992).

occurred over the period from the third quarter of 1992 to the third quarter of 1995 have more than compensated for the previously recorded losses in some cases (Sweden) and have partially compensated for the losses in others (Spain). For Greece and Portugal, these nominal changes have not led to any improvement in cost competitiveness, which has continued to worsen (Commission of the European Communities, 1995, p. 4).

7.6   A summary

In this chapter we have reviewed several popular interpretations of the ERM crisis, casting the analysis within the unifying framework introduced in Chapter 6. Even though external shocks, originating outside the Periphery, represent the key macroeconomic disturbance in the exchange rate system, all these interpretations emphasize the role played by domestic credibility (that is, the interactions between public and private sectors in each single Periphery country). We summarize here our main conclusions.

By its nature an adjustable peg creates the possibility of multiple equilibria. Radically different forecasts of future monetary policies may be model consistent, that is, compatible with rational predictions by private agents, to the extent that they are ex post validated by the behavior of the policy maker. In turn, optimal monetary policies are determined taking market participants' expectations as a datum. This element of circularity underlies the possibility of self-fulfilling prophecies. Thus, a sudden shift in expectations may force the government to abandon the peg, even in the absence of any prior or concurrent deterioration in macroeconomic fundamentals. This analysis has been offered as an explanation of why ERM credibility suddenly vanished in September 1992. Despite the fact that only a few weeks before interest rate differentials were narrowing (the argument goes), the private sector's coordination suddenly shifted from one (favorable) expectation regime to another (unfavorable) one.

The explanation based on multiple instantaneous equilibria fits by construction the evidence of low interest rate differentials and low nominal wage increases in the period leading up to the crisis. As we have seen, the crucial empirical argument in its favor is the absence of any apparent worsening of current macroeconomic indicators before the crisis. For this very reason, however, this explanation faces a conceptual problem when it comes to identifying the switch from a "tight" to a "loose" policy regime that should follow a crisis, validating ex post the shift in expectations. Such regime breaks are not easily detectable after the 1992–93 crisis.

According to the empirical literature on the crisis, an explanation based on fundamentals appears to be wanting. A scrutiny of the domestic macroeconomic stance in each ERM country suggests no clear conclusion about the contribution of specific domestic imbalances to the generation of such a widespread crisis, although in a number of countries (notably Italy and possibly also the United

Kingdom) country-specific tensions had been building up. We have focussed on three stories that undoubtedly contribute, each from its own particular perspective, to our understanding of the 1992 puzzle. These interpretations, whether viewed individually or collectively, appear incapable of explaining satisfactorily (either empirically or theoretically) why a large-scale systemic crisis did occur. They do, however, shed light on possible sources of exchange rate tension in the ERM during the period leading up to the crisis and thus complement our systemic perspective to be formalized in the next chapter.

First, insofar as the perception of a failing political consensus in favor of Maastricht softened the policy makers' commitment to the ERM, the first Danish referendum led to a downward revision of the costs of a devaluation. In exploring this effect, we have related the magnitude of the sunk costs of a realignment to the stability of the exchange rate parity.

Second, the analysis in this chapter addressed a major problem in disentangling the role of German reunification in the ERM crisis, namely the long delay between the unprecedented reunification shock and the currency turmoil. By allowing for private sector learning about the nature and the magnitude of the shock, we have shown that there could be significant lags between the realization of a persistent disturbance to aggregate demand in the Center and the eruption of tensions in the foreign exchange markets.

Moreover, when dealing with unprecedented shocks, agents' knowledge of the structure of the relevant stochastic processes may not be complete. Because future developments and scenarios are hard to forecast, the precise degree of persistence over time of the underlying shocks is uncertain, and the possibility of drastic revisions in beliefs concerning the distribution of the shock should not be ruled out. The perception of fundamental imbalances that require a general realignment in the system may therefore be the result of such an updating of agents' beliefs, rather than the outcome of sizable modifications in the current fundamentals.

Third, competitiveness problems can result from imperfect credibility as reflected in the level of domestic money wages, weakening the incentives to maintain a peg. The structure of the model could be enriched to allow for alternative mechanisms through which competitiveness may deteriorate, such as inflation inertia, multiperiod contracts, or hysteresis in unemployment. A short section of the chapter also dealt with exchange rate misalignments due to overambitious price targets.

In our opinion, these stories are important pieces of a fundamentals model of the crisis that has not yet revealed all of its interpretative potential. As pointed out in the beginning of this chapter, the relevant source of macroeconomic uncertainty, from the vantage point of each Periphery country, includes the policy strategies adopted in the rest of the system. The implications of this view are developed fully in the next chapter.

CHAPTER 8

Policy coordination and currency crises

8.1 Introduction

In our view, most readings of the 1992–93 events miss the following crucial element: the ERM crackup has been the crisis of an exchange rate *system*, rather than the collapse of a collection of unilateral pegs individually pursued by a number of countries. The thesis we develop in this chapter is that the conclusions reached within the conceptual framework of the "unilateral peg" may be incomplete or misleading, since they both ignore the key role played by structural policy spillovers among European countries and overlook the effects of coordination (or lack thereof) of monetary and exchange rate policies within the system.

In this chapter and the next we argue that, while domestic private–public sector interactions are certainly an important part of the process that brought down the ERM, the 1992–93 crisis was in the first instance a conflict among monetary authorities and a failure of the European system as a policy coordination mechanism. In contrast to an approach that focuses exclusively on country-specific issues, ultimately only a systemic view is able to provide a comprehensive reading of the ERM crisis.

Our analysis thus fits the category of "fundamental" explanations, provided the set of fundamentals is augmented to include the cooperative (or noncooperative) design of monetary and exchange rate policies in the system, that is, to include the "rules of the game" that characterize the behavior of the Periphery countries and the Center vis-à-vis each other. The model we present is fully consistent with the logic of exchange rate crises as discussed in Chapters 5 through 7. Yet, in order to stress and analyze the specific role of international policy coordination, we choose to downplay the importance of cross-country differences and idiosyncratic features at the core of the analysis of Chapter 7.

In particular, throughout this chapter we make a set of (admittedly unrealistic) assumptions that rule out cross-country differences in economic structure, inherited economic conditions, domestic credibility, and subjective expectations. All policy-makers in the Periphery are assumed to the same level of employment and face the same realignment costs:

$$\bar{n}_i = \bar{n} \quad \text{and} \quad c_i = c, \qquad i = 1, 2, \ldots, N. \tag{8.1}$$

Consistently, we assume that the private sectors coordinate their expectations on the same (multicountry) equilibrium, that is,

$$w_{i,t} - \bar{s}_{i,t} = w_{j,t} - \bar{s}_{j,t} = w_t - \bar{s}_t \qquad i, j = 1, 2, \ldots, N. \qquad (8.2)$$

These two assumptions together imply that all countries in the Periphery are *ex-ante* identical.[1]

As our historical reconstruction in Chapter 3 makes clear, asymmetries between European countries in the early 1990s were by no means negligible, and there is no doubt that a comprehensive assessment of the ERM crisis should not ignore such differences in national fundamentals. Nevertheless, during the twelve months spanning September 1992 to August 1993, a wave of crises was witnessed within the EMS which appears to be only weakly related to visible divergences in macroeconomic policy stance and economic performance among European economies. To the extent that the 1992–93 events in Europe represent the breakdown of a system rather than the demise of the unilateral exchange rate policies undertaken by a collection of isolated countries, the analysis of intra-Periphery asymmetries does not help solve the puzzles of the ERM crisis.[2]

In the light of these considerations, the assumptions of symmetry (8.1) and (8.2) are meant only to facilitate the understanding of the crucial issue at stake – the role of policy coordination in an exchange rate crisis. The analysis gains in clarity by focusing on a model that abstracts from many other (by no means irrelevant) determinants that are specific to particular countries.

In what follows, we reconsider the model presented in Chapter 6 from a new perspective. In comparison to Chapter 7, we shift the core of the analysis from the role of domestic private agents to the interplay among national policy makers. Wages are taken as given parameters, that is, we do not explicitly address the problem of determining market expectations.[3] For these reasons, there is no need to emphasize further the time dimension of our model; for notational convenience, we will drop time subscripts throughout the rest of our model.

Moreover, in this chapter the relevant price level for the Center country is the CPI, rather than the GDP deflator. The latter assumption was introduced in Chapter 7 for the sake of analytical tractability. In this chapter, our analysis returns to the original framework of Chapter 6, which allows for structural interdependence between Center and Periphery as a whole, as well as among Periphery countries.

---

1. Joint conditions (6.30) and (8.2) imply that $w_t - \bar{q}_t$ are also equalized in the Periphery.
2. See Buiter, Corsetti and Pesenti (1997).
3. It is worth emphasizing that, while our approach does not rule out the possibility of multiple instantaneous equilibria for given fundamentals, it works even if the domestic equilibrium is unique.

The outline of the chapter is as follows. First, we will concentrate on the monetary game and the reaction functions of each country in the system, discussing the nature and magnitude of international spillovers of domestic policies, that is, the intra-Periphery externalities underlying our model. Then, for given wages, we characterize the noncooperative (Nash) equilibrium of the monetary policy game between the Center and the N countries in the Periphery of the system. This will provide the analytical benchmark describing the behavior of an exchange rate system where all Periphery countries independently and unilaterally pursue a peg against the currency of the Center. Next, we will introduce cooperation in the Periphery of the system and discuss its rules. Finally, we will compare the properties of the system when Periphery countries coordinate their policies with respect to the Nash benchmark. A nontechnical summary of the main conclusion of the analysis is presented at the beginning of Chapter 9.

8.2   Noncooperative equilibrium

8.2.1   Reaction functions in the Center and the Periphery

In this section we characterize the monetary policy game between the Center and the N countries in the Periphery of the system, for given market expectations (embedded in the predetermined money wages). For each country, we are interested in determining the "reaction function", that is, the optimal monetary response to external shocks taking the behavior of the other monetary authorities in the system as a datum.

Consider first the reaction function in the Center country.[4] Taking the first-order condition for loss minimization in (6.24), the Center's optimal monetary policy is given by

$$n^* = H \left[\beta \phi \frac{1}{N} \sum_i n_i + \beta \epsilon - w^* \right] \tag{8.3}$$

where

$$H \equiv \frac{\sigma (\alpha + \beta \phi)}{1 + \sigma (\alpha + \beta \phi)^2}. \tag{8.4}$$

Equation (8.3) reveals that, *ceteris paribus*, the Center will always find it optimal to react to a monetary expansion (contraction) in the Periphery by increasing (reducing) its own money supply. In other words, from the vantage

---

4. It is worth emphasizing that the Center is not assumed to be a Stackelberg leader. Throughout this section, the Center and each individual member of the Periphery play Nash vis-à-vis all other players. However, alternative specifications regarding the nature of the strategic game between Center and Periphery as a whole would not alter the main results of our model.

point of the Center, its monetary policy action and the monetary policy actions of each of the Periphery countries are strategic complements.[5]

The intuition is straightforward. Given its preferences (6.24), the Center always equates, at the margin, the costs of price fluctuations to the benefits from bringing employment closer to the natural rate level. To the extent that, say, a monetary expansion in the Periphery brings about a depreciation of the Periphery's effective real exchange rate z,[6] the CPI in the Center will fall together with the price of imported goods. The Center's employment is of course affected only by its own monetary policy. Therefore, as a result of the monetary expansion in the Periphery, the benefit from a more expansionary monetary stance in the Center (to stabilize domestic employment) exceeds, at the margin, the cost of increasing the CPI.

Consider now the optimal monetary policy in a representative Periphery country i. Due to the presence of sunk, lump-sum realignment costs, the reaction function for country i is discontinuous. If $\Delta \tilde{s}_i \leq \tilde{c}$,

$$n_i = \frac{1}{[\alpha + \xi(1 - \theta)]} \left[\bar{s} - w + w^* + \xi\theta \sum_{j \neq i} n_j + (\alpha + \phi)n^* - \epsilon \right]$$

(8.5)

while if $\Delta \tilde{s}_{i,t} \geq \tilde{c}$,

$$n_i = \frac{1}{[\alpha + \xi(1 - \theta)]} \left[\bar{s} - w + \Delta \tilde{s}_i + w^* + \xi\theta \sum_{j \neq i} n_j + (\alpha + \phi)n^* - \epsilon \right]$$

$$= \frac{1}{A[\alpha + \xi(1 - \theta)]} \left[\bar{n} - \Lambda \left(w - \bar{q} + \beta\epsilon - \beta\xi\theta \sum_{j \neq i} n_j - \beta\phi n^* \right) \right].$$

(8.6)

5. Player a's action n_a is a strategic complement with respect to player b's action n_b if the magnitude of the optimal action of player a increases whenever player b increases the magnitude of her action, that is, if and only if $\partial n_a / \partial n_b > 0$. In the two-player case the reaction curve of player a would slope upward. When $\partial n_a / \partial n_b < 0$, country b's action is instead a strategic substitute with respect to country a's action. On the game-theoretical implications of strategic complementarity and substitutability, see Bulow, Geanakoplos, and Klemperer (1985).

6. A real depreciation of z is a straighforward result when all Periphery countries simultaneously expand, because every currency depreciates vis-à-vis the Center (6.37). At first sight, less obvious is the case in which only a few countries in the Periphery increase their money supply. A monetary expansion in country i brings about, *ceteris paribus*, a depreciation of its bilateral real exchange rate $z_{i,t}$ (6.39). However, an expansion in one country will have repercussions on all other Periphery countries, even if they defend their nominal exchange rate parity against the Center. More precisely, an expansion in country i tends to appreciate country j's real exchange rate against the Center if $\theta > 0$, and to depreciate it if $\theta < 0$. At any rate, by (6.37), these indirect effects of a monetary expansion in country i do not prevail over its direct effect, independently of the sign of θ, and the Periphery real effective rate z unambiguously depreciates as a consequence of a monetary expansion by any subset of countries in the Periphery.

These expressions reveal that the money stocks of any pair of countries j and i are not necessarily strategic complements, depending on the sign of the parameter θ. They are strategic complements if and only if the parameter θ is positive. In this case the best response to country j's monetary expansion is a monetary expansion in country i as well. Conversely, if $\theta < 0$, Periphery countries' policy money stocks are strategic substitutes. In this case the best response to country j's monetary expansion is a monetary contraction in country i. Note that for each Periphery country, its money stock and the Center's money stock are unambiguously strategic complements.

The sign and the magnitude of the coefficient θ are central to our interpretation of the Periphery reaction functions, and the Nash equilibrium they support. In the next section, we will show that θ can be thought of as a synthetic indicator of intra-Periphery externalities and structural policy spillovers.

8.2.2   International policy spillovers

Consider a monetary expansion in a representative Periphery country, indexed by j, which brings about a real depreciation of its currency against the Center.[7] The impact of such a monetary expansion on the economy of any other Periphery country, indexed by i, can be split into two components of opposite sign, an expenditure-switching effect and an expenditure-changing effect.

To understand these effects, consider the equilibrium condition in the goods market of the Center (6.8). Other things equal, a real depreciation of the Periphery country j's currency shifts demand in the Center away from the goods produced either in the Center or in the rest of the Periphery (that is, in any country $i \neq j$) and toward country j's goods. This is the *expenditure-switching effect*, associated with a monetary expansion in country j that lowers aggregate demand in the rest of the Periphery and in the Center. However, output supply in the Center is unchanged (since this depends only on the Center's own money stock), so equilibrium requires a fall in the Center's real interest rate. *Ceteris paribus*, the fall of r^* lowers the real interest rate in all other countries and boosts demand for the Periphery's output. This is the *expenditure-changing impact* of a monetary expansion in country j: it increases global demand by lowering the "world" interest rate.

What matters here is the sign and the magnitude of the elasticity of the real interest rate in country i, r_i, with respect to country j's real exchange rate, z_j,

---

7. Given the constant velocity money demand function $m_{j,t} = p_{j,t} + y_{j,t}$ and the output supply function $y_{j,t} = \alpha(m_{j,t} - w_{j,t})$, it follows that with $\alpha < 1$ (and predetermined wages), country j's GDP deflator increases with its nominal money stock but less than proportionally, and its real output expands. The increase in aggregate demand (6.16) that matches the increase in supply requires a real depreciation and a fall of the real interest rate. The elasticity of the bilateral real exchange rate with respect to the money supply is, in fact, equal to $\xi(1 - \theta)$, which is unambiguously positive for $\beta < 1/2$.

implicitly given by (6.32). This elasticity is equal to $\beta - (\delta/\nu)$, and by (6.40) it is proportional to the negative of θ. Consider a parameter configuration such that θ is positive. Since in this case the elasticity of demand with respect to the real exchange rate δ is relatively large, the depreciation of j's bilateral real exchange rate with the Center brings about a large fall in demand for Center output. For a given domestic supply in the Center the real interest rate will have to fall substantially to clear the market for the Center's output. This decline in the real interest rate is transmitted to the other Periphery countries. They now face excess demand at their old bilateral real exchange rate with the Center and will experience a real appreciation. Although in our model all goods market interaction among the Periphery passes through the Center, similar considerations also apply in the more general case in which intra-Periphery trade is considered.

Summarizing, if $\theta > 0$, the expenditure-changing effect of a monetary expansion by one Periphery country prevails over the expenditure-switching effect: expansionary policies somewhere in the Periphery bring about a real appreciation and a fall in real interest rates in the other Periphery countries.[8] On the other hand, if $\theta < 0$, the spillovers associated with a monetary expansion by one country have the opposite sign. The real interest rate must increase in all Periphery countries that do not expand their money stocks, while their bilateral real exchange rates depreciate against the Center. This is the case of a prevailing expenditure-switching effect.[9]

An important implication of a dominant expenditure-changing effect is that a monetary expansion in one country tends to enhance the stability of the peg in all other Periphery countries, because it lowers the shadow devaluation rate for any level of the Center shock. In fact, from (7.6) we have

$$\frac{\partial \Delta \tilde{s}_i}{\partial n_j} = -\left(\frac{A - \beta \Lambda}{A}\right)\xi\theta < 0 \qquad \text{if } \theta > 0. \tag{8.7}$$

Conversely, if $\theta < 0$, the SDR in one country increases with a monetary innovation in any other country.

8.2.3   Are national monetary policies strategic complements?

In the vast majority of two-country theoretical models of monetary interdependence, monetary instruments are assumed to be strategic comple-

8. Ultimately, if $\theta > 0$, the impact of country j's devaluation is a reduction of the international competitiveness of country i. However, this result stems from the increase in demand for country i's goods (brought about by the fall in the world real interest rate), so that the recessionary spillovers that typically characterize beggar-thy-neighbor policies do not materialize here.

9. Qualitatively similar results are often found in the literature on international monetary transmission. For instance, in Obstfeld and Rogoff (1995a), the effects of foreign money supply increases on home output are found to be ambiguous, since they depend on the size of the consumption elasticity of money demand.

ments.[10] However, as discussed in the previous section, the sign and size of the strategic linkages between national policy makers are theoretically ambiguous. Ultimately, whether expenditure-switching effects prevail over expenditure-changing effects or vice versa is an empirical question, which can be addressed only by using a multicountry econometric model. The problems in carrying out empirical estimates of these effects are well known. It does not come as a surprise that on the basis of the simulation exercises in the literature, the evidence on the nature of worldwide policy spillovers is far from conclusive.

Rather than directly estimating the reaction functions of national monetary authorities, the empirical literature on macroeconomic interdependence and global cooperation typically focuses on the "policy multipliers" of a multicountry econometric model, that is, the effects (over a pre-specified period of time) of a change in the policy mix of a given country on the economies of the other countries, holding constant the policy mix (or policy rules) in the other countries.[11]

A representative example of such simulation exercises is the estimate of the repercussions (after a two-year lag) of a 1% increase in the money supply of the United States on output and inflation in the rest of the world, and the analogous effects of a 1% increase in the money supply of the rest of the world on output and inflation in the United States. This is the case considered by Frankel (1988), who reports results based on twelve global econometric models.[12] Six out of twelve models forecast that a monetary expansion in the United States reduces foreign output; the other six models predict instead a nonnegative impact on foreign output. With only one exception, all models predict a fall in inflation in the rest of the world following the increase in US money supply. A monetary expansion in the rest of the world increases US income according to most models, and it generally has a deflationary impact in the United States.

10. In the textbook case, when two countries face a global inflationary shock, a monetary contraction in the home country depreciates the foreign country's exchange rate, magnifying the inflationary impact of the original shock on the foreign economy. As a reaction to home country's policy, the foreign monetary authority also tightens its money supply.

11. The results of such counterfactual simulations are, of course, sensitive to what is assumed about the behavior of the policy authorities in the other countries. Even if strategic reactions by the foreign authorities are ruled out, it will, for instance, make a significant difference whether the foreign authorities peg the short-run nominal interest rate, the exchange rate, or the growth rates of some monetary aggregate. In some simulations the monetary authorities are assumed to use a policy reaction function linking monetary growth, the short nominal interest rate, and/or the exchange rate. Similarly, the details of the specification of a "constant" fiscal policy in the rest of the world will influence the outcome of the simulations, and even the simulations of monetary impulses. Plausible candidates include keeping public spending and tax revenues constant (in nominal or in real terms or as a proportion of GDP) and keeping the public sector financial deficit constant (in nominal terms, in real terms, or as a fraction of GDP), either through variations in spending or through variations in revenues.

12. See also Ghosh and Masson (1994, Ch. 2).

The disagreement across different models is to a large extent the obvious consequence of sharply contrasting assumptions, especially regarding the nature of market expectations.[13] There exist, however, subsets of models that share a large number of key features. For instance, both the International Monetary Fund's MULTIMOD (Masson, Symansky, and Meredith, 1990) and the MSG model (McKibbin and Sachs, 1991) build upon a Mundell-Fleming framework which incorporates rational expectations, asset dynamics, and intertemporal budget constraints.

A common framework does not necessarily lead to identical results. According to MULTIMOD, an unexpected permanent increase in the US stock of base money has on impact a positive effect on the GNP of European countries (Germany excluded); the effect turns negative two to three years following the US monetary impulse; it is positive thereafter (United Kingdom excluded). Repeating the same experiment using the MSG model leads to the conclusion that there is almost no international transmission of US monetary policy. Output of the other countries in the model, as well as the trade balance of the United States, remain virtually unchanged. As McKibbin and Sachs put it, "floating exchange rates effectively insulate the output of countries from monetary policies abroad."[14]

Nonetheless, when these two models are simulated with the goal of estimating the impact of a German monetary expansion on the key macroeconomic variables of the other European countries, their results tend to converge. Notably, both provide strong support for our maintained hypothesis: a German monetary expansion increases output and decreases real interest rates in the Periphery. Specifically, in the MSG model, a sustained 1% monetary expansion in Germany is associated with a persistent increase in the GDP of the other EMS countries,[15] a transitory expansion in their exports, an improvement in their trade balance, and a prolonged fall in both short- and long-term real interest rates.[16] These results are to a large extent confirmed by the simulations of the MULTIMOD:[17] a 10% increase in the German money supply target in 1990 increases French output (in percentage terms) by 3.3 in 1990, 4.2 in 1991, 3.4 in 1992, and 1.6 in 1993; the corresponding figures for Italy are respectively

---

13. The models considered in Frankel (1988) include both the DRI, EEC and Wharton, which assume adaptive expectations, and the LIVERPOOL model, which assumes fully forward-looking behavior by wage setters without relevant nominal rigidities.
14. McKibbin and Sachs (1991, p. 84).
15. See McKibbin and Sachs (1991, Table B-10, p. 241). According to the simulation results for the five years following the German expansion, real GDP in the rest of the EMS increases by 0.52, 0.32, 0.24, 0.22, and 0.21 percent, respectively.
16. The absolute deviations of real short-term interest rates from the baseline levels over a five-year horizon are –0.6, –0.28, –0.14, –0.08, –0.06. The analogue deviations of real long-term rates are –0.14, –0.08, –0.05, –0.04, –0.04.
17. Masson, Symansky, and Meredith (1990, Table 14, p. 31).

3.8, 4.5, 3.7, 2.0; for the United Kingdom (the only EMS country not assumed to maintain a peg against the D-mark during the time span of the simulation exercise) the positive impact is short-lived: 1.6 on impact, zero or negative thereafter. Given the sharp divergence in predictions regarding international interdependence at a global level, we consider these converging results regarding the Center–Periphery interdependence in Europe extremely encouraging.

The available empirical evidence on the intra-Periphery spillovers is less direct. Ideally, the appropriate simulation exercise would trace the effects of a monetary expansion in one Periphery country on output, interest rates, and exchange rates of the other Periphery countries, while these peg their currency against the D-mark. It bears emphasizing that in the light of our model, a positive output multiplier (and a negative interest rate multiplier) would be evidence in support of a prevailing expenditure-changing effect.[18]

Few studies in the existing literature provide an evaluation of intra-EC policy multipliers. Masson, Symansky, and Meredith (1990) consider the effects of a 10% increase in the UK money supply target on France, Italy, and Germany, starting in 1990.[19] They find that the UK monetary expansion has a positive effect on French and Italian outputs, both on impact and after a one-year lag, whereas the impact on German output is nonnegative.[20] The effects on short-term interest rates are negligible in the Periphery, although German interest rates fall by ten basis points in the two years following the UK monetary expansion.

McKibbin and Sachs (1991) consider the effects of a monetary expansion in the "rest of the OECD" (the OECD countries minus United States, Japan, and the EMS countries) on the EMS countries. Assuming that the policy multipliers for rest of the OECD represent an acceptable proxy for the policy multipliers of the subset of ERM countries that adopt a monetary expansion, real interest rates at any maturity are found to be persistently lower (relative to the baseline) both in Germany and in the rest of the EMS following the increase in money supply. The effects on output are temporarily negative but become positive after a one-year lag.

More recently, Hughes-Hallet and Ma (1995) use an updated version of MULTIMOD to run a number of simulation exercises on costs and benefits from coordination for the period 1990–1996. Particularly interesting from our

---

18. This can be seen by using (6.44) Keeping s_i constant and observing that n_i and v are negatively related, a monetary expansion in the Periphery country j decreases v if and only if $\theta > 0$. By the same token, the model (6.42) predicts that a monetary expansion in Periphery country j lowers interest rates in the rest of the Periphery when $\theta > 0$.

19. The authors consider the United Kingdom as the only EMS/non-ERM country, and they do not include France, Italy, and smaller industrial countries in their assessment of monetary multipliers, since "monetary policies in these countries are constrained by the need to limit deviations of their exchange rate vis-à-vis the Deutsche mark" (p. 23).

20. The percentage deviations of real GNP from baseline are 0.4 in 1990 and 0.2 in 1991 for France, 0.3 and 0.2 for Italy, 0.2 and 0.0 for Germany (see Table 16, p. 33).

vantage point is the comparison of two of their scenarios. The first is the "reference" solution, run under the assumption that both Italy and the United Kingdom realign their currencies in 1992; the second is a no-realignment scenario in which United Kingdom and Italy target, respectively, DM $2.95 \pm 2.5\%$ per pound and DM $1.33 \pm 2.5\%$ per 1000 lira.

The results are unambiguous. The absence of realignments in 1992 leads to "massive increases in instability ... as recession, an overvalued exchange rate and high interest rates, and hence losses in real credibility, drive things downward. There are no inflationary problems (prices fall by 2%–3% each year), but interest rates have to rise to levels not seen since the late 1970s. Real interest rates are very high therefore. That generates a persistent recession."[21] More important for our purposes, the monetary tightening associated with the defense of the Italian and British currency bands leads to a generalized increase in real short-term interest rates, both in Germany and in France.[22]

We summarize the review of the empirical evidence on policy spillovers as follows. In general, there is considerable disagreement on the sign and the size of international spillovers. However, the extent of the disagreement is smaller when we look at studies on the interdependence of European countries. The available evidence on spillovers among the ERM countries best fits the pattern of a prevailing expenditure-changing effect.

We believe that the results of the simulation exercises based on multicountry econometric models can only be approached with the necessary and appropriate reservations – perhaps with some degree of skepticism. However, these simulation results provide empirical support for the widely held view that the ERM devaluations in 1992 substantially contributed to the fall of interest rates both in Germany[23] and in the rest of the system (France and the United Kingdom represent particularly spectacular cases) between 1992 and 1993.

To the extent that the impact of the "swing" of German interest rates on the economies of the European Periphery is considered the predominant macroeconomic issue in the unfolding of the ERM events (the consensus view), there is strong evidence in support of the assumption that, on balance, the net effect in the transmission of monetary policies in Europe was positive ($\theta > 0$). It is worth noticing that this assumption does not rule out the possibility of intra-Periphery shifts in demand – from strong-to weak-currency countries' goods – following a devaluation; it only de-emphasizes their relevance vis-à-vis the impact of a system-wide fall in real interest rates.[24]

21. Hughes-Hallett and Ma (1995, p. 32).
22. France is assumed to maintain the peg under both scenarios. See Hughes-Hallett and Ma (1995, Tables 3 and 4, pp. 46–47).
23. A striking visual representation of this point is provided by Figures 3.1 and 3.2, which show the plot of short-term nominal and real interest rates in Germany in the 1990s (the spike in Figure 3.2 corresponds to September 1992).
24. See the discussion in Chapter 3 above.

8.2.4   Timing, number, and size of realignments in the Periphery

Having determined that the relevant pattern of intra-Periphery spillovers is consistent with strategic complementarity of monetary policies in Europe, we can now characterize the Nash equilibrium of our Center-Periphery system. It is summarized by the proposition below.

> **Proposition 1.**   *A Nash equilibrium is described by two threshold values of the shock ϵ, denoted by $\underline{\epsilon}^d$ and $\bar{\epsilon}^d$, with $\underline{\epsilon}^d < \bar{\epsilon}^d$, that split the support of the shock into three segments: all Periphery countries jointly devalue their currencies by a common percentage (increasing with the size of the shock) when the shock is larger than the higher threshold $\bar{\epsilon}^d$; all Periphery countries maintain the peg when the shock is below the lower threshold $\underline{\epsilon}^d$; a fraction f of Periphery countries (with $0 \leq f \leq 1$) devalue their currencies while a fraction $1-f$ maintain the peg when the shock falls between the two threshold $\underline{\epsilon}^d$ and $\bar{\epsilon}^d$.*

In a related paper (Buiter Corsetti and Pesenti (1997)), we delve into a full characterization of the N–country Nash equilibrium, also allowing for the possibility of country-specific asymmetric macroeconomic conditions. In what follows, we find it convenient to convey the most important point of our construct by reducing the degree of complexity induced by strategic interactions among monetary authorities. The most parsimonious means to this end is to assume that the number of countries in the exchange rate system is large. This admittedly unrealistic assumption implies that the impact of the monetary stance of a single country on the system-wide monetary average is negligible. Thus, as each monetary authority will react to the system-wide average stance (now independent of the country behaviour), the fraction of countries that devalue in equilibrium, f, is uniquely determined. Moreover, all countries that choose to realign devalue their currency by a constant common percentage.

The simplified version of the Nash equilibrium is illustrated by Figure 8.1. The graph at the top plots the fraction of countries abandoning the peg against the support of the shock ϵ.[25] The second graph plots the devaluation rate chosen by each country that abandons the peg. The graph at the bottom presents the information contained in the first two graphs in a different way, by plotting the average depreciation rate of the Periphery as a whole vis-à-vis the Center.

25. If we had not ruled out *a-priori* the possibility of revaluations in the Periphery, the support of the shock would be split into five segments, defined in terms of four thresholds (denoted $\underline{\epsilon}^d$, $\bar{\epsilon}^d$, $\underline{\epsilon}^a$ and $\bar{\epsilon}^a$, and such that $\underline{\epsilon}^a < \bar{\epsilon}^a < \underline{\epsilon}^d < \bar{\epsilon}^d$). In addition to the previous devaluation rules, in equilibrium all Periphery countries would jointly revalue their currencies when the shock is lower than $\underline{\epsilon}^a$; all Periphery countries would defend the peg when the shock ϵ falls between $\bar{\epsilon}^a$ and $\underline{\epsilon}^d$; a fraction f of Periphery countries would revalue their currencies while a fraction $1-f$ maintain the peg when the shock falls between $\underline{\epsilon}^a$ and $\bar{\epsilon}^a$. In this equilibrium, no Periphery country would find it optimal to devalue against the Center when some other Periphery country revalues instead.

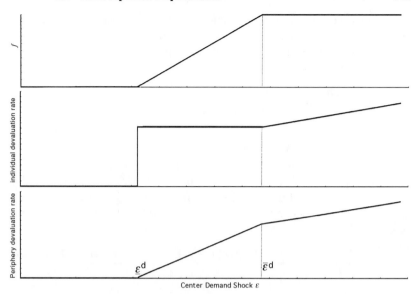

Figure 8.1. Individual and average devaluation rates in the absence of cooperation.

We offer a three-step proof of our proposition. To begin with, focus on some equilibrium outcome involving a devaluation by at least some countries. We conjecture the existence of a realization of the shock, $\epsilon = \hat{\epsilon}$, such that *each* Periphery country is indifferent between maintaining the peg and abandoning it. In other words, at $\hat{\epsilon}$, it must be the case that the deflationary and recessionary implications of the defense of the peg are just equal (in terms of domestic welfare) to the impact of a realignment, which improves external competitiveness and boosts aggregate demand but increases domestic inflation and entails a lump-sum loss of social utility. By conditions (7.9), it is obvious that this is possible if and only if the SDR, evaluated at $\hat{\epsilon}$, is equal to $\tilde{c}$ for each country in the Periphery:

$$\Delta\tilde{s}_i[\hat{\epsilon}] = \tilde{c} \qquad i = 1, 2, \ldots, N. \tag{8.8}$$

Given that the Periphery countries are indifferent between a peg and a float, denote by f the fraction of countries that decide to realign. Since the countries that choose to abandon the peg devalue (optimally) by a percentage $\tilde{c}$, the average actual depreciation rate is

$$\frac{1}{N}\sum_{i=1}^{N}(s_i - \bar{s}_i) = f\,\Delta\tilde{s}_i[\hat{\epsilon}] = f\tilde{c}. \tag{8.9}$$

Second, we determine average employment in the Periphery, as well as total employment in the Center, at $\epsilon = \hat{\epsilon}$. Consider the aggregate reaction function for the Periphery as a whole. This is obtained by rearranging (8.5) and (8.6) as follows:

$$\frac{\sum_{i=1}^{N} n_i}{N} = \frac{1}{\alpha + \xi(1-\theta)} \left[\frac{\sum_{i=1}^{N} s_i}{N} - \epsilon + \xi\theta \frac{N-1}{N} \sum_{i=1}^{N} n_i \right.$$
$$\left. + (\alpha + \phi)n^* - w + w^* \right]. \tag{8.10}$$

From this expression, we eliminate employment in the Center n^* by substituting the reaction function of the Center (8.3). Then, using (8.9), we can solve for the average employment rate in the Periphery, conditional on the shock ϵ being equal to $\hat{\epsilon}$:

$$\frac{\sum_{i=1}^{N} n_i[\hat{\epsilon}]}{N} = \frac{f\tilde{c} - [1 - \beta H(\alpha + \phi)]\hat{\epsilon} + [1 - H(\alpha + \phi)w^* + (\bar{s} - w)]}{(\alpha + \phi)(1 - H\beta\phi)}. \tag{8.11}$$

An analogous expression for the level of employment in the Center is obtained by substituting (8.11) into the Center reaction function:

$$n^*[\hat{\epsilon}] = H \left[\beta\phi \frac{\sum_{i=1}^{N} n_i[\hat{\epsilon}]}{N} + \beta\hat{\epsilon} - w^* \right]. \tag{8.12}$$

Note that, since we know the common individual devaluation rate of the countries that abandon the peg, the average monetary stance in the system (and hence average employment) is known up to the determination of the percentage of countries that devalue in equilibrium f. This percentage is determined in the next step of the solution.

Third, consider the shadow devaluation rate of a representative Periphery country (7.6). In our conjectured equilibria at $\epsilon = \hat{\epsilon}$, each individual country is indifferent between devaluing and keeping the peg, so that its shadow depreciation rate is equal to the cost $\tilde{c}$. Clearly, for our conjecture to be true, it must be the case that the average shadow depreciation rate in the Periphery, evaluated at $\epsilon = \hat{\epsilon}$, is also equal to the cost $\tilde{c}$.

$$\frac{\sum_{i=1}^{N} \Delta\tilde{s}_i[\hat{\epsilon}]}{N} = \tilde{c} = \frac{1}{A} \left\{ \bar{n} + (A - \beta\Lambda)\hat{\epsilon} - (A - \beta\Lambda)\xi\theta \frac{N-1}{N} \sum_{i=1}^{N} n_i[\hat{\epsilon}] \right\}$$
$$- \frac{1}{A} \{[A(\alpha + \phi) - \Lambda\beta\phi]n^*[\hat{\epsilon}] + \Lambda(w - \bar{q})$$
$$- A(w - \bar{s} - w^*)\}. \tag{8.13}$$

Table 8.1. *Parameter definitions for Eq. (8.14).*

$$\Omega_1 \;=\; (A - \beta\Lambda)\{1 + [1 - \beta H(\alpha + \phi)]\omega_1\} - \alpha\beta H\omega_2$$

$$\Omega_2 \;=\; \Omega_1 + \beta\Lambda + \beta H(\alpha + \phi)[(A - \beta\Lambda)\omega_1 + \omega_2]$$

$$\Omega_3 \;=\; \Omega_2 - A$$

$$\Omega_4 \;=\; \Omega_2 - H(\alpha + \phi)[(A - \beta\Lambda)\omega_1 + \omega_2]$$

where

$$\omega_1 \;=\; \frac{\xi\theta(N - 1)}{(\alpha + \phi)(1 - H\beta\phi)}$$

$$\omega_2 \;=\; \frac{A(\alpha + \phi) - \beta\Lambda\phi}{(\alpha + \phi)(1 - H\beta\phi)}$$

Equations (8.11)–(8.13) determine the percentage of countries that in equilibrium must abandon the peg at $\epsilon = \hat{\epsilon}$,

$$f = \frac{1}{\tilde{c}\Omega_3}[\bar{n} + \Omega_1\hat{\epsilon} - \Omega_2(\bar{s} - w) - \Omega_4 w^* - \Lambda(w - \bar{q}) - A\tilde{c}].$$

$$(8.14)$$

The coefficients Ω_k, $k = 1, \ldots, 4$, in this expression are functions of the parameters of the model, as summarized in Table 8.1. The proportion of countries abandoning the peg, f, is a linear function of target exchange rate, the target price level, the predetermined wage rates, and the realization of the shock.[26]

Equation (8.14) implies that – as we conjectured – at $\epsilon = \hat{\epsilon}$ each country is indeed indifferent between abandoning or maintaining the announced exchange rate parity, provided that a proportion of countries f devalue in the aggregate. Note that with ex ante identical countries it is not possible to determine which particular countries will implement a devaluation.

Nonetheless, the range of shocks for which our conjecture is valid is limited by the fact that f must lie between zero and 1. The boundaries of this range can thus be determined by setting $f = 0$ and $f = 1$ in (8.14), and then solving for the corresponding threshold values, $\underline{\epsilon}^d$ and $\bar{\epsilon}^d$. For shocks larger than $\bar{\epsilon}^d$, all countries in the Periphery will devalue by the same optimal rate $\Delta\tilde{s}_i \geq \tilde{c}$. For shocks smaller than $\bar{\epsilon}^d$, the Periphery countries will jointly maintain the peg.[27]

To understand the economic intuition underlying our results, compare Figure 8.1 with Figure 7.1, where the shadow devaluation rate is plotted against

---

26. It can be easily shown that the coefficient of the latter variable, Ω_1/Ω_3, is unambiguously positive.

27. In the absence of restrictions on the support of the shock, the case of an equilibrium involving a revaluation by (possibly) some countries but a devaluation by none would be perfectly symmetric. For a shock $\epsilon = -\hat{\epsilon}$, the average actual appreciation rate in the Periphery would be $\sum_{i=1}^{N}(s_i - \bar{s}_i)/N = -\tilde{c}f$, while expression (8.14) would still define the number of countries abandoning the peg in equilibrium.

the country-specific shock v_i. In Figure 7.1, the higher the country-specific shock, the higher the devaluation rate if the Periphery country finds it optimal to abandon the peg. At the point $v_i = \bar{v}_i$, the country is indifferent between devaluing and not devaluing by the percentage $\tilde{c}$. In other words, at the threshold $\bar{v}_i$, the welfare benefits of a devaluation in terms of higher employment are exactly offset by the political cost of a loss of anti-inflationary reputation.

Now recall that the country-specific shock is a combination of the global shock ϵ and the monetary stance in the rest of the system. Thus, v_i can be equal to $\bar{v}_i$ when the global shock is relatively low and when no other country – inside or outside the Periphery – expands its money supply. Equally, v_i can be equal to $\bar{v}_i$ when the global shock is sufficiently large but when many Periphery countries follow expansionary policies and devalue. We conclude that there is a continuum of combinations of ϵ and f for which a Periphery country remains indifferent between maintaining the peg and devaluing at the rate $\Delta \tilde{s}_i = \tilde{c}$. Thus, when we plot the shadow devaluation rate $\Delta \tilde{s}_i$ against the support of the shock ϵ, as in Figure 8.1, the point corresponding to $v_i = \bar{v}_i$ in Figure 7.1 stretches over some range of ϵ; the edges of this range in Figure 8.1 are $\underline{\epsilon}^d$ and $\bar{\epsilon}^d$.[28]

8.2.5   Asymmetric exchange rate policies

Each country, taking as given the behavior of all other countries, will independently determine whether it is preferable to peg or float according to the (by now familiar) rule (7.9), that is, by comparing the country-specific shadow devaluation rate with the devaluation threshold. The model determines the proportion of countries that will find it optimal to devalue in equilibrium. Which countries will actually abandon the peg is not determined.

Only when the shock ϵ is either extremely high or extremely low will the exchange rate behavior be identical across ex ante symmetric countries (either they will all peg, or they will all devalue by the same amount). It is important to stress that in the simplified Nash equilibrium we constructed, Periphery countries that start off identical also share the same level of welfare ex post for any realization of the shock, even when their exchange rate policies differ.

This latter point deserves special attention. In order to stress how international factors influence the behavior of the national policy authorities, we have abstracted from structural differences at the national level and assumed perfectly symmetrical countries. Yet, in a noncooperative equilibrium, for some

---

28. An important difference between this equilibrium and one that does not assume a large number of countries is the fact that the devaluation rate in equilibrium need not be constant between $\underline{\epsilon}^d$ and $\bar{\epsilon}^d$. As the impact of the monetary policy pursued by each country on the system-wide average monetary stance cannot be neglected, the equilibrium devaluation rates will vary with ϵ. Yet, with or without the assumption of a large number of countries, the equilibrium is characterized by a partial realignment: only a fraction f of countries devalue for intermediate realizations of the shock.

intermediate range of the shock, there will be a number of Periphery countries which find it optimal to abandon the peg, while the other countries optimally maintain the defense of their exchange rate parities. In other words, identical Periphery countries facing the same global shock will act in a highly asymmetric way.

Ex ante, the policy makers in the Periphery countries are all equally credible in their commitment to keep the exchange rate fixed; the fundamentals of each economy are exactly the same, except for differences induced by the behavior of other countries. However, because of the international spillovers from domestic policy making, the macroeconomic outlook of ex ante identical countries may vary considerably ex post. Some economies will have higher inflation, lower unemployment, and a depreciated currency, while some other economies will keep inflation down at the cost of relatively higher unemployment without devaluing their currencies.

The sustainability of the exchange rate regime in the second group is helped by the behavior of the first group. This is because, under our assumption on the sign of international policy spillovers ($\theta > 0$), the monetary expansion induced by a devaluation in country j (say, the United Kingdom) lowers the real interest rate in the Center country and everywhere in the system, reducing financial tensions in country i (say, France) that does not devalue. At the same time, the devaluation of the first group of countries reduces CPI inflation in the second group.

The presence of intra-Periphery spillovers creates strategic interactions among policy makers. Heuristically, the devaluation of country j's currency will affect the decision of country i through a shift to the right of this country's SDR for any level of the shock to fundamentals ϵ. Should the Periphery countries try to internalize these effects in their policy making? What are the implications of policy coordination for the stability of the exchange rate system? This question is addressed in the next section.

8.3   Cooperation in the Periphery

8.3.1   *Feasible policy agreements and national horizontal equity*

In this section we look at a behavioral alternative to Nash, involving international policy coordination. The scenario we consider makes three descriptively realistic (in the context of the ERM) assumptions about the nature of the game played by the Periphery countries and the Center. First, the Center never coordinates its monetary policy with the Periphery, while the Periphery countries can cooperate among themselves. Second, intra-Periphery cooperation is subject to a national horizontal equity constraint. This constraint requires all cooperating countries (which are identical ex ante) to be equally well off ex post. Third, we rule out side payments among the Periphery countries. In this section we briefly discuss the rationale underlying these assumptions.

In what follows, the Center's monetary policy always represents the optimal reaction to policies in the Periphery, independently of whether these are coordinated or not, and we abstract from issues regarding cooperation between the Center and the Periphery. Of course, the historical reconstruction of the ERM crisis as presented in Chapter 3 underlies our modeling strategy. Our maintained hypothesis is that cooperation is perceived in the Center as an unacceptable compromise on internal objectives. Some authors have even pointed out that Center–Periphery coordination may not be in the interest of the Periphery either, to the extent that international cooperation undermines the anti-inflationary credibility of the conservative central bank in the Center country.[29]

The case we focus on has all Periphery countries cooperating to maximize their joint welfare.[30] Even though all Periphery countries are structurally identical, this need not automatically imply that in a cooperative equilibrium they would either achieve equal welfare or adopt the same policies. Obviously, the existence of the fixed (sunk) per-country cost of abandoning the parity implies that, for small shocks ϵ, it might be efficient (regarding the sum of the national welfare levels) to have but a few countries devalue, even if ex post this would make the "scapegoat" countries worse off than the remaining countries that stick to their fixed parities.

Of course, schemes of cooperation with the property that ex ante identical countries are not guaranteed to be equally well off ex post are not likely to suit actual policy making in Europe. Albeit technically possible and economically efficient, such schemes would hardly be considered politically acceptable. First, there could be considerable disagreement about the nature and the magnitude of the common shock, as well as about the severity of the domestic credibility problem. Second, because of uncertainty regarding the shock and difficulty in monitoring individual policy makers' behavior, complex cooperation schemes might create incentives to misbehave that substantially reduce the gains from cooperation.

For this reason, in what follows we will impose as a "primitive" a *national horizontal equity constraint* in the joint maximization problem defining the cooperative agreement.[31] This constraint states that, if the Periphery countries are symmetric before the shock is observed, no Periphery nation would agree on implementing a cooperative action that would, ex post, make it worse off than

---

29. See for instance Alesina and Grilli (1993).
30. This is measured by (the negative of) the sum of their domestic loss functions,
$$-\sum_{i=1}^{N} E_{t-1} L_{i,t}.$$
31. Such assumption is obviously based on positive, not normative, considerations.

any other Periphery nation.[32] In other words, no discrepancy in welfare levels among symmetric Periphery countries is permitted under any circumstances.[33]

Does the restriction of identical ex post utility levels translate into a restriction of symmetric use of policy instruments in the system? In principle, a system of redistributive international transfers could remove asymmetries in welfare levels generated, on impact, by nationally differentiated policy measures within a cooperative framework.[34] Contingent transfers could therefore be used to compensate for the declining competitiveness of the countries that do not devalue. Such a view neglects the costs associated with the loss of reputation and anti-inflationary credibility accompanying a realignment. It may well be that, under a national horizontal equity constraint, transfers would paradoxically run in the opposite direction, from the countries that maintain the peg to those that devalue (and lose credibility).

We believe that ruling out these kinds of transfers or side payments as a maintained hypothesis captures a realistic feature of the actual working of the ERM. While there exist many intra-EU transfers, with a wide variety of motivations and goals – many of which are designed to meet specific distributional or restructuring objectives – the only transfer flows contingent on the implementation of exchange rate policy are the Monetary Compensatory Amounts of the CAP, which are limited to the agricultural sector, and played no role whatsoever in the unfolding of the 1992–93 events.

It is worth recalling that the possibility of introducing redistributive transfers in the EMS has been discussed in 1995, when French and Belgian export-competing firms – and a number of leading politicians from these two countries – argued that the "competitive devaluations" by United Kingdom, Italy,

32. A discussion of the historical role of a (strong form of) national horizontal equity is in De Cecco (1988). The author focuses on the hypothesis according to which cooperative actions are pursued only if they preserve the relative positions, in terms of economic and political power, of the four main members of the EMS. A general discussion of distributive issues and economic integration is in Guerrieri and Padoan (1988).

33. If the Periphery countries were not all equal ex ante, this constraint could be generalized to the requirement of "fair" outcomes (ex post), such that no Periphery country would tolerate a cooperative action that reduces its welfare (relatively to other countries) below some predetermined level, unanimously agreed upon.

34. Note that the literature on EMU mainly discusses international transfers in the framework of the theory of optimal currency areas (see Chapter 10). International transfers contingent on relative aggregate demand shocks can help reduce the short-run cost of IS shocks due to domestic nominal rigidities in a fixed exchange rate system, thus increasing the stability and viability of the system. At a theoretical level, our model highlights a different role of contingent international transfers: as side payments that could make asymmetric coordinated policies feasible by compensating the countries that sustain the largest adjustment costs in a realignment. While in principle sound, however, the assumption of intra-Periphery side payments of the kind required to support cooperation with nationally differentiated policy actions would hardly be defensible on empirical grounds.

and Spain since September 1992 sanctioned the imposition of countervailing duties within the EU. Rebutted forcefully by several economists (including the EU Commissioner Mario Monti) as inconsistent with the Single Market legislation, the case for "devaluation aid" and compensatory transfers failed to convince the officials of the Commission, who in the fall of 1995 concluded that, if anything, strong-currency countries such as France, the Benelux, and Germany had gained in competitiveness through low inflation, lower interest rates, and low labor costs.[35]

In our symmetric context, when all intra-Periphery externalities are taken into account and side payments are ruled out, the behavior of each single Periphery country must be equal to the average behavior of the Periphery as a whole: if a realignment occurs, all Periphery countries realign simultaneously and by the same amount. We provide an admittedly extreme but instructive scenario in which distributional conflicts in designing joint exchange rate policies may actually inhibit desirable policy initiatives.

Insofar as the realism of our framework is concerned, it is worth recalling that generalized devaluations represented an institutional reality in the history of the ERM since its very early stages. Six out of eleven realignments between 1979 and 1987 involved all ERM currencies (excluding the Dutch guilder, which was realigned only in two cases). The other realignments, which involved only one or two currencies, were typically triggered by specific national contingencies rather than representing the collective response to global shocks, such as a sharp fall of the US dollar.[36]

Summarizing, we restrict cooperative behavior in the Periphery to be symmetric. In our framework, countries can agree only on symmetric devaluation, that is, devaluation at a common rate, or else no devaluation. As we will show, under some circumstances (i.e., when national horizontal equity becomes a binding constraint) it may be collectively rational to give up cooperation. If there is no feasible way to solve the distributional conflicts involved in coordination, then uncoordinated Nash behavior may be welfare-improving for both individual countries and the ERM as a whole, as long as it leads to a higher overall degree of monetary expansion in response to the Center shock.

8.3.2   *Optimal monetary policy under cooperation*

If all Periphery countries coordinate and act symmetrically, they effectively behave as if they where a single currency area vis-à-vis the Center, that is, they internalize all the cross-country effects on employment and inflation of their national monetary policies. Consider first the optimal monetary policy

---

35. See *Financial Times*, September 18, 1995.
36. See the discussion in Giavazzi and Giovannini (1989).

conditional on a coordinated symmetric abandonment of the peg. Given that the common objective function is the equally weighted sum of domestic objective functions, the optimal money supply in the representative Periphery country i satisfies

$$n_i^{CS} - \bar{n} + \sigma[\alpha + \beta\phi](q_i^{CS} - \bar{q}_i) = 0 \tag{8.15}$$

where the superscript CS refers to coordinated symmetric behavior by the Periphery countries. The optimal money supply implies the following shadow depreciation rate, different from the SDR under Nash behavior – as it corresponds to a different optimal monetary policy – and identical in all Periphery countries (thus, not indexed by i):

$$\Delta\tilde{s}^{CS} = \frac{1}{A^{CS}}[\bar{n} + (A^{CS} - \beta\Lambda^{CS})\epsilon + A^{CS}(w - \bar{s} - w^*)]$$

$$- \frac{1}{A^{CS}}\{[A^{CS}(\alpha + \phi) - \beta\phi\Lambda^{CS}]n^* - \Lambda^{CS}(\bar{q} - w)\} \tag{8.16}$$

where

$$A^{CS} \equiv \frac{1 + \sigma(\alpha + \beta\phi)^2}{\alpha + \phi}, \qquad \Lambda^{CS} \equiv \sigma(\alpha + \beta\phi). \tag{8.17}$$

By analogy with our analysis of the Nash equilibrium, policy makers will resort to a coordinated symmetric devaluation of the domestic currencies if and only if

$$\sum_{i=1}^{N} \frac{1}{2}\left\{\left[(n_i^{FX} - \bar{n})^2 + \sigma(q_i^{FX} - \bar{q}_i)^2\right]\right.$$

$$\left. - \left[(n_i^{CS} - \bar{n})^2 + \sigma(q_i^{CS} - \bar{q}_i)^2\right]\right\} \geq Nc. \tag{8.18}$$

Following the steps outlined in Chapter 7, this policy rule can be written in terms of the SDR under symmetric cooperation:

$$\Delta\tilde{s}^{CS} \geq \sqrt{\frac{2c(\alpha + \phi)}{A^{CS}}} \equiv \tilde{c}^{CS}. \tag{8.19}$$

As in the case where individual countries play Nash, the optimal choice of an exchange rate regime requires the comparison of the SDR with the cost of abandoning the peg, where the latter expressed in the appropriate metric.

8.3.3 The cooperative equilibrium

The optimal monetary policy in the case of coordinated symmetric behavior of the N countries in the Periphery is implemented according to the following

Table 8.2. *Definitions of parameters used in Equation (8.22).*

$$\Psi_1 = (A^{CS} - \beta\Lambda^{CS}) - \alpha\beta H\omega_3$$
$$\Psi_2 = \Psi_1 + \beta\Lambda^{CS} + \beta H(\alpha + \phi)\omega_3$$
$$\Psi_3 = \Psi_2 - A^{CS}$$
$$\Psi_4 = \Psi_2 - H(\alpha + \phi)\omega_3$$
$$\omega_3 = \frac{A^{CS}(\alpha + \phi) - \beta\Lambda^{CS}\phi}{(\alpha + \phi)(1 - H\beta\phi)} = \frac{1 + \alpha\Lambda^{CS}}{1 - H\beta\phi}$$

reaction functions. If $\Delta\tilde{s}^{CS} \leq \tilde{c}^{CS}$, then

$$n = \frac{\bar{s} - w + w^* + (\alpha + \phi)n^* - \epsilon}{\alpha + \phi}. \tag{8.20}$$

If $\Delta\tilde{s}^{CS} \geq \tilde{c}^{CS}$, then

$$n = \frac{\bar{s} - w + \Delta\tilde{s}^{CS} + w^* + (\alpha + \phi)n^* - \epsilon}{\alpha + \phi}. \tag{8.21}$$

As the Center country always plays Nash vis-à-vis the Periphery, its reaction function is the same as that given in (8.3).

The characteristics of a symmetric coordinated equilibrium are summarized by the following proposition.

Proposition 2. *The cooperative equilibrium under a national horizontal equity constraint and no side payments can be described in terms of a unique threshold value for the shock ε, denoted by $\bar{\epsilon}^{CS}$. The Periphery will resort to a coordinated symmetric devaluation if and only if the Center demand shock is larger than the threshold $\bar{\epsilon}^{CS}$.*

The proof can be derived by using the methodology discussed in Chapter 7 and is therefore omitted. We give hereafter the expression determining the equilibrium threshold value $\bar{\epsilon}^{CS}$ as

$$\bar{\epsilon}^{CS} = \frac{1}{\tilde{c}^{CS}\Psi_1}[-\bar{n} + \Psi_2(\bar{s} - w) + \Psi_3\tilde{c}^{CS} + \Psi_4 w^* + \Lambda^{CS}(w - \bar{q})] \tag{8.22}$$

where the parameters Ψ_k are defined in Table 8.2.

8.4   Does cooperation in the Periphery make a difference?

8.4.1   Welfare with positive monetary externalities in the Periphery

This section is devoted to a comparison of the two equilibrium allocations discussed in the previous sections. The comparison is carried out under the maintained assumption that nominal wages (i.e., the private sector's predetermined expectations) are the same across equilibria. Of course, this assumption does not violate the analytical consistency of the model, insofar as wages are set before the national authorities determine their optimal policies and choose whether to cooperate or not.

We have already seen that, under the maintained assumption that the expenditure-changing effects of a monetary expansion prevail over its expenditure-switching effects in the rest of the Periphery ($\theta > 0$), monetary instruments are strategic complements in the policy game. We now turn to the key welfare implication of the international transmission of monetary policies, on which most of our results are based: In the presence of shocks to aggregate demand in the Center, a monetary expansion in country j has a positive external effect on welfare of country i.

To see this, consider first the case of a shock to aggregate demand in the Center that is high enough to trigger a common devaluation in the Periphery when all countries play Nash. On one hand, higher values of the shock ϵ translate (other things being equal) into a higher depreciation rate and therefore into a higher domestic price level (CPI) for country i. On the other hand, under our hypothesis about the international transmission of monetary policy, a devaluation by any other Periphery country will induce an appreciation of country i's currency vis-à-vis the Center, partly offsetting the inflationary consequences for country i of the shock to aggregate demand in the Center. As the international spillovers of a monetary expansion in country j bring country i's CPI closer to its current target value, the optimal monetary policy (conditional on abandoning the peg) in country i becomes more expansionary, increasing its employment and welfare.

Formally, the response of country i's welfare to a monetary expansion in country j conditional on both countries' letting their currencies float can be calculated by differentiating country i's loss function with respect to country j's employment, and then evaluating this expression at the equilibrium level of employment and prices under a float:

$$\partial \ell_i^{FL} / \partial n_j = -\sigma \left(q_i^{FL} - \bar{q}_i\right) \beta \xi \theta. \tag{8.23}$$

For sufficiently large values of ϵ, the Nash equilibrium price level will be above its target level $\bar{q}_i$, and Nash equilibrium employment will be below its target level $\bar{n}$. Expression (8.23) is therefore negative when θ is positive: a monetary expansion in country j increases welfare in country i.[37]

In a cooperative equilibrium, the determination of the optimal money supply in the Periphery will take into account the existence of these external effects. So, for any realization of the shock that is large enough to trigger a common

---

37. The opposite holds in the presence of large negative shocks ϵ. As q_i^{FL} is now below the CPI target, a contraction in country j will be associated with a welfare improvement in country i.

devaluation, the Periphery as a whole will tend to expand more in a symmetric cooperative equilibrium than in a Nash equilibrium.[38] As Canzoneri and Henderson put it, "when policy makers impose positive externalities on one another, cooperation calls for doing more, rather than less."[39]

8.4.2   Equilibrium realignments under alternative policy regimes

This section contrasts the behavior of the exchange rates in the two equilibrium allocations, both at an individual country level and for the Periphery as a whole. The differences in the behavior of the exchange rates under the two policy regimes are summarized by Propositions 3 through 6 and illustrated by Figures 8.2 and 8.3. For different sets of parameter values,[40] these figures plot the share of countries that abandon the peg (f), the optimal individual devaluation rates $(s_i - \bar{s}_i)$, and the effective devaluation rate vis-à-vis the Center $(\sum_i (s_i - \bar{s}_i)/N)$ against the support of the demand shock ϵ. In all graphs, the solid line refers to the Nash equilibrium and the dashed line to the cooperative allocation.[41] The graphs are all derived under the maintained assumption of a large number of countries. It will be clear, however, that all the propositions to follow hold in the general case.

Consider first the two thresholds $\tilde{c}$ and $\tilde{c}^{CS}$. By definition, these variables measure the smallest jump in the exchange rate of any Periphery country that

38. We can also consider the case in which country j expands its money supply but country i maintains a fixed nominal exchange rate vis-à-vis the Center. With the money supply in country i adjusting endogenously to peg the current parity, both employment and the CPI in this country will increase with a monetary expansion by country j, provided $\theta > 0$. In terms of country i's loss function, the good news of an increase in the level of activity should therefore be set against the bad news of a higher price level. Over the relevant range of realizations of the shock (that is, those values of the shock for which a common devaluation is optimal in a symmetric cooperative equilibrium), the good news will dominate the bad news. This result can easily be established by noting that the square of the SDR is proportional to the difference between the loss under a peg and the loss under a float (net of the sunk cost of realignment). The effect of country j's monetary policy on a country i that pegs its currency can thus be assessed as follows:

$$\frac{\partial \ell_i^{FX}}{\partial n_j} = \frac{\partial \ell_i^{FL}}{\partial n_j} + \Delta \tilde{s}_i \left[\frac{A}{c[\alpha + \xi(1-\alpha)]} \right] \frac{\partial \Delta \tilde{s}_i}{\partial n_j}.$$

As discussed above, the first term on the left-hand side is negative over the relevant range of the shock. Also, by (7.6), the SDR of a Periphery country is a negative function of employment in the other Periphery countries. Therefore, the expression above is unambiguously negative over the range of the shock associated with $\Delta \tilde{s}_i \geq 0$.

39. Canzoneri-Henderson (1991, p. 72).
40. In particular, the inflationary bias in the Periphery is "worse" in Fig. 8.2 compared to Fig. 8.3.
41. The two allocations (and therefore the two lines) would necessarily coincide if there were no external effects of one country's policy actions on other countries' welfare (i.e., $\theta = 0$).

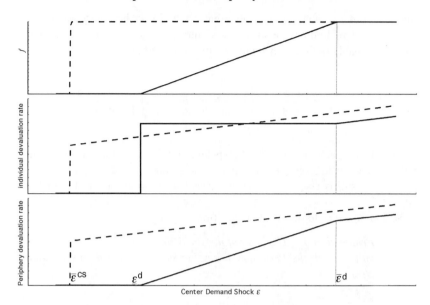

Figure 8.2. System-wide policy behavior and currency crises: the case in which constrained cooperation dominates no-cooperation.

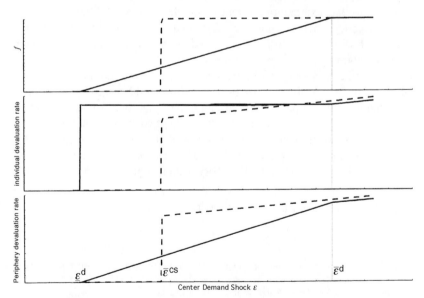

Figure 8.3. System-wide policy behavior and currency crises: the case in which no-cooperation can dominate constrained cooperation.

finds it optimal to abandon the peg (that is, the lower boundary on the size of a bilateral realignment against the Center). It is easy to show that the smallest possible optimal devaluation rate is unambiguously higher in a Nash allocation:[42]

$$\tilde{c} \equiv \sqrt{\frac{2c[\alpha + \xi(1 - \theta)]^2}{1 + \sigma[\alpha + \beta\xi(1 - \theta)]^2}} \geq \tilde{c}^{CS} \equiv \sqrt{\frac{2c(\alpha + \phi)^2}{1 + \sigma(\alpha + \beta\phi)^2}}.$$

$$(8.24)$$

This result is apparent in the second graph of Fig. 8.2 when comparing the jumps in the actual devaluation rate for a shock at thresholds $\bar{\epsilon}^d$ and $\bar{\epsilon}^{CS}$, respectively. The same result is also illustrated in Fig. 8.3 for a different set of parameter values.[43]

We can now turn to our third proposition.

> **Proposition 3.**   *The level of the shock that triggers a generalized devaluation in the Periphery is smaller under cooperation than under Nash:*
>
> $$\bar{\epsilon}^{CS} \leq \bar{\epsilon}^d.$$
> $$(8.25)$$

This result depends on the mechanism of international monetary transmission. In the previous section we have shown that within the Periphery, there is a positive welfare externality associated with the international transmission of monetary policy when θ is positive. Under our assumptions, monetary policy under Nash will be too restrictive compared to a symmetric cooperative policy that fully internalizes such externalities.

Consider the threshold value of the shock that, in a Nash equilibrium, triggers a devaluation by $\tilde{c}$ in all countries ($\epsilon = \bar{\epsilon}^d$). Since at the margin every country is indifferent between pegging or devaluing by $\tilde{c}$, the sum over all Periphery countries of the welfare differential between the two regimes (net of realignment costs) is exactly equal to the total cost of abandoning the peg, Nc. By construction, however, for the same level of the shock, the welfare gains from a generalized devaluation in the Periphery would be higher in the coordinated

---

42. To prove the inequality in the text, consider the function

$$f(x) \equiv \frac{(\alpha + x)^2}{1 + \sigma(\alpha + \beta x)^2}$$

and note that $\tilde{c}$ and $\tilde{c}^{CS}$ are monotonic transformations of $f(\phi)$ and $f(\xi(1 - \theta))$, respectively. Observe that $f(x)$ is monotonically increasing in x. Since $\phi \equiv \xi(1 - N\theta) \leq \xi(1 - \theta)$, it follows that $f(\phi) \leq f(\xi(1 - \theta))$, verifying the inequality.

43. By construction, the variables $\tilde{c}$ and $\tilde{c}^{CS}$ measure the national welfare costs of abandoning the peg. Accordingly, the minimal welfare cost per country of abandoning the peg is always higher in a Nash equilibrium than in a coordinated symmetric equilibrium.

symmetric equilibrium: when $\theta > 0$, the sum of welfare differentials across countries is never lower than Nc.

Therefore, using inequality (8.24) and expressing the welfare differential in the two exchange rate regimes in terms of the shadow devaluation rate, we have

$$\Delta \tilde{s}^{CS}[\bar{\epsilon}^d] \geq \tilde{c} \geq \tilde{c}^{CS} = \Delta \tilde{s}^{CS}[\bar{\epsilon}^{CS}]. \tag{8.26}$$

Because the shadow devaluation rate is increasing in the size of the shock, the threshold value for ϵ that triggers a coordinated symmetric devaluation must be lower than $\bar{\epsilon}^d$; for any distribution of the shock, a realignment by all countries simultaneously is more likely under symmetric cooperative behavior than under Nash.

However, symmetric coordination need not imply more frequent realignments *tout court*, as uncoordinated devaluations by a subset of countries are possible also for $\epsilon \leq \bar{\epsilon}^d$. In Figure 8.3, for instance, when ϵ is between $\underline{\epsilon}^d$ and $\bar{\epsilon}^{CS}$, some countries will devalue in a Nash equilibrium, while all Periphery countries will maintain the peg under a cooperative agreement. It bears emphasizing that this is not a general result. Figure 8.2 shows the possibility that, for some different configuration of parameters, the trigger point for a generalized devaluation under symmetric cooperation is lower than the threshold at which at least one country realigns under Nash.[44] In this case, a cooperative agreement delivers less exchange rate stability for any level of the shock in the Center.

The next proposition focuses on the magnitude of realignments rather than on their "timing".

> **Proposition 4.**   *There exists a range of realizations of the shock for which a Periphery country that abandons the peg devalues more in a Nash equilibrium than in a coordinated symmetric equilibrium. In other words, the subset of countries that devalue in a Nash equilibrium do so at an individual rate higher than the common devaluation rate in a symmetric coordinated equilibrium.*

Consider a realization of the shock such that the Periphery is indifferent between a coordinated peg and a coordinated symmetric devaluation, that is, $\epsilon = \bar{\epsilon}^{CS}$. By (8.24), to the extent that the Nash equilibrium has some countries devaluing, the depreciation rate for those countries under Nash is higher than the depreciation rate in a coordinated symmetric equilibrium. As Figure 8.2 shows, this result may hold also when Periphery countries resort to coordinated devaluations much before any country would devalue in a Nash allocation $(\underline{\epsilon}^d > \bar{\epsilon}^{CS})$.

---

44. Policy makers will benefit in this case from "smooth" and frequent realignments (a familiar pattern during the early stages of the ERM).

Nevertheless, in the aggregate, the following proposition holds:

Proposition 5.   *Provided that a coordinated realignment occurs ($\epsilon \geq \bar{\epsilon}^{CS}$), the effective average devaluation is higher in a coordinated symmetric equilibrium than in a Nash equilibrium:*

$$\frac{1}{N} \sum_{i=1}^{N} \left(s_i^{CS} - \bar{s}_i \right) \geq \frac{1}{N} \sum_{i=1}^{N} (s_i - \bar{s}_i), \quad \text{for } \epsilon \geq \bar{\epsilon}^{CS}. \tag{8.27}$$

This proposition can be verified immediately by taking the average of the Periphery exchange rates vis-à-vis the Center (6.44):

$$\frac{1}{N} \sum_{i=1}^{N} s_i = (\alpha + \phi) \left(\frac{1}{N} \sum_{i=1}^{N} n_i - n^* \right) + \left(\frac{1}{N} \sum_{i=1}^{N} w_i - w^* \right) + \epsilon. \tag{8.28}$$

Propositions 4 and 5 together state that, for realizations of the shocks to the right of $\bar{\epsilon}^{CS}$ ($\epsilon \geq \bar{\epsilon}^{CS}$), the average devaluation rate is unambiguously higher in a coordinated symmetric allocation, even when the individual country's optimal depreciation rate (conditional on it abandoning the peg) is higher in a Nash equilibrium. The nature of the external effect of a Periphery country's monetary policy on the other Periphery countries' welfare provides the rationale for these propositions.

For shocks large enough to make all countries devalue in both equilibria, the average money supply in the Periphery will be larger in a symmetric cooperative equilibrium than in a Nash equilibrium. The average devaluation rate for the Periphery as a whole will therefore be higher in the symmetric cooperative equilibrium. For smaller shocks (not large enough to make all countries devalue under Nash, yet large enough to make all countries devalue in a coordinated symmetric equilibrium), a Nash equilibrium also results in a suboptimally low average monetary expansion in the Periphery, implying an average depreciation lower than in the case of symmetric coordination.

The explanation of this result is to be found in the differential impact of coordinated and noncoordinated devaluations on the real interest rate in the system as a whole. An uncoordinated devaluation by a few countries has a limited impact on the real interest rate in the system. Thus, output stabilization by the countries that opt for a float requires a relatively large jump in their exchange rates. A coordinated devaluation by many countries, instead, brings down the system-wide real interest rate substantially. The benefit from a large individual country exchange rate depreciation for output stabilization purposes is much lower, compared to its costs in terms of inflation.

Consider now Figure 8.3 for values of the shock between $\underline{\epsilon}^d$ and $\bar{\epsilon}^{CS}$, for which no symmetric devaluation is possible, while some Periphery countries would find it optimal to devalue when playing Nash. In this range of values for the shock, a Nash equilibrium is associated with a more expansionary monetary policy than a cooperative equilibrium. Thus, we can state our last proposition.

> ***Proposition 6.*** *Because of the horizontal equity constraint, there may exist a range of realizations of the shock for which no country devalues in a coordinated symmetric equilibrium, while some countries devalue in a Nash equilibrium. Monetary policy in the system is correspondingly less expansionary in a coordinated equilibrium than in a Nash equilibrium.*

The implications of this result deserve special attention because they point to the possibility that, for given wages, ex post welfare could be higher in a Nash equilibrium than in a coordinated symmetric equilibrium. This will be the case for values of ϵ that are not large enough to trigger a coordinated symmetric devaluation, but large enough to induce an uncoordinated devaluation by some countries in a Nash equilibrium. For such values of the shock, noncooperation dominates symmetric (constrained) cooperation, from the point of view of the Periphery countries as a group and indeed from the point of view of the system as a whole.[45]

Proposition 6 shows that symmetric cooperation is not necessarily the best choice for the Periphery under any circumstances. On the one hand, common policy actions by the Periphery internalize all the indirect effects of each individual Periphery country's monetary policy on the other Periphery countries' welfare; by definition, these external effects are not taken into consideration by the policy makers in a Nash equilibrium. On the other hand, the maximization of the Periphery joint objective function is subject to an equity constraint. Because of the requirement of (ex post) symmetry, devaluations are implemented only when the shock is sufficiently large to justify the "payment" by each country of the political sunk costs of a coordinated abandonment of the peg. Thus, against the gains from cooperation, stemming from the internalization of intra-Periphery spillovers, must be set the lack of flexibility of an agreement subject to a symmetry constraint.

In other words, it could be the case that the Periphery countries do not abandon the peg for "relatively small" shocks in a (constrained) symmetric equilibrium. This outcome could be socially inefficient (in terms of the sum of the Periphery

---

45. Lewis (1989) considers a model in which monetary coordination, rather than an exchange rate realignment, is socially costly. According to her analysis, although in general governments find it optimal to adopt noncooperative policies, the benefits of stabilization outstrip the costs required to institute temporary schemes of cooperation in the presence of sufficiently large output disturbances in the global economy.

countries' loss functions) compared to the (unconstrained) Nash equilibrium in which a subset of the Periphery countries would abandon the peg. It would a fortiori be socially inefficient when compared to the hypothetical equilibrium under unconstrained cooperation, which would also involve abandonment of the peg by a subset of the Periphery countries. Ultimately, for reasons different from those usually pointed out in the literature, (constrained) policy coordination may be counterproductive here. This is an important result for our interpretation of the ERM crisis. We will return to this point in the next chapter.

What caused the system to crumble?

9.1 Building blocks of a systemic theory

By focusing the analysis on the role of international spillovers and policy games, Chapter 8 has concluded our journey through the conceptual and analytical dimensions of the literature on currency crises. The goal of Chapter 9 is to assess the ERM crisis from the perspective of our Center–Periphery model. We start in this section by reviewing our analysis of the role of policy coordination in a currency crisis. In Section 9.2, we provide a detailed reinterpretation of the 1992–1993 events in the light of our results. While the formal analysis in Chapters 6 through 8 will instruct our reading of the crisis, in what follows we will widen the scope of the discussion beyond the strict boundaries of our model and consider additional elements that, for the sake of analytical tractability, were not incorporated into our formal analysis.

It may be helpful to restate the main features of our theoretical framework. Our construction conforms to the traditional view of the ERM as a way of borrowing or importing anti-inflationary credibility from Germany (the consensus view at the time of the crisis). Since individual Periphery countries are affected by an inflationary bias, they agree on the desirability of limiting exchange rate flexibility. The international exchange rate agreement provides the commitment technology that policy makers cannot find at home, although such a commitment is known to be less than perfect and market participants perceive the abandonment of the peg as a possible policy option in the presence of domestic or external shocks.

The Center provides nominal stability to the entire system by targeting a time-invariant price level. Policy makers in the Center are inward-looking, so that the Center ends up always playing Nash vis-à-vis the Periphery (and vice versa). The system is hit by a large, asymmetric disturbance in the form of a real demand shock in the Center, generating pressure for an effective real appreciation of the currency of the Center. The Periphery as a whole would benefit from a monetary expansion in the Center, which would absorb at least part of the domestic demand surge and dampen the increase in interest rates. However, the resulting level of domestic inflation would be unacceptable to the authorities of the Center. The Center would of course benefit from a realignment of the Periphery, offsetting the original demand shock, but a realignment would entail high reputation and credibility costs for the policy makers of the Periphery countries.

In addressing the issue of the impact of such a disturbance on the system, our starting point is where other contributions to the literature stop: the exchange rate crisis as the outcome of a conflict of interest between the Center and the Periphery rooted in the fact that each side would benefit from a costly monetary expansion by the other side. The policy options we focus on are those open to the Periphery countries individually and collectively, when the relations between Center and Periphery are assumed to be frozen in noncooperative behavior.

While the Periphery countries can cooperate among themselves, intra-Periphery cooperation is subject to a national horizontal equity constraint. This assumption draws on the idea that ERM members would implement coordinated realignments only if the distribution of the implied costs and benefits was considered fair. Technically, the constraint requires that cooperating countries that are identical ex ante also be equally well off ex post. If the Periphery countries were not all equal ex ante, this constraint could be generalized to the requirement of fair outcomes (ex post) from jointly determined exchange rate initiatives. On the basis of the European experience, side payments contingent on realignments among the Periphery countries are ruled out as politically questionable and institutionally infeasible.

We considered two scenarios characterizing the possible policy responses of the Periphery countries to the Center demand shock. In the first scenario, Periphery countries coordinate their exchange rate policies – subject to the aforementioned institutional constraints – so as to maximize a common social welfare function. In the alternative scenario, there is no cooperation, and each country unilaterally maximizes its own objective function.

Our model shows that, given a realistic hypothesis about the sign of international policy spillovers (expansionary monetary policy in any Periphery country contributes to lower real interest rates in the system as a whole, and causes a real appreciation of the currencies of all other Periphery countries), these scenarios differ in the following ways. The minimal size of the Center shock required to bring about a coordinated (symmetric) devaluation by the Periphery is smaller than the minimal size of the shock required to induce general devaluation under Nash (loosely speaking, a general devaluation occurs "sooner" under restricted cooperation than under Nash). Also, whenever the Center shock is large enough to trigger a generalized devaluation in the Periphery under symmetric cooperation, the effective average devaluation is larger under cooperation than under Nash (loosely speaking, general devaluations are larger under restricted cooperation than under Nash). At the same time, there exists a range of Center shocks for which the subset of countries that devalue in a Nash equilibrium do so at individual rates that are higher than the common rate in a symmetric coordinated equilibrium (loosely speaking, when a few countries devalue in an uncoordinated way, the size of their individual realignments is relatively large).

In sum, in response to the demand shock in the Center, the coordinated response of the Periphery would be likely to consist of a realignment scheme including many currencies, or no realignment at all. This is a direct implication of the equity constraint (the expression of the requirement of political fairness in the Periphery). Conversely, in a scenario without cooperation, provided that some countries devalue and therefore lower real interest rates in the system, some other countries may avoid realignment altogether. The average monetary stance is less expansionary than in a scenario with a coordinated realignment, because the subset of devaluing countries has only a limited impact on the average system-wide equilibrium real interest rate. Nonetheless, for this very reason, if a country abandons the peg, its individual devaluation rate turns out to be very large.

9.2 Lessons from the theory

A crisis of the exchange rate system is primarily a crisis of the cooperation agreement that defines and sustains it. In our theoretical framework, there are at least two ways in which a crisis may emerge.

9.2.1 Opportunistic behavior at individual-country level

First, to the extent that the coordination scheme lacks an effective enforcement mechanism, individual countries always have an incentive to renege on the agreement and play according to their individual reaction functions. Although the hypothesis of an exchange rate crisis stemming from individually deviant behavior raises an issue of logical consistency (Why did the deviant countries accept to be part of the system in the first place?),[1] it is not unrealistic. Consider a realization of the shock slightly larger than $\underline{\epsilon}^d$ in Figure 8.2. While coordination requires a generalized devaluation, national policy makers may be tempted to "save" their currency. After all, as Figure 8.2 suggests, in a Nash equilibrium just to the right of $\underline{\epsilon}^d$, it may take the devaluation of just one currency to absorb the shock and save the rest of the Periphery from the embarrassment of reneging on the announced exchange rate targets.

If market participants' beliefs are based on the assumption of symmetric cooperative behavior, they will expect, for a shock in the range under consideration, to observe a sizable appreciation of the Center's real exchange rate, to be achieved through cooperative small uniform devaluations of all currencies in the Periphery. In such a situation, a large devaluation by one country (or a

---

1. This question of course points at political economy considerations, stressing the role of policy makers' changing attitudes towards the international agreement.

small number of countries) provides a strong signal to market participants that national policy makers are no longer acting cooperatively.

If the Periphery as a whole reverts to undiluted Nash, some countries will maintain their exchange rate parity vis-à-vis the Center. For the others, the equilibrium devaluation rate must be large. Since on average the monetary stance of the system is not as expansionary as under coordination, real interest rates do not fall as much: devaluing countries will use their exchange rate instruments to target a sustained increase in the level of aggregate demand. Ultimately, large-scale currency crises in a number of countries will be required to modify appreciably the effective terms of trade of the Center. Note that, in this first interpretation of a currency crisis, $\underline{\epsilon}^d$ falls to the right of ϵ^{CS}; therefore, the national horizontal equity constraint is not binding and plays no role in the story.[2]

9.2.2   *Abandoning cooperation as a collectively rational choice*

A second interpretation of the emergence of a crisis is illustrated in Figure 8.3. Consider a realization of the shock in the range $(\underline{\epsilon}^d, \bar{\epsilon}^{CS})$. When national horizontal equity is an issue, a Center shock that is large but not large enough to justify a collective devaluation puts the system under considerable stress. If a cooperative defense of the peg prevails, the Center is worse off because it cannot benefit from the positive external effects of a more expansionary monetary policy in the Periphery. At the same time, Periphery countries perceive that the individual gains from a unilateral devaluation are high.

Implementing a coordinated but selective (that is, nonuniversal) devaluation is problematic when there are no instruments to distribute its costs and benefits evenly across nations. For realizations of the shock in the range $(\underline{\epsilon}^d, \bar{\epsilon}^{CS})$, the loss in welfare from constrained cooperative behavior is partly avoided in a Nash equilibrium. A Nash equilibrium would accomplish what symmetric coordination cannot: some subset of countries would devalue, making the monetary stance in the system more expansionary (although not by enough to maximize the sum of the national welfare functions).

If policy makers realize that the system is in such a state, it could be collectively rational to revert to Nash, and thus to implement uncoordinated devaluations. Even if in the eye of an observer these devaluations look like a disorderly response by domestic policy makers to market pressures, they would

---

2. When all countries in the Periphery are ex ante identical, which particular set of countries devalue (or revalue) in a Nash equilibrium is indeterminate. Now introduce a (small) difference between country structures, say, in the determinants of the inflationary bias of country i ($\bar{n}_i \geq \bar{n}$). Then, extending the logic of our model, in equilibrium country i would not necessarily be part of the set of devaluing countries, in spite of its stronger inflationary bias. See Buiter, Corsetti and Pesenti (1997).

nonetheless be consistent with (constrained) welfare maximization both at the level of the individual Periphery country and from the point of view of the Periphery as a collective. Yet again, a realignment involving only one country would signal to the private markets that the exchange rate mechanism as a coordination device has ground to a halt.

9.2.3   Financial markets and systemic effects

What is the role of markets in a crisis of the exchange rate system? The answer to this question is complex, because markets play both an active and a passive role. Regarding their active role, in our theoretical framework, private sector expectations are reflected in the level of the predetermined nominal variables. Higher nominal wages, *ceteris paribus*, reduce the stability (and viability) of a peg: all threshold values for the shock determining both coordinated and unco-ordinated optimal switches between exchange rate regimes are functions of the predetermined nominal variables. On the other hand, once private expectations are formed, exchange rate policies are the outcome of rational (discretionary) decision making by the national authorities, who assess the costs and benefits of defending the peg, given the current realization of the shock to the fundamental. In this sense, the behavior of the financial markets may be seen as a passive response to policy makers' choices, and a currency crisis would be nothing but the expression in the financial markets of the tensions that lead to the breaking up of the international agreement on policy coordination.[3]

Can a system of fixed exchange rates survive a crisis that puts into question its viability as a policy coordinating mechanism? The answer to this question depends on two considerations. First, in the light of the crisis, private agents may modify their beliefs about the likelihood of future cooperative behavior in the policy game. The levels of wages and domestic interest rates vary with the market's perception of the nature of the ongoing game among policy makers. The post-crisis fixed exchange rate system may be intrinsically more or less fragile, depending on the perceived changes in the nature of the game.

Second, as a result of a crisis, policy makers may form coalitions, that is, new agreements among subsets of the players replace the old agreement. For example, a subset of the Periphery countries may either join an enlarged Center or establish a unilaterally fixed exchange rate area vis-à-vis the Center (the *Core*) which excludes the other Periphery countries (the *Outsiders*). Our discussion

---

3. An extreme view on this issue is given by Tommaso Padoa-Schioppa (1994, p. 19), "The relationship between markets and central banks . . . is similar to that between tigers and their tamers. The latter can bend the former to his will if he uses superior skills, great care, and intelligence. If, instead, the tamer excites and irritates the tigers, they will win. . . . Having more than one tamer in the cage does not help: it may lead to quarrels and in any case creates a problem of coordination such as has been encountered during the last year."

of the Nash allocation points out a mechanism through which the stability of the bilateral exchange rates in the Core benefits from the free float of the Core vis-à-vis the Outsiders' currencies.

9.3   The interpretation of the 1992–93 ERM crisis in a Center–Periphery model

As seen in Chapters 3 and 5, the literature on the ERM crisis has stressed the lack of cooperation between the (Frankfurt-based) Center and the Periphery (the rest of the ERM) as an important factor in the collapse of the system. What our theory in Chapter 8 emphasizes is the crucial role of the lack of cooperation in the system as a whole, in transforming the tensions between Center and Periphery into a large-scale crisis of the European exchange rate system.

The idea that at the roots of the ERM crisis was a policy coordination failure has been expressed by many. The implications of coordination failure for exchange rate stability, however, cannot be properly understood without developing a systemic model. A full-fledged systemic theory of exchange rate crises needs to address at least two issues. First, what difference do cooperation and noncooperation make regarding both the international and the country-specific macroeconomic equilibria? Second, what are the beliefs of the private sector regarding the nature of the international monetary game? On the basis of our theoretical elaboration on these issues, we now provide a novel interpretation of the eruption of the ERM crisis. Our thesis is that this coincided with a discrete change in markets beliefs on intra-ERM policy cooperation prompted by the modalities of the first ERM realignment on September 14.

9.3.1   Fundamental imbalances and tensions in the currency markets

Our reconstruction of the crisis in Chapter 3 highlights a few key elements in the buildup of tension in the ERM between the end of 1991 and the summer of 1992. The first is the Center–Periphery conflict stemming from the German reunification shock. In that period it became clear that, absent a realignment in the ERM, the Bundesbank would pursue the goal of domestic price stability by using its interest rate instruments with little regard for the consequences for the domestic real economy, and with utter disregard for the international implications of such a policy. As shown in Figures 3.1 and 3.2, interest rates in Germany increased relentlessly in the period leading up to the crisis.

Regarding domestic imbalances, competitiveness and fiscal problems were apparent in Italy. The downturn in the level of economic activity, coupled with the notorious fiscal problems, were fueling doubts about the desirability of a strenuous defense of the exchange rate. Evidence on a negative trend in the amount of international reserves held by Bank of Italy suggests that speculative pressures started as early as the spring of 1992.[4] While Spain and Portugal too were experiencing some deterioration of competitiveness, the strength of the pound was being undermined by a severe contraction that generated internal pressures for a relaxation of UK monetary policy.

For the EU as a whole, the average gap between actual public debt and deficit performance and the Maastricht fiscal criteria widened.[5] In part, this could be attributed to the operation of the automatic fiscal stabilizers during a fiscal downturn, but doubts were also growing regarding the political feasibility of the budgetary tightening required to satisfy the deficit criterion by the critical EMU deadlines. Regarding the debt criterion, even an inner core country like the Netherlands was obviously unable or unwilling to make a serious adjustment effort, with the debt-GDP ratio of that country hovering tenaciously around 80 percent. Finally, there is little doubt that the results of the first Danish referendum led to an extensive downward revision of the perceived costs of leaving the ERM. A shrinking political support for Maastricht was confirmed by the results of the polls in the weeks preceding the French referendum.

9.3.2   A policy coordination shock

During the summer of 1992, these elements (reinforced by the dollar crisis in August) halted the trend of improving credibility that had characterized the ERM since the late 1980s.[6] According to the evidence on interest differentials, expectations of devaluation vis-à-vis the D-mark increased virtually everywhere. The highest differentials were observed for Italy, Spain, and Portugal. However, the size of these differentials was small relative to the magnitude of the depreciations that actually occurred following Black Wednesday.

At the beginning of September, a massive speculative attack against the lira took place. It intensified after the EC meeting in Bath on the 5th and 6th of September, on which occasion the conflict on exchange rate matters among European policy makers was widely reported by the press. During the week following the event, Bundesbank and Bank of Italy put forward a proposal for a generalized realignment involving a 3.5% revaluation of the D-mark, and a 3.5% devaluation of the lira against all other currencies in the ERM (that is, a 7% devaluation of the lira against the D-mark).

Part of the proposal involved a cut in the German interest rates by a magnitude that would depend on the number of countries joining in the realignment, as well as on the size of the devaluation. This aspect of the proposal was widely interpreted as a bargaining scheme, with the Bundesbank willing to trade interest rate cuts in exchange for a generalized devaluation of the ERM currencies

4. See Goldstein et al. (1993, p. 53).
5. See Table 3.1.
6. See Chapter 4.

vis-à-vis the D-mark. Our model suggests that such an interpretation may be quite misleading. In a standard augmented Mundell-Fleming model (such as ours), a decrease in the Community-wide interest rate following a generalized realignment is an equilibrium (endogenous) outcome and does not require the Center (Germany) to modify its noncooperative policy strategy vis-à-vis the Periphery. There need not be any quid pro quo involved. After the realignment, it is in the interest of Germany to accompany the fall in the equilibrium interest rate with a revision of its key rates.

Since the realignment proposal did not receive any formal consideration, on September 14 only the lira was devalued against the D-mark by 7%. Peter Kenen writes apropos this issue:

> The Germans were apparently interested in a more general realignment but pursued the matter rather casually – too casually perhaps to impress the French with the urgency of the issue .... It may be objected that France would have vetoed a general realignment, even if Germany had pressed for one, because the French believed that the franc was immune to contagious speculation. What would have happened, however, if the German chancellor had warned the French president that the Bundesbank could not be expected to support the franc – if he had called attention to the so-called Emminger letter?[7] (One might also ask what would have happened if the German chancellor, not the Italian prime minister, had telephoned John Major about the devaluation of the lira – and added the same sort of warning about future Bundesbank support for the pound).[8]

After less than 24 hours of stability, market expectations of devaluation jumped upward, including the lira, the sterling, and the peseta. On Black Wednesday, the United Kingdom and Italy withdrew from the ERM, the peseta was devalued by 5%, and several other currencies were quoted near the floors of their ERM bands.

One key test for any interpretation of the ERM crisis is the ability to provide a plausible and coherent explanation of the sudden loss of credibility experienced by virtually all currencies in the system between the Bath Meeting and Black Wednesday. The theory of currency crises reviewed in Chapter 7 meets this challenge by attributing the timing of the crisis to a manifestation of essentially arbitrary self-fulfilling prophecies. The possibility of sudden shifts in market expectations, unrelated to fundamentals, is intrinsic to the flexible peg models of the ERM reviewed in Chapter 7, but the theory underlying this view does not address the causes of such shifts in expectations. Supporters of this interpretation raise the point that the coordination of markets on a particular equilibrium may be driven by publicly observable events. Yet, these events are left unidentified.

The theory presented in Chapter 8 instead relies on a mechanism generating shifts in expectations that is independent of the existence of multiple equilibria

7. See Chapter 3.
8. Kenen (1995, p. 160).

and self-fulfilling prophecies. The underlying idea is rather uncontroversial. Expectations of domestic monetary and exchange rate policies are conditional on information on the nature of the international monetary game. Our model implies that, with monetary cooperation, restoring equilibrium after a large system-wide shock requires a generalized realignment of limited size. Without cooperation, restoring equilibrium requires large devaluations, but only by a few countries. Consistently, the perception of a regime switch in monetary policy-making – from cooperation to noncooperation – would in itself lead market participants to revise their beliefs and anticipate sizable realignments in some countries. These predictions elucidate the logic of the ERM crisis as a systemic crisis.

The notion that a cooperative response to the underlying tensions consists of a generalized realignment involving small devaluations sheds light on the behavior of intra-ERM interest differentials during the Summer of 1992, up to the dawn of the crisis. Periphery countries were expected to engineer domestic monetary expansions and depreciate their currencies to protect their economies against the adverse domestic implications of high German interest rates. To the extent that markets perceived the ERM as a coordination device, forecasts reflected the idea that Periphery countries would have loosened their monetary stances in a cooperative way.

Following this line of reasoning, it is worth stressing that if the German–Italian proposal had been implemented, to a large extent policy makers would have validated market expectations of a generalized devaluation of modest overall size. This is not to say that the German–Italian proposal was indeed the only (or even an effective) solution to the ERM problems. Perhaps a better coordinated realignment scheme would also have included differentiated rates of exchange rate devaluation for countries other than Italy.

Nevertheless, regardless of its technical features, the central goal of a coordinated realignment was a substantial reduction of the real interest rates in the system. Our model stresses that, from the standpoint of the Periphery as a whole, this goal is best achieved by extending the number of currencies involved in a devaluation, rather than implementing largely asymmetrical monetary policies.

For this very reason, the solitary realignment of the lira on September 14, 1992, conveyed a crucial piece of information to the markets. The new parity grid, without a generalized revaluation of the D-mark, could hardly have been regarded as consistent with Periphery-wide cooperation in monetary policy. Notably, the lira devaluation rate was 7 percent, the same figure that had been proposed in the context of a general realignment two days earlier, which would have had all Periphery countries joining Italy in devaluing their currencies. Rather than absorbing the tension in the system, the realignment of the lira – in a period of rampant rumors, leaks about disagreements, and polemics among ERM member countries – represented an additional, largely unanticipated shock to the ERM fundamentals, insofar as it conveyed bad news concerning the ongoing noncooperative policy game in the ERM. As Padoa-Schioppa (1994) puts it:

> [The cause of the ERM crisis] was plainly traceable to what in the academic jargon is called a 'coordination failure' .... There was the refusal to accept a general realignment and even to call a meeting of the Monetary Committee or of the ministers and central-bank governors when, in September 1992, a general realignment might have calmed the markets. The general procedure, once embarked on, did not produce a credible new grid. At various times, and in various ways, through unhelpful declarations that excited markets as well as through policy decisions that caused unnecessary friction, the system was destabilized by its very custodians.[9]

The news on the degree of cohesion among the ERM countries led private markets to revise their views on the persistence of high interest rates in Europe. Our model shows that uncoordinated realignments deliver less system-wide monetary expansion than coordinated realignments, even if all of the devaluations that characterize the new Nash equilibrium are implemented fully. In the light of this result, the generalized shift in expectations in mid-September was the rational response of the markets to the perceived regime switch in Europe-wide policy-making.

9.3.3   Scenarios for the crisis

The policy conflict underlying the lack of Center–Periphery cooperation has been widely analyzed by the literature. There is plenty of evidence that Germany utterly opposed any revision of its own monetary policy. Considerable pressure was put on Germany to do exactly what it did not want to do. The climax of this conflict occurred during the Bath Meeting a few days before the crisis. In the reconstruction of Muehring (1992),

> Near the end of the conference in the British spa town of Bath on Saturday, September 5, British Chancellor of the Exchequer Norman Lamont asked Bundesbank president Helmut Schlesinger once more for a commitment to cut German interest rates, which could be included in the postmeeting communiqué. Schlesinger, containing his mounting anger, replied that it was impossible. When Lamont continued to press him, the normally unflappable Bundesbank president suddenly stood up to leave, only to be restrained by an almost equally annoyed Theo Waigel, the German finance minister. "My dear Norman", Waigel snapped, "you have asked us that question four times, and

---

9. Padoa-Schioppa (1994, pp. 14–15). While we share many of the arguments of Padoa-Schioppa (1994), who also stresses the role of (the lack of) policy cooperation in the crisis, there are a few differences in our analysis, an important one being the analysis of the conflict between Germany and the rest of the Periphery. Padoa-Schioppa holds the view that France did match or outperform Germany in terms of price stability. Fundamentally, therefore, the conflict was about the choice between the alternatives of (German) hegemony and joint (Franco-German) decision-making in determining the ERM-wide monetary stance.

four times we have given you the same answer. We do not see the need for wasting any more time. So if you ask again, I will get our helicopter ready to take us back."[10]

Germany was keen on implementing a generalized ERM realignment, but apparently no country (with the exception of Italy) was willing to discuss the terms of an ERM-wide realignment. In the EC meeting of Bath at the beginning of September 1992:

> Schlesinger was not so much ignored as scorned, says a participant [to the EC meeting in Bath], for his apparent willingness to "so easily put monetary union at risk" with the first ERM realignment since 1987.... "Realignment was a dirty word in Bath", Schlesinger was later bitterly to complain to a German colleague.[11]

As it became absolutely clear that Germany would not give in to the other ERM countries' request to loosen its monetary policy, there were two possible courses of action open to the Periphery countries. The first one was to engage in a possibly painful defense of the existing parities, at the cost of further domestic deflation and worsening fiscal imbalances. The second one was to engineer some monetary expansion in the Periphery. This could have been achieved either in a coordinated way (implying bargaining and compromising on whether, and by how much, each particular country should have devalued), or in a noncoordinated way ("each for himself").

Why were European countries unable to agree on coordinated policy action? At a theoretical level, our model addresses this issue by focusing on potential conflicts regarding how the costs and benefits of a coordinated realignment are to be distributed among the members of an exchange rate system. We have characterized plausible scenarios in which a realignment may be socially desirable, yet there is no distribution of costs and benefits that is equitable in the eyes of the Periphery countries. When the national horizontal equity constraint is binding, a joint defense of the existing parities is the only feasible coordinated exchange rate policy. The inability of the Periphery to implement a monetary expansion is socially costly in terms of output and employment.

As regards the Center, it should be stressed that its unwillingness to coordinate its policy with the rest of the system by no means implies indifference with respect to the conduct of policy in the Periphery. To the extent that the coordinated response of the Periphery to the fiscal shock in the Center is a large monetary expansion, coordination in the Periphery helps stabilize both the price level and output in the Center. However, when the only politically acceptable coordination is on a strenuous joint defense of the existing parities – the case just referred

---

10. In private conversations with the authors of this book, Schlesinger explained in detail his explicit position during the meeting: "The Bundesbank committee decided the day before not to lower, but authorized me to say that we would not increase."
11. Muehring (1992, p. 7).

to – then uncoordinated behavior with some large devaluations is welcomed by both the Center and the Periphery as a whole.[12]

In the new uncoordinated scenario, the first wave of speculative attacks hit a set of currencies that appeared weak on the basis of conventional indicators. This set included the lira, the pound, and the peseta. The uncertainty regarding the political support for the Maastricht Treaty may have played a role in delaying the speculative attack on the French franc until after the referendum result – a tiny majority for the *oui* to Maastricht.

Many observers were puzzled by the attack against the French franc in September 1992, as they argued that the traditional arguments emphasizing the role of weak fundamentals in triggering a currency crisis did not apply to the French case. The puzzle worsened when the French franc came again (and repeatedly) under pressure in the 1992–93 period. The "paradoxical" attacks on the French franc have been proposed as a central piece of empirical evidence supporting the view that, at the root of the ERM crisis, were self-fulfilling prophecies.

It is worth stressing that the French franc puzzle need not be regarded as evidence in support of self-fulfilling prophecies. According to the systemic logic of our model, a strong domestic performance – as measured by the standard set of macroeconomic indicators – is no guarantee against the possibility of a currency crisis. Restoring international equilibrium after a sizable shock to the Center requires a sizable fall in the system-wide real interest rate, and a sufficiently large real appreciation of the Center's effective exchange rate against the Periphery. Both real interest and exchange rates are functions of the average size of the realignment in the Periphery – that is, the average monetary stance in the system.

Absent cooperation, if not enough countries have already devalued by a sufficient amount to restore system-wide equilibrium, both "weak" currencies (such as the pound and the peseta) and "strong" currencies (such as the French franc) are potential candidates for speculative attacks. Our model predicts that a noncoordinated equilibrium requires a few countries to devalue by a sizable amount; it cannot predict which currencies will be devalued. Each currency is a potential candidate for a large-scale devaluation, regardless of how sound its domestic fundamentals look.[13]

---

12. Among the possible scenarios depicted by our model, there also is one where uncoordinated behavior leads to a strenuous defense of existing parities, while the optimal policy under coordination is a generalized devaluation. If this is the correct interpretation of the 1992 September crisis, the unwillingness of the Periphery countries to accept the German–Italian proposal for a coordinated devaluation plainly was a mistake. In this case too, the 7% realignment of the lira, motivated by a deterioration of Italian domestic credibility, would have signalled a lower-than-expected level of policy coordination.

13. Because of international monetary spillovers, this prediction of the model holds also in the presence of some (moderate) initial heterogeneity across countries.

We stress two caveats. The first one regards the definition of the Center of the system. This, of course, may include more than one country, provided that their monetary policies are fully coordinated. This is the case for Germany, the Netherlands, and to a certain extent Belgium. The second caveat concerns the evidence of a coalition or cooperative arrangement between Germany and France. France clearly cannot, for the period under consideration, be considered part of the (hard) Center. Yet, unlike all other Periphery countries, which were effectively left to fend for themselves, France benefited in the defense of its parity from massive German support, putting it in the special position of belonging to the extended Center or "soft Core" of the system.

With the exception of France, once the crisis had started, the survival of the ERM was clearly linked to each individual country's willingness to peg its exchange rate to the D-mark, with little or no intracommunity support. The difficulty of this task was magnified by a widespread feeling that the strength of the political support for Maastricht had dwindled with the first Danish referendum. From September 1992 to August 1993, the operation of the ERM is well described in terms of uncoordinated attempts to determine the new equilibrium exchange rates, that is, by the (somewhat messy and staggered implementation of the) Nash scenario of our model.

The defense of the French franc, in particular, implied that the average monetary stance in Europe was relaxed at a relatively slow pace, with the contribution of other European currencies that underwent repeated realignment or sustained depreciation. Expectations of future interest rates in a noncoordinated monetary system consequently were relatively high, with a significant degree of persistence.

Outside the ERM, high interest rates were creating problems to the Scandinavian countries that kept their currencies pegged against the D-mark, exacerbating already severe country-specific problems (the breakup of its trading arrangements with the FSU for Finland, and the collapse of domestic consumption demand for Sweden).

According to our interpretation, the enlargement of the band in August 1993 represented explicit recognition that the ERM had lost its ability to be a coordination device for the domestic policies of the ERM members. In this sense, the width of the bands accurately reflected the weakness of international ties in the remains of the monetary system in Europe. The enlargement of the band created room for an assessment of the new equilibrium exchange rate parities. At the same time, it urged European policy makers to launch a new round of negotiations in preparation for the next step of European monetary cooperation.

CHAPTER 10

Rebuilding the system: What next?

10.1   Introduction

In the central chapters of this book, most of our analysis of the European currency crisis was centered on the standard paradigms of a credibility game between a national policy maker and the private sector, and of strategic interaction among policy makers of different countries. In particular, we have built a novel interpretation of the 1992–93 events by developing a multicountry model of output and inflation stabilization with short-run nominal rigidities. Besides its application to the fall of the ERM, however, our theoretical construction has a number of additional implications for the design of a monetary union that are bound to be increasingly important as the final collective and individual decisions on EMU approach.

Following our discussion of the quest for exchange rate stability in Europe and our historical and analytical evaluation of the causes of the breakdown of the ERM in 1992–93, we now devote the final chapter of this book to the analysis of some key economic issues that have, so far, been only implicitly treated in our work. This involves a reexamination of the considerations that should guide the design of monetary, exchange rate, and fiscal policy by a group of nations considering monetary union and a brief discussion of a few issues in the transition to monetary unification. Much of it is a review of the theory of optimal currency areas, one of the murkiest and most unsatisfactory areas of macroeconomic and monetary theory. The focus throughout is on the policy implications of the various strands of this literature, each of which addresses (albeit often only indirectly) the question of what a nation (or group of nations) gains or loses by giving up monetary sovereignty.[1] This includes a brief discussion of the microeconomic arguments in favor of a common currency.

Should the EU pursue monetary union? In Chapter 2, we argued that each fundamental step in the recent monetary history of Europe was taken more on political than technical economic grounds. The answer to the above question is no exception to this rule. Yet, as the deadline for the final decision on EMU

---

1. Once it is clear what is actually given up, it is a fairly straightforward matter to determine what changes are required (in the fiscal policy instrumentarium and/or in other aspects of the capacity to adjust) to compensate for the loss of the national monetary instrument(s), or at least to minimize the welfare consequences of such a loss.

approaches, there is an urgent need for a deeper understanding of the economic issues involved in such an important monetary reform. The aim of this chapter is to point out what we still need to know – identifying areas for improving the current state of economic analysis – hoping to contribute to the definition of a proper policy-related research agenda.

The outline of the chapter is as follows. Section 10.2 reviews microeconomic arguments for a common currency. Section 10.3 reviews neoclassical public finance arguments against a common currency. Section 10.4 considers the implications of nominal rigidities. Section 10.5 looks at what kinds of additions to the policy arsenal or institutional capacity for adjustment to shocks are required to make up for the loss of the exchange rate instrument. Section 10.6 reviews the role of capital mobility. Section 10.7 focuses on the current debate on the transition toward EMU. Section 10.8 concludes our monograph by summarizing the case for EMU in the light of the arguments discussed in the previous chapters.

10.2   Microeconomic efficiency arguments for a common currency

The microeconomic efficiency arguments for a common currency are well known and don't require restating at length. A medium of exchange or transactions medium is subject to an obvious network externality (see for example Dowd and Greenaway, 1993). This is most easily seen in the case of intrinsically valueless (or fiat) money: the usefulness of a medium of exchange (i.e., the likelihood of it being accepted in exchange for intrinsically valued goods and services by any economic agent) is increasing in the number of other economic agents that are likely to accept it as a medium of exchange, since what determines the liquidity or "moneyness" of the medium of exchange is the probability of being able to dispose of it when desired, at short notice, at little cost, and at reasonably stable and predictable terms of trade.

The public good properties of money should be characterized carefully. They relate to the social utility derived from the adoption as *numéraire*, medium of exchange, and means of payment, of one particular currency (or set of currencies) rather than another. This issue is quite distinct from that of how the (indirect) utility enjoyed by an individual agent varies with the quantity of a particular currency held by that agent, holding constant the pattern of currency use by all other agents.

The use of a given stock of money balances in transactions is obviously rival: I can only spend a given dollar bill once. However, since the usefulness to me of any particular currency for effecting transactions (the "moneyness" of any given currency) is strictly increasing in the frequency, scale, and scope of that currency's use by others, there is an ultra-non-rivalness in the choice of which currency to use. This creates the public good aspects of money. Social transactions costs are minimized with a single currency. There is a direct parallel here with the social gains from having a common language (or a common measurement system):[2] apart from aesthetic considerations, the value to me of learning another language is increasing in the number of other people that know the language.

Although the theoretical principle is compelling, complex measurement problems make it difficult to assess empirically the order of magnitude of the microeconomic efficiency gains that might be achieved by monetary union, in the EU or elsewhere. The Cecchini Report tried to estimate the real resource savings from the bid-ask spreads in the foreign exchange markets. This, the value added in the foreign exchange business, represents the competitive rentals of the physical and human resources currently tied up in the exchange of currencies that would be liberated by monetary union, plus any pure rents, enjoyed either as monopoly profits or as X-inefficiency (organizational slack).

This approach is problematic for a series of reasons. To the extent that currency markets are imperfectly competitive, the equilibrium spreads may overstate the social opportunity costs incurred by banks and other foreign exchange traders, of exchanging one currency for another. On the other hand, the spread ignores altogether the real resource costs incurred by the other (non-bank) parties in the foreign exchange markets, the so-called in-house costs in Emerson et al. (1990). Also, the increasing returns associated with the public good aspects of money imply that the value of the technological network externalities is not captured by the bid-ask spread in the foreign exchange markets, even if the latter are competitive and efficient. In sum, it seems fair to say that the existing estimates are either inconclusive or arbitrary, and there is no consensus regarding the true magnitude of the net benefits from monetary harmonization.[3]

If one could redesign the world from scratch, microeconomic efficiency would clearly suggest the optimality of a single currency. It does not follow, however, that it is necessarily efficient (from a microeconomic point of view) to move to a common currency from an initial situation involving many currencies. Switching currencies (i.e., moving to the use of a different currency as *numéraire*

2. An updated analogy would emphasize the social gains of adopting common or compatible software systems.
3. The resources savings from having a common currency are of course not restricted to those obtainable from closing a number of spot markets foreign exchange. Many other markets for exchanging financial instruments denominated in the to-be-defunct currencies would also disappear (currency futures markets, currency swap markets, and many organized exchanges and over-the-counter markets for foreign exchange derivatives).

and medium of exchange) is costly because, as Down and Greenaway put it, in a world of boundedly rational agents with limited computational data-gathering and data-processing capacity, "we must learn to reckon in the new currency, we must change the units in which we quote prices, we might have to change our record, and so on."[4]

In addition, there are the real resource costs of introducing a new currency (or of extending the use of an existing currency to previous non-users), the costs of converting contracts denominated in old currencies into the new currency (which will provide a great windfall for the legal profession) and a variety of other costs that can be labelled "vending machine costs". To sum up, the on-off cost of switching must be set against the continuing gains from operating with a single currency, meaning that the microeconomic case for moving to a common currency from a preexisting multiple currency system is not a priori self-evident. On the other hand, unless one has a very high discount rate, on-off switching costs are likely to be dominated by the permanent flow of transaction cost savings.[5]

Leaving aside the microeconomic efficiency arguments for a common currency, there are just two fundamental reasons why the nominal exchange rate regime might matter for real economic performance. These are the same reasons why money matters in any economy, open or closed: seigniorage and nominal rigidities. We consider these in turn in the next two sections. Note that, once we abstract from the microeconomic efficiency arguments, the arguments for a common currency (or monetary union) are the same as those for any credible fixed exchange rate regime. As elaborated in detail in the previous chapters, it may of course be the case that the only truly credible fixed exchange rate regime is a common currency. For most of the arguments that follow, however, the key issue is whether the peg is fixed and is believed to remain fixed now and in the future.

---

4. Dowd and Greenaway (1993, p. 1180).
5. An interesting point, noted in Dowd and Greenaway (1993), is that from the point of view of efficiency, a move to a single currency should be a move towards the universal use of one of the preexisting currencies (say the D-mark in the EU) rather than the adoption of a new currency (such as the ECU). That way, at least the Germans will be spared the switching costs, and even non-Germans will be dealing with a common currency that will at least be somewhat familiar. By the same token, English, Spanish, or Mandarin would make a better world language than Esperanto. Note that it is only the name and other phenotypical superficialities like the appearance of notes and coins that should be adopted universally in order to minimize switching costs. Even if the name "mark" were retained, the Bundesbank would, as provided in the Maastricht Treaty, lose its ability to conduct monetary policy in Germany or anywhere, and would become just the German branch office of the ECB. Needless to say, the institutional solution actually adopted in Europe – the name of the common currency will be, rather anonymously, "euro" – is nothing but a further consequence of the national horizontal equity principle at work.

10.3   Seigniorage and exchange rates

10.3.1   *Tax distortions and the efficiency-related argument against a common currency*

Governments[6] can appropriate real resources by issuing intrinsically value-less (fiat) money, provided private agents believe that fiat money will offer them a competitive rate of return – including saved transactions costs – over the planned holding period. A government can raise the attractiveness to private agents of its fiat money by paying interest on it, by declaring it legal tender, by requiring certain transactions (say, tax payments) to be made with it, and by making the use of other transactions media costly or even illegal. Since the private (and social) marginal cost of producing fiat money is approximately zero, the government must have some monopoly power over its issuance if it wishes to gain command over real resources by varying its quantity.

There are several ways of measuring the resources accruing to the government through its monopoly on the issuance of base money. The three important ones are seigniorage, the inflation tax, and the interest burden foregone.[7]

Seigniorage is the resources the government appropriates by expanding the nominal monetary base. Let the nominal quantity of government fiat money (henceforth base money) outstanding at the end of period t be denoted H_t. For simplicity, assume that base money (currency plus banks' balances with the central bank) is non-interest-bearing. Let P_t be the general price level during period t, Y_t be the real GDP, $h_t \equiv H_t/(P_t Y_t)$ be the monetary base-GDP ratio

6. In this section, "government" refers to the consolidated public sector (general government and central bank).
7. A fourth measure of government revenue from base money issuance is the Central Bank's budgetary contribution to the general government. This is effectively the tax levied by the Treasury on the Central Bank. In principle, it could be anything up to the maximal feasible resource transfer of the Central Bank to the Treasury, that is, the Central Bank's net worth. For our purposes, the intrapublic sector transfer of resources between the central bank and the general government is of no interest. What we are interested in is the transfer of resources between the public sector as a whole (that is, the consolidated general government and central bank) and the remaining economic actors (the domestic private sector, the state enterprise sector, and the rest of the world). The same applies to other proposed measures of the resource transfer between the general government and the central bank, such as the fiscal seigniorage favored by Klein and Neumann (1990, 1992), and by Rovelli (1994). Klein and Neumann define fiscal seigniorage as central bank profits transferred to the general government, plus the net increase in central bank credits to the government, minus interest payments of the government to the central bank. As pointed out by van Ewijk (1992), there are questions about the appropriateness of this definition even as a measure of the contribution the general government gets from the central bank's monopoly over base money. Drazen (1985) consolidates the general government sector with the central bank and consequently has a measure of seigniorage that corresponds to our own (see also Buiter, 1983a,b).

(the reciprocal of the income velocity of circulation of base money), $\pi_t \equiv \Delta P_t/P_{t-1}$ be the rate of inflation, and $g_t \equiv \Delta Y_t/Y_{t-1}$ be the growth rate of real GDP; Δ is the backward difference operator. As a fraction of GDP, seigniorage (denoted σ) is defined as

$$\sigma_t = \frac{\Delta H_t}{P_t Y_t}. \tag{10.1}$$

The *inflation tax* is the reduction in the real value of the outstanding stock of base money due to increases in the general price level. As a fraction of GDP, the inflation tax (denoted τ^π) is given as

$$\tau_t^\pi = \pi_t \frac{H_{t-1}}{P_t Y_t}. \tag{10.2}$$

The inflation tax and seigniorage are related by the identity[8]

$$\sigma_t \equiv \tau_t^\pi + \left(\frac{g_t}{1+g_t}\right) h_{t-1} + \Delta h_t. \tag{10.3}$$

Seigniorage exceeds the inflation tax if there is positive real GDP growth and if the base money–GDP ratio is increasing (the income velocity of circulation of base money is declining).

By being able to issue non-interest-bearing base money, the government avoids having to issue a corresponding amount of interest-bearing debt. The *interest burden foregone* (as a fraction of GDP), denoted ω_t, is

$$\omega_t = i_t \frac{H_{t-1}}{P_t Y_t} \tag{10.5}$$

where i denotes the short nominal rate of interest.[9]

---

8. To obtain this identity, rewrite seigniorage as

$$\sigma_t \equiv \left(\frac{(1+\pi_t)(1+g_t) - 1}{(1+\pi_t)(1+g_t)}\right) h_{t-1} + \Delta h_t$$

and the inflation tax as

$$\tau_t^\pi \equiv \frac{\pi_t h_{t-1}}{(1+\pi_t)(1+g_t)}.$$

9. The flows of current and future seigniorage and the flows of current and future interest burden foregone are related by the following identity:

$$\sum_{j=0}^{\infty} \left(\prod_{k=0}^{j} \frac{1}{1+i_{t+k}}\right) \Delta H_{t+j} = \sum_{j=1}^{\infty} \left(\prod_{k=0}^{j} \frac{1}{1+i_{t+k}}\right) i_{t+j} H_{t+j-1} - \frac{H_{t-1}}{1+i_t}. \tag{10.4}$$

Thus, the present discounted value of current and future seigniorage equals the present discounted value of the current and future interest burden foregone (roughly the operating profits of the central bank), minus the initial stock of base money (the liabilities of the central bank).

If there exists a stable base money demand function, and if we are able to predict the arguments in the base money demand function for the period of interest, we can provide a map between the seigniorage revenue extracted by the government and the rate of inflation.[10] When the demand for money is sensitive to the rate of inflation, the inflation tax is distortionary, like every other real-world tax, transfer or subsidy. The normative neoclassical theory of public finance recognizes that, in general, a (constrained) optimal design of fiscal policy will require the use of all distortionary tax instruments. Efficiency requires that the excess burdens imposed by the various distortionary taxes be equalized at the margin.

This might seem to create a presumption that countries with well-developed direct and indirect tax systems would make less use of the inflation tax than countries with less efficient revenue administrations and more relaxed public attitudes towards tax evasion. The (constrained) optimal inflation rates might be expected to vary across time and across countries as tax bases, tax administration, and tax ethics vary. This would constitute an efficiency-related argument against a common currency.

Nonetheless, the empirical evidence shown in Table 10.1[11] makes clear that in recent years there has been very little recourse to the inflation tax or to

10. We can illustrate this point with a simple log-linear money demand function. Let h_t be a negative function of the domestic short nominal interest i:

$$\ln(h_t) = \alpha_t - \beta i_t, \quad \beta \geq 0.$$

By the standard Fisher equation, the domestic nominal interest is the domestic real interest rate plus the expected rate of inflation π_t^e, that is,

$$1 + i_t = (1 + r_t)\left(1 + \pi_t^e\right).$$

For a given domestic real interest rate, the monetary base–GDP ratio is uniquely (and negatively) related to the domestic expected rate of inflation. To determine the amount of seigniorage σ according to (10.1), however, we have to project the growth rate of real GDP and base money velocity as well, and consider both actual and expected rates of inflation. In a steady state, with α_t, r_t, and g_t constant and exogenous, and $\pi^e = \pi$, seigniorage as a function of the rate of inflation exhibits the familiar Laffer-curve pattern:

$$\sigma = \{1 - [(1+\pi)(1+g)]^{-1}\}\exp(\alpha' - \beta'\pi)$$

with $\alpha' = \alpha - \beta r$ and $\beta' = \beta(1+r)$.

11. Source: IFM. Base money is measured as reserve money. The inflation rate is the annual (year-over-year) rate of growth of the GDP deflator. Interest rates are TB rates except for the Netherlands, where the call money rate is used, and Finland, for which the money market rate is used. In the 1990s, the averages are over 1990–94, except for Austria, Belgium, Greece, Ireland (1990–93), Italy (1990–92), and Portugal (1990–92). The 1985–89 measure of seigniorage in the United Kingdom excludes 1986 data, since there is a break in the UK series between 1985 and 1986. Similarly, the 1985–89 measure of seigniorage in Portugal excludes 1989, since there is a major break in the monetary base series for Portugal between 1988 and 1989.

Table 10.1. *Seigniorage in the EU*

	Seigniorage as % of GDP Average over annual figures		Inflation tax as % of GDP Average over annual figures		Interest forgone as % of GDP Average over annual figures	
	1985–89	1990–94	1985–89	1990–94	1985–89	1990–94
Austria	0.39	0.44	0.28	0.33	0.53	0.76
Belgium	0.16	−0.07	0.30	0.21	0.62	0.58
Denmark	0.60	0.62	0.21	0.10	0.47	0.50
Finland	1.09	0.73	0.31	0.21	0.64	0.79
France	0.35	−0.24	0.24	0.12	0.52	0.43
Germany	0.67	0.56	0.21	0.34	0.42	0.73
Greece	2.24	1.91	2.55	2.38	2.71	2.60
Ireland	0.53	0.20	0.37	0.07	0.93	0.89
Italy	1.56	0.86	0.98	0.92	1.77	1.81
Netherlands	0.67	0.50	0.06	0.19	0.51	0.60
Portugal	1.92	2.93	2.21	2.90	2.24	2.87
Spain	1.89	−0.42	1.34	0.82	1.86	1.61
Sweden	0.74	1.52	0.40	0.34	0.66	0.86
United Kingdom	0.30	0.15	0.20	0.17	0.40	0.34

seigniorage for most EMU countries, and that the interest-burden foregone is likewise small. Notable exceptions are Spain, Italy, and especially Greece and Portugal (see also Grilli, 1989a, b). It seems extremely unlikely that the imposition of a common (low) rate of inflation on the EMU countries would significantly increase the excess burden associated with the financing of the public spending program.[12]

As the EU is only a relatively small subset of the set of all nations, there is an additional international seigniorage dimension. Member currencies (especially the D-mark) are used as reserves, intervention currencies and vehicle currencies by official and private agents outside the EU. The total amount of external seigniorage raised by all EU members from non-EU members is likely to change as a result of monetary union. It is quite possible that a new European currency

12. In addition to this empirical argument, it is worth mentioning that recent theoretical developments in the field of dynamic optimal taxation since Chamley (1986) have questioned the optimality of using seigniorage in the long run. The Friedman rule, that optimal monetary policy is characterized by satiation in real money balances and a zero nominal interest rate (at any rate, in the long run), emerges quite naturally in the standard Ramsey optimal taxation problem with money as an argument in the direct utility function. See the discussion in Roubini and Milesi-Ferretti (1994), and Buiter (1995).

could become, in relatively short order, a more effective competitor for the US dollar as an international store of value than the D-mark is today.[13] This good news must, however, be balanced by the recognition that the rules that will be followed by the European Central Bank for the distribution of its seigniorage (including its external seigniorage) among the various member states is unlikely to mimic the current distribution across countries. Scope for conflict is clearly present.[14]

10.3.2   A broader view of the inflation tax

The inflation tax considered in the theory of public finance is perhaps more accurately referred to as the (narrowly defined) *anticipated* inflation tax. It bears emphasizing that, besides seigniorage revenues, anticipated inflation can influence the government's budgetary position through other channels. The most important of these is the so-called Olivera-Tanzi effect, through which a higher rate of inflation erodes the real value of taxes paid in arrears. The reason is that such arrears often are neither index linked nor subject to a market interest rate reflecting anticipated inflation.

In addition to using anticipated inflation (broadly defined to include the Olivera-Tanzi effect and similar phenomena), the government can improve its real financial net worth by reducing the real value of its outstanding nominally denominated debt through unanticipated changes in the rate of inflation. This was discussed in Chapter 5. The effect of an unexpected increase in the current and/or future rate of inflation on the market value of the domestic currency–denominated, nonindexed, fixed-rate debt increases with the remaining term to maturity of the debt.[15] Short-term, floating-rate debt can have its real value eroded by an unanticipated increase in the price level.

It has been argued that, for a number of countries with high public debt/GDP ratios and a doubtful capacity for generating significant and sustained primary surpluses, giving up the ability to have nationally differentiated unanticipated inflation tax levies on the national debt may be more serious than the loss of the discretionary use of the anticipated inflation tax. The need for a de-jure (through a partial "consolidation" or default by some other name) or de-facto (through an inflation surprise or an unexpected devaluation) capital levy on the

13. We are talking potentially serious money. A recent Bundesbank study, reported in the *Financial Times* (June 21, 1995, p. 2), estimated that some 30 to 40 percent of the total currency circulating outside the banking system (between DM65bn and DM90bn) was probably abroad. The corresponding figure for the US dollar was estimated to be between 60 and 70 percent.
14. See Casella (1992) and Sibert (1994).
15. To the extent that the Fisher hypothesis does not hold and higher anticipated inflation reduces the real rate of interest, the real value of the debt is eroded even by higher anticipated inflation.

public debt may well become irresistible. If a de-jure public debt repudiation turns out to be politically unacceptable, a fierce burst of monetary and exchange rate irresponsibility may be the only way to reimpose ex post consistency on the public accounts.

Needless to say, for such a group of countries, the odds on being able to join EMU would worsen drastically, and indeed fatally. In principle, the optimal time to undertake de-facto debt repudiation would be just before joining EMU, since in that case there would be no cost (in terms of the credibility of the country's commitment to future noninflationary policies) from having a last fling with inflation. Nevertheless, whatever the merits of these considerations, the exchange rate, inflation, and interest rate criteria of the Maastricht Treaty rule out such a public debt "endgame". Note that the mere possibility of an inflationary solution to fiscal crisis can make fiscal corrections more difficult outside the monetary union than inside it. Through its effects on interest rate differentials, the inflation risk increases the debt burden.[16] Fiscal convergence would therefore be easier if the countries not satisfying the Maastricht criteria were nonetheless accepted in the monetary union. Paradoxically, delaying their participation could undermine their "convergence", in terms of both the interest rate criterion and the debt and deficit criteria.

10.4 Nominal rigidities and the Keynesian arguments for an optimal currency area

In this section, we focus on the implications of short-run Keynesian nonneutralities associated with various nominal rigidities and sluggishness in wage and/or price-setting behavior.[17] Nominal rigidities can represent the result of the empirically common practice of setting wages and prices in money terms for several periods in advance, since these multiperiod nominal contracts are often not index linked, that is not contingent on nominal wage and price developments elsewhere in the economy. Incomplete indexation also accounts for the redistributions of income and wealth often associated with unanticipated changes in the rate of inflation. Needless to say, such a nominal rigidity (money wages set one period in advance) was a central ingredient of the unilateral peg and Center–Periphery models discussed in Chapters 6 through 8.

---

16. If there is only the risk of inflation but not the reality of inflation, the real (inflation-corrected) interest burden would increase. If inflation expectations are realized, the higher nominal interest rates (reflecting expected inflation) would be offset by the reduction in the real value of the oustanding nominally denominated debt due to actual inflation.

17. They are to be distinguished from the nonneutralities that would be present even in a world without nominal rigidities, and that reflect the effects of anticipated inflation on consumption demand and portfolio allocation.

10.4.1   Monetary nonneutralities, exchange rate flexibility, and real economic performance

The first issue that must be settled is whether there is any long-run (steady-state) effect of monetary policy on such real variables as the level of capacity utilization or the rate of unemployment. In the Phillips-curve paradigm, long-run nonneutrality of inflation requires at least one of two phenomena to be present: either the long-run Phillips curve is nonvertical, or there is hysteresis in the natural rate of unemployment.

The argument is no doubt familiar, so we will only restate it briefly in terms of the simplest expectations-augmented Phillips curve, as a straightforward variant of our setup in Chapter 6.[18] The actual unemployment rate is denoted u and the natural rate of unemployment u^N. The core inflation rate or underlying rate of inflation is denoted $\hat{\pi}$, and ζ denotes some exogenous process driving the natural rate of unemployment. Specifically, ζ is a process independent of past, current, and anticipated future values of the rate of inflation, the growth rate of nominal money, or the actual unemployment rate.

$$\pi_t = -\alpha\left(u_t - u_t^N\right) + \gamma\hat{\pi}_t, \quad \alpha > 0, \quad 0 \le \gamma \le 1 \tag{10.6}$$

$$\hat{\pi}_t = \eta E_{t-1}\pi_t + (1 - \eta)\pi_{t-1}, \quad 0 \le \eta \le 1 \tag{10.7}$$

$$u_t^N = \delta u_{t-1} + (1 - \delta)u_{t-1}^N + \zeta_t, \quad 0 \le \delta \le 1 \tag{10.8}$$

In a long-run steady state, expectations are realized ($E_{t-1}\pi_t = \pi_t$) and the inflation rate is constant. Consider first the case where the natural rate is exogenous, that is, $\delta = 0$. In that case,

$$\pi = \frac{\alpha}{\gamma - 1}(u - u^N). \tag{10.9}$$

There is no long-run inflation–unemployment trade-off if and only if $\gamma = 1$; that is, core inflation feeds one-for-one into actual inflation, and the long-run Phillips curve is vertical at the exogenous natural rate of unemployment.

Now maintain the vertical long-run Phillips curve, that is, $\gamma = 1$, but allow path dependence or hysteresis in the natural rate by assuming $\delta > 0$. The current natural rate now depends (with exponentially declining weights) on the entire past history of the actual unemployment rate (and, of course, on the entire past history of the exogenous process ζ). While the Phillips curve is vertical in steady state, it can be vertical at any level of the unemployment rate, depending on the past history of the actual unemployment rate. With hysteresis, any temporary shock, including a temporary nominal shock in the presence of nominal rigidities, can have permanent, irreversible real effects.

18. Many other formalizations are possible. See for example Buiter (1985) and Buiter and Miller (1985).

If the long-run Phillips curve is vertical and there is no hysteresis in un-employment – as considered in most studies in the economics of optimal currency areas – any monetary nonneutralities are strictly short-run only. This has important implications for what exchange rate flexibility (or more generally, exchange rate management) can achieve, particularly for its ability to influence the real interest rate, the real exchange rate, real output, and other aspects of real economic performance. Monetary policy can temporarily influence the short-term real interest rate in the presence of nominal inertia; given the myopia, herd-instinct, and bandwagon effects that often dominate financial markets on a day-to-day basis, monetary policy may also have a transitory effect on the long-term real interest rate (although not necessarily in a very predictable manner). But ultimately monetary policy cannot influence either the short-term or long-term real rates in steady state – pace frequently heard claims about the properties of optimal currency areas – unless the economy is hysteretic (or the long-run Phillips curve is nonvertical).

The consensus view that monetary nonneutrality vanishes in the long run has important implications for what a country actually gives up when it inexorably fixes the external value of its currency, and thus for what it would have to gain or recoup in other dimensions of policy – or in the degree of flexibility of market and non-market institutions – in order to restore the capacity to respond to internal and external shocks that it had before it gave up its monetary sovereignty. With money nonneutral in the short run but neutral in the long run, nominal exchange rate flexibility can make only a transitory difference to the way in which the real variables of the economy[19] respond to shocks, regardless of whether these shocks are real or nominal, and regardless of whether they are permanent or transitory.[20]

The classic analysis by Poole (1970) on the stabilization properties of alternative monetary regimes, as well as a careful reading of the original piece on optimal currency areas by Mundell (1961), suggests that positive and negative aspects of exchange rate flexibility in the presence of nominal rigidities are tightly interlinked. The "good news" is that nominal exchange rate flexibility facilitates international relative price and cost adjustments that are warranted by developments in – and shocks to – real fundamentals. Although such adjustments will eventually occur, regardless of the nature of the nominal exchange rate regime, under flexible rates they will be achieved more quickly, and with smaller transitional or adjustment costs. The "bad news" about nominal exchange rate flexibility in the presence of nominal price or cost rigidities is that

---

19. Including the rate of inflation, which is of course a real variable.
20. As we shall see below, the transitory difference made by nominal exchange rate flexibility to the real adjustment path of the economy is potentially desirable in the case of shocks to goods market demand, but it is potentially undesirable in the case of monetary shocks.

it will cause financial shocks and other nominal shocks to result in temporary changes in international relative prices and costs – changes that are unnecessary and harmful from the point of view of the underlying real fundamentals, and that involve real, albeit transitory, adjustment costs.

To the list of the bad news, one could add a traditional argument against exchange rate flexibility that (as pointed out in Chapter 1) periodically reappears in the policy debate. In a world with incomplete markets, the existence of multiple currencies with (potentially) flexible conversion rates creates additional markets through which extrinsic, nonfundamental volatility can be injected into the financial system, and thus into the economic system as a whole. Exchange rate flexibility may breed excess volatility and temporary (but possibly persistent) misalignment, rather than merely filtering an exogenously given amount of irreducible, fundamental uncertainty.

10.4.2   *Asymmetric shocks*

The considerations mentioned above help in assessing the results of the theoretical and empirical literature on whether Western Europe is an optimal currency area. The optimal currency area literature[21] has emphasized that if the preponderance of shocks hitting a potential common currency area are idiosyncratic or asymmetric (i.e., region-specific or nation-specific), then the case for a common currency is weakened. Much of this literature may not have been sufficiently diligent in pointing out that nominal rigidities are a necessary condition for this conclusion to follow. But even having granted nominal rigidities their central place in the argument, the presumption that asymmetric shocks tout court favor independent currencies and floating exchange rates is seriously misleading.

Mundell's theory of optimal currency areas points out the disruptive effects of asymmetric real (IS) shocks in the presence of nominal rigidities and low labor mobility. Within the same analytical and conceptual framework considered by Mundell, monetary and financial (LM) shocks are actually best dealt with in a fixed exchange rate regime (through a straightforward application of the analysis of Poole (1970) to Mundell's open economy model). In the Appendix to this book, we provide a discussion of this issue based on a variant of the model presented in Chapters 6 through 8.

---

21. The classic references are Mundell (1961); McKinnon (1963); Kenen (1969); Ingram (1969, 1973); and Ishiyama (1975). Among recent contributions see Melitz (1991); De Grauwe and Vanhaverbeke (1991); Masson and Taylor (1992); Krugman (1992, 1993); De La Dehesa and Krugman (1993); Eichengreen (1990, 1992); Bayoumi and Eichengreen (1993); Bayoumi and Thomas (1995); Bini-Smaghi and Vori (1993); Eichengreen and Wyplosz (1993); Leeftinck (1994); Bayoumi (1995); von Hagen and Hammond (1995); Muet (1995); and Rubin and Thygesen (1996).

With few exceptions, in the literature dealing with the empirical assessment of Western Europe as an optimal currency area, this simple truth has routinely been ignored. The standard empirical procedure for evaluating the desirability of retaining nominal exchange rate flexibility has normally involved the decomposition of demand and supply shocks into idiosyncratic (asymmetric) vs. common (symmetric) shocks. Finding a preponderance of asymmetric shocks was then interpreted as an argument against monetary union. Ironically, the standard identifying restrictions commonly imposed in order to distinguish supply shocks from demand shocks imply quite the opposite.

Specifically, the commonly adopted identifying restriction that demand shocks have no long-run effects makes sense only for monetary (LM) shocks, and if asymmetric monetary shocks are important, a fixed exchange rate is in fact optimal. The restriction that there be no long-run real effects certainly is untenable on theoretical and empirical grounds for fiscal policy shocks or other IS shocks. Absent debt neutrality, even the redistribution over time (through borrowing) of the lump-sum tax financing of a given exhaustive public spending program will affect saving and capital formation. Likewise, permanent variations in exhaustive spending will, have long-run real effects, except in the simplest representative-agent models. Changes in private saving behavior brought about by shocks to the subjective discount rate, the parameters characterizing the intertemporal substitution rate or the parameters characterizing risk aversion likewise will tend to have long-run real effects. Yet, the long-run effects of IS shocks of this kind are surprisingly assumed away in much recent empirical work.

It is clear that demand shocks in turn have to be decomposed into financial (LM) and goods market (IS) shocks for it to be possible to draw sensible inferences about the appropriate exchange rate regime. Empirical evidence (based on credible identifying restrictions) about the relative importance of IS vs. LM shocks in the EU would be most welcome.[22]

Among the few recent empirical investigations in this direction, Nikolakaki (1996) attempts to identify separately the contributions of LM, IS, and supply shocks to the variability of output and the real exchange rate in a number of EU countries[23] in the post–Bretton Woods period, using structural VAR

---

22. An equally serious qualification to many of the findings in the literature is that the nature and magnitude of the disturbances perturbing the system may be a function of the exchange rate regime itself, as asserted above. That is, different exchange rate regimes not only transmit given fundamental (real and nominal) shocks differently, but they also may generate different kinds and amounts of extrinsic, nonfundamental noise.

23. Austria, France, Italy, Germany, the Netherlands, Portugal, Spain, Sweden, and the United Kingdom (all relative to Germany).

methods.[24] When the identification scheme allows only supply shocks to have long-run effects on real output, supply shocks account for most of the variability in output for six countries (and IS shocks account for very little), even in the short run. In France and Italy, however, LM shocks typically account for between 45 and 68 percent of output variability over a 1- to 10-quarter horizon. IS shocks account for the bulk of real exchange rate variability at all horizons, (and supply shocks account for very little) except in the Netherlands and Germany, where LM shocks dominate. The relevance of IS shocks as a source of output volatility increases significantly when the identification scheme allows both aggregate supply shocks and IS shocks to have long-run real effects.

Clearly, even if these results are taken at face value, their interpretation must be informed by the Lucas critique. It is by no means obvious that the reduced-form relationships between (on one hand) output and the real exchange rate and (on the other hand) the three shocks will remain invariant under the changes in the stochastic processes driving these three shocks that might result from a major regime change such as a move to a monetary union. Nevertheless, some interest attaches to the finding that LM shocks were a nonnegligible source of real output variability during the post–Bretton Woods era for several of the countries considered.

To summarize, it can be argued that asymmetric shocks, far from being an argument against, are an argument in favor of a fixed exchange rate or a common currency if the shocks in question are financial shocks, and if the degree of international financial capital mobility is very high.

10.4.3   Openness and production diversification

Two further characteristics of a country's economic structure have been argued to be important for the choice of exchange rate regime. These are the openness of the country to trade in goods and services and the degree of diversification of its production and demand structures.

Regarding openness to trade, it is argued that if imports and exports (or more generally importables and exportables) are large relative to domestic absorption and production, then variations in the nominal exchange rate will tend to be translated swiftly and comprehensively into increases in domestic consumer and producer prices, without any changes in key indices of international competitiveness. The limiting case would be that of the small open economy with only traded goods. Note, however, that even in this case nominal wage rigidity would cause (short-run) changes in real wages and real unit labor costs to result from variations in the nominal exchange rate, thus influencing an important

---

24. Related results are discussed by Cavallari (1996).

dimension of international competitiveness, even without any changes in the relative prices of different traded goods.[25]

As for diversification of the production and demand structures, this is best viewed as a determinant of the likelihood that shocks to the demand for or supply of goods and services are symmetric (general) or asymmetric (nation-specific). If goods demand or supply shocks are more symmetric, fewer and smaller international relative price or cost adjustments are required, and nominal exchange rate flexibility is less valuable. If two nations have well-diversified production structures, an industry-specific supply shock is more likely to affect both countries in a similar manner. Similarly, if their demands are well diversified, shocks to demand (say, fiscal policy shocks) are likely to impact more symmetrically on the domestic and foreign economies.

10.5   What makes up for loss of exchange rate flexibility?

If money is neutral in the long run, what is gained through exchange rate flexibility is an instrument with strictly temporary or transitory real effects: it facilitates adjustment to goods market shocks and complicates adjustment to financial shocks. Compensating for the loss of the exchange rate instrument, therefore, requires only an alternative instrument with strictly temporary or transient real effects.

It is true that the word *temporary* can cover any interval of real time from one nanosecond to anything short of eternity. How long is the short run relevant for assessing the real effects of variations in the nominal exchange rate? There obviously can be no universally valid answer to this question; it depends on the nature of the shocks hitting the system, on the collective institutional arrangements that have evolved and are in place in a particular country at any given point in time, and on the decision rules adopted by private agents.

A conventional wisdom going back at least to Milton Friedman holds that in a low-inflation OECD-type economy, rather closed to international trade like the United States, it may take as long as two years for monetary changes to feed through into prices rather than quantities. If capital formation has been affected in the meantime, real consequences of nominal shocks may last and linger even longer than that. For more open economies and for economies undergoing higher and more variable rates of inflation, the real consequences of nominal shocks may be significantly less persistent. There is some evidence to support the view that most of continental Europe has significant real price

25. In the model under consideration, labor services (and leisure) are of course nontraded goods, so variations in the nominal exchange rate still work by influencing the relative price of traded and nontraded goods. The only other transmission channel would be the asset revaluation effects of nominal exchange rate changes, including real balance effects.

and cost rigidities, but no nominal inertia of much consequence. The loss of the exchange rate instrument would be of little significance, if that were the case.

The optimal currency area literature has discussed at length the issue of what policy, institutional, or other behavioral changes are necessary to compensate for the loss of the nominal exchange rate instrument. The focus has been on the roles of international factor mobility, underlying divergent or convergent real economic behavior (such as productivity growth, real earnings growth, and demographic developments), and international fiscal transfers. We shall deal with them in turn. The discussion takes us some distance away from the safe ground of the formal models considered in the rest of our book, but the points are so central to an appreciation of the pros and cons of monetary union that they must be addressed here. Rather than reiterating arguments and conclusions, we choose to pursue the specific task of presenting a constructive critique of the less satisfactory results in the literature.

10.5.1   Factor mobility

International factor mobility, including labor mobility, may be very valuable from the point of view of adjusting to asymmetric goods market shocks. Its usefulness as a substitute for nominal exchange rate flexibility, however, is questionable.

The standard argument goes as follows. When a country is hit by an asymmetric shock to the demand for or supply of its output, there are two international adjustment mechanisms consistent with the maintenance of full employment: a change in the relative price of the domestic good, and international factor mobility. If there is a high degree of international factor mobility, international relative prices will have to change only little in response to a given asymmetric goods market shock. Since international relative price changes are costly with a fixed nominal exchange rate (because they require a phase of deviations from full capacity utilization and full employment), a high degree of international factor mobility, by obviating the need for any (significant) international relative price adjustment, reduces the cost of giving up nominal exchange rate flexibility.

The problem with this argument is that international factor mobility, especially labor mobility, is costly. International relocation of real factors of production is an investment subject to sunk (irreversible) costs. It is therefore efficient only in response to permanent (or at least very persistent) real shocks. Net migration flows that are (efficiently) reversible over the period of a typical business cycle are rare. As a substitute for nominal exchange rate flexibility, international factor mobility therefore delivers both too much and too little.

It delivers too much, insofar as international factor mobility is a mechanism for achieving permanent real adjustments. Nominal exchange rate flexibility cannot do that; it has only transitory real effects. International factor mobility delivers too little, insofar as does not possess the self-liquidating, transient properties of nominal exchange rate adjustment.[26]

In response to a temporary real shock, factors should not move internationally. A temporary international relative price change represents a better solution in terms of social welfare, and the cost of achieving this will be lower with a (well-managed) flexible nominal exchange rate. In response to a permanent real shock, international factor mobility may be optimal. With low international mobility costs, relative price changes will be unnecessary. With high international mobility costs, factors will not move even in response to permanent real shocks and international relative prices will have to adjust significantly. Monetary policy (and nominal exchange rate adjustments) will again lower the transitional costs of achieving the required relative price adjustment.

Another way of putting this is that international labor mobility is not an effective cyclical stabilization mechanism. It is a means for achieving long-term structural change. Since the exchange rate regime affects only the behavior of the real economy at cyclical frequencies, labor mobility is not a substitute for nominal exchange rate flexibility.

The point is often made that the states of the United States are better candidates for a common currency area than the members of the EU, because interstate labor mobility is significantly higher in the United States than intercountry labor mobility in the EU.[27] It is true that in the United States there is rather more permanent or long-term interstate labor mobility, but only little of this occurs at cyclical frequencies. The kind of temporary, reversible, or cyclical international labor mobility required to compensate fully for the loss of monetary autonomy is not found anywhere in the world, not even in the United States, or in other federal states with a common currency.

---

26. Note that net international migrations flows can be reversible without this requiring the reversal of any individual migration decision. Only in a representative agent model, gross flows equal net flows, and reversal of the net migration flow requires individual migrants to reverse their earlier migration decisions, that is, to engage in strictly temporary migration. In a model with a heterogeneous potential migrant population and positive gross flows in both directions, sign reversal in the net flow of migrants between countries does not require any individual migration decision to be reversed, that is, it does not require temporary migration by any individual migrant. By itself, however, recognition of migrant heterogeneity and positive two-way gross flows does not invalidate the presumption that, because migration is subject to sizeable sunk costs, it is neither an effective mechanism for adjusting to temporary shocks, nor an effective substitute for an adjustment mechanism that has only temporary real effects.

27. See for example Eichengreen (1990, 1992); Muet (1991, 1995); Blanchard and Katz (1992); and Mantel (1994).

10.5.2   Convergent real developments

The discussion of real convergence in a monetary union provides a record number of fundamental misunderstandings of what nominal exchange rate flexibility can deliver.[28] To put it bluntly, most contributors to this debate forget that real convergence or divergence is to a large extent irrelevant in an assessment of the pros and cons of monetary union.

Asserting the contrary would mean attributing to monetary policy (under which we include exchange rate policy) power and significance well beyond what it can deliver. Does anyone really believe that the problems of Italy's Mezzogiorno would have been alleviated if Southern Italy had been given its own currency and had decided to float the Southern Lira independently of the Northern Lira? Or that Appalachia would have been more prosperous if it had been granted its own currency? How would real wage rigidities be alleviated by having an independent currency and a floating exchange rate? How are the competitiveness problems associated with excessive nonwage labor costs mitigated by having a floating exchange rate? Why would international differences in the severity of intergenerational distribution problems, and in the strains put on public sector budgets by graying populations and emerging "youth deficits", be any less with a floating exchange rate than under a fixed rate? Is there any reason why regions characterized by persistent differences in total factor productivity growth or by persistent differences in real earnings growth unrelated to productivity growth differentials cannot be locked together in a common currency area? No doubt real economic performance would be dismal in a region whose real earnings growth systematically exceeded its productivity growth, but it would be equally dismal with a fixed exchange rate, a floating exchange rate, or bilateral barter.

---

28. The following quote from a speech of the Governor of the Bank of England is representative of a widespread opinion on the role of divergent real economic structures, behavior and developments:

> This longer-term problem of unemployment reflects, at least in part, structural features of the European labour market, which also differ from one country to another – for example in the degree of flexibility in wages and other conditions of employment, or in the degree of nonwage, social costs of employment. It is being addressed, variously, through structural policies nationally and through measures such as those that are being explored by the European Commission and debated by the European Council. But it will not easily go away. And it could in fact become more difficult to resolve within monetary union as a result of ongoing differences between member countries, for example, as a result of differences in rates of productivity growth, or unrelated differences in earnings growth, or as a result of divergent demographic trends and associated differences in dependency ratios (George, 1995).

The foregoing discussion apparently runs against arguments such as those made by Krugman (1992, 1993) and by Dehesa and Krugman (1993) about increasing returns, thick market externalities, conglomeration, and the processes of regional specialization and concentration. If money is neutral, even in the short run, then the exchange rate regime is obviously irrelevant. If money is nonneutral at least in the short run, the hysteretic features of many of these new economic geography models imply that transitory shocks, including monetary and exchange rate shocks, can have permanent effects. But so can any other transitory shock, including the most transitory of fiscal shocks. As these models make it so easy to influence the long-run course of history (just tweak any instrument temporarily), neutralizing the undesirable real effects of the absence of nominal exchange rate flexibility (or the undesirable real effects of its presence) would not necessarily pose a significant challenge to policy makers.

10.5.3   International fiscal transfers

What is lost by giving up nominal exchange rate flexibility can be recouped through international fiscal transfers that are strictly temporary or transitory (and indeed reversible – in present value terms – if there is no Ricardian equivalence). There is no need for any permanent fiscal transfers to make up for the loss of national monetary autonomy. The fact that the EU budget is tiny and engages in a negligible amount of international redistribution is therefore irrelevant from the point of view of monetary union. By the same token, the fact that the US federal budget is responsible for a significant amount of interstate redistribution (when state GDP varies) represents massive overkill from the point of view of establishing the presumption that the United States is an optimal currency area.[29]

All the EU needs in order to compensate for the loss of national monetary sovereignty and nominal exchange rate flexibility is an international transfer mechanism that is capable of making temporary (i.e., self-liquidating) transfers between countries. It may well be that much greater permanent or structural international and interregional redistribution will be required within the EU in order to render the system politically viable. However, that is a quite separate matter from the issue of what needs to be done to make up for the loss of the national exchange rate instrument.[30]

---

29. In the empirical analysis of Sala-i-Martin and Sachs (1992), there is a large area of ambiguity between insurance against certain kinds of transitory shocks (which is all that nominal exchange rate flexibility can provide) and permanent redistribution through the federal budget. See also Eichengreen (1990); Van Rompuy (1991); Abraham and Heremans (1991); von Hagen (1992); Courchene (1993); Goodhart and Smith (1993); Bayoumi and Masson (1994); and Muet (1995).
30. On the fiscal implications of a common currency see also Buiter and Kletzer (1991).

10.6   Capital mobility as an argument for a common currency

Many arguments given in Emerson et al. (1990) to the effect that the logic of market integration implies the need for a common currency seem to derive from fears that competitive nominal devaluations can buy a country a lasting comparative advantage, thus distorting the competitive level playing field.

These fears are misplaced. Even if a lasting gain in cost competitiveness could be achieved in this manner (which it cannot), they ignore the inflationary consequences that would result from a systematic policy of pursuing a weaker real exchange rate through repeated attempts at keeping nominal exchange rate devaluations ahead of domestic price and cost increases. They ignore the historical evidence, which supports the view that it is not possible to gain any enduring competitive advantage by pursuing deliberately inflationary policies. The model in Chapters 6 to 8, like most of the rest of the literature, shows that in equilibrium anticipated devaluations don't buy improved competitiveness. Unanticipated devaluations may buy a temporary improvement in competitiveness, but if they result in a loss of anti-inflationary credibility, they will result in a permanently higher rate of inflation.

Arguments against exchange rate flexibility based on the complications it creates for managing the CAP (through the wedges it drives between market exchange rates and "Green currency values") are very far into the realm of the Nth-best. It makes no sense to tie the EU's choice of currency regime to the fate of a moribund agricultural welfare state.

Only one aspect of market integration does indeed point in the direction suggested by the "one market, one money" school of thought. That aspect is financial market integration, specifically the removal of fiscal and administrative obstacles to the international movement of financial capital. The arguments supporting the idea that free capital mobility makes a single currency highly desirable (or perhaps even unavoidable) are both theoretical and empirical but are by no means universally accepted. Central to the argument is the view that floating exchange rate regimes, whether the exchange rates float cleanly or dirtily, are frequently likely to have undesirable operating characteristics, such as excess short-term volatility and persistent medium-term misalignment, in the presence of large-scale reshuffles in international portfolios. Whether or not this belief is supported by thorough empirical evidence, it is shared by a large fraction of the European policy makers. The second key plank in the argument is that managed exchange rate regimes, including fixed-but-flexible exchange rate systems such as Bretton Woods, or target zones with hard barriers such as the ERM of the early 1990s, appear to break down with probability one in finite time. They are not sustainable, and therefore, except in the short run, they are infeasible.

The latter point requires a brief discussion. While technically any solvent government facing a speculative attack in the absence of capital controls should be able to borrow infinite amounts of foreign exchange (simply by swapping it for its own currency or debt), in reality there is a limit to the credit lines that any monetary authority can draw on. As long as such limits on a country's ability to acquire reserves can be challenged by private speculators in reasonably efficient financial markets (or as long as the cost of acquiring additional reserves by raising domestic interest rates ultimately rises to unacceptable heights, due to lack of credibility), unrestricted international capital mobility will be a dagger pointed at the heart of any adjustable peg system.

According to this view, the completion of one component of the single market program – the elimination of (virtually) all remaining restrictions on the intra-EC mobility of financial capital – was sufficient to seal the fate of the EMS and the ERM. With all legal restrictions removed and much of the accumulated inefficiency of the previously protected private financial sectors swept away, a market mechanism was created that could shift literally hundreds of billions of dollars worth of financial claims between currencies in a matter of minutes, and at very little cost.

From these two considerations, the argument concludes that EMU represents the only possible regime consistent with both the widespread policy aversion toward currency instability and capital mobility. The only potential alternative to EMU would require a return to a regional system of managed exchange rates, putting the capital flight genie back in the bottle through fiscal or administrative capital controls. Would such a solution work? We do not think so. The scope and efficiency of the global industry ready to take on the authorities by supplying the means to avoid and evade controls is awesome. The rewards from taking on the monetary authorities are too high. Given the ineffective penalties likely to be imposed and the low risk of being caught evading the controls, the odds on capital controls working within the European Union effectively are virtually nil.

Proposals for imposing non-interest-bearing reserve requirements on balances used for taking open positions to attack currencies are naive, because they ignore key developments of the last two decades in the international financial markets. Attacking a currency through the spot markets represents nowadays only one – and not the most sophisticated or profitable one – of the myriad strategies available to financial speculators. Taxes[31] on foreign exchange transactions would likewise have to be expanded in their coverage to include transactions in the option markets and in markets for all other kinds of derivatives. They would also require virtually world-wide implementation in order to avoid disintermediation out of the controlled areas. By the mid 1990s,

---

31. Capital controls based on transaction taxes are sometimes referred to as "Tobin tax". This is incorrect. Tobin taxes were meant to "throw sand" – not stones – "in the excessively lubricated wheels of financial markets". They were not conceived as tools for implementing capital controls (see Tobin, 1982).

hypothetical proposals and blueprints suggesting such extensions have been met with widespread skepticism both in the academic and political milieu.[32]

10.7   Issues in the transition to EMU

In early 1998, the decision will have to be taken on which countries qualify for EMU. Stage 3, involving the irrevocable locking of exchange rates, is supposed to begin no later than January 1, 1999. However, the recent Green Paper of the European Commission (Commission of the European Communities, 1995a) suggests that up to a year may pass between the date on which it is decided which countries qualify for EMU and the date on which the currencies of the countries in question are actually locked together permanently and the final conversion parities are actually chosen.

The proposed introduction of a single currency involves three phases. The start of Phase A, (the "Launch of EMU") is assumed to produce the following: the list of participating member states, the date of the start of EMU announced (or confirmed), the deadline for the final changeover to the single currency, the setting up of the European System of Central Banks (ESCB) and the European Central Bank (ECB), and the start of production of notes and coins. Phase B (the "Start of EMU"), which must begin no later than 12 months after Phase A, is when economic and monetary union actually enters into force, with the irrevocable fixing of parities. During this phase, a "critical mass" of Euro-denominated financial transactions will have to be built around a single monetary policy and the issue of new public debt. Phase C ("Single currency fully introduced"), which will commence no later than three years after Phase B, will see the completion of the transitional phases, with the rapid introduction of new bank notes and coins and the general changeover of means of payment.

The key point to note is that although the European Council will decide to launch the single currency and will designate the countries that meet the convergence criteria – and thus may take part in this process in accordance with Article 109j (3) and (4) of the EC Treaty – the actual fixing of the parities and the choice of conversion rates will not occur until the beginning of Phase B, which could be as long as twelve months after the beginning of Phase A. In the light of the 1992–1993 events, this interval between Phase A and B seems designed to wreck the process of monetary unification. The Green Paper even recognizes the problem of endgame instability:[33]

> Once the date for the starting of the third stage is known, markets would make guesses about the final conversion rates and they would switch between

32. See Haq, Kaul, and Grunberg (1996).
33. See for example Froot and Rogoff (1991) and Bayoumi (1995).

possible outcomes; markets could also push exchange rates significantly away from levels justified on the basis of fundamentals.

The only way around this difficulty would be to commit credibly, right from the starting date of the third stage, to the final conversion rates. How such credible commitment can be achieved without formally abandoning monetary sovereignty (i.e., without subordinating national monetary authorities to a European Central Bank) unfortunately is unclear.

The practical difficulties involved in switching from national currencies to a new common currency and the public relations problem of selling the new currency to the people of Europe are real but not very significant or interesting. Fortunately it does not take much imagination to handle the legal problem of extending and enforcing contracts previously written in terms of national currencies or the engineering problem of refitting vending machines. The only interesting economic and political issues concern the membership of the group of countries that will irrevocably fix their exchange rates, its relationship to the EU members that are not in the group, and the conduct of monetary policy by the ECB.

A scenario consisting of a transitory arrangement with a Center (the "ins") and a Periphery raises many questions regarding both feasibility and desirability of a new ERM. A first issue is the already mentioned instability problem associated with the endgame condition: maintaining the peg in the face of a goods market shock makes sense only if there are reputational (credibility) costs associated with the abandonment of the fixed parity. National monetary policy reputational capital is scrapped when a nation joins a monetary union. Hence a last-minute devaluation or revaluation will always be individually rational. This argues in favor of an exchange rate convergence criterion with narrow bands in the period leading up to monetary union.[34]

We also previously mentioned the possibility that coalitions among the "ins" would make entry harder for the "outs" (who are typically less disciplined on fiscal and inflationary matters). At the very least, the interest rates of the more inflation-prone "outs" would exceed those of the "ins" by the expected currency depreciation premium. This would make it harder for them to meet the interest rate criterion for admission to EMU. Building up domestic credibility outside the monetary union could require costly repeated deflationary policy responses to internal and external shocks. Joining EMU would be a costless way to eliminate the expected currency depreciation premium and avoid this version of the Tantalus syndrome.

Although considerable analytical effort has been devoted to the analysis and design of EMU institutions, the literature so far has failed to present a consistent model of the transition. We believe that the Center–Periphery model discussed in Chapters 6 through 8 represents a natural starting point for developing a formal

---

34. See also the discussion in Thygesen (1996).

model capable of addressing some of the key issues raised by the coexistence of "ins" and "outs" in a new EMU-centered ERM.

The first of these issues is an empirical assessment of both the signs and the magnitudes of intra-EU structural external policy spillovers. The second issue is the possible strategic monetary and fiscal interaction between the "ins" and the "outs" of the union. Our model implies that, under reasonable assumptions on the sign of the structural external spillovers from monetary policy (that a devaluation by any Periphery country lowers the system-wide real rate of interest and causes an appreciation of the currencies of the other Periphery countries), the weakness of the Periphery-wide exchange rate undermines the disinflationary policy of the "outs", while permitting the Center to pursue its anti-inflationary objectives at a smaller unemployment cost. This should strengthen the political cohesion of the "ins".

What would be the response of the ERM to asymmetric shocks (to the Center as a whole, to individual Center countries, or to an individual country in the Periphery)? Is it conceivable that the "outs" will experience a trend appreciation of their currencies in response to a Center that is now interested in buying competitiveness for its weakest regions (the "weak Euro" scenario)? Or will the "outs" be pushed into instability and devaluations that would help to consolidate price stability in the Center, but at the cost of preventing the "outs" from becoming "ins" for some considerable period (the exclusionary "strong Euro" scenario)? While this study does not provide the answers to these important questions, it does provide the first step toward an analytical framework capable of addressing these issues in a systematic manner.

10.8   Reconstructing the monetary system in Europe through EMU

Most economic arguments for or against monetary union are misconceived and overstated. Opponents of monetary union tend to overestimate what is gained by retaining monetary sovereignty and what is given up by surrendering it. Advocates of monetary union tend to overstate the joys of a common currency and the damage inflicted by nominal exchange rate flexibility, through excessive short-run volatility and persistent misalignment.

While we would be the first to point to the significance of the international monetary and exchange rate system for the design and effectiveness of stabilization policy in the EU as a whole and in its individual members, we should not be blind to the fact that it is merely monetary policy – or rather the international dimension of monetary policy – that we are dealing with. Monetary policy is not unimportant from the point of view of short-run, cyclical stabilization, but neither is it the stuff of which the wealth of nations is made.

Since the narrowly economic case for or against monetary union is so inconclusive (or finely balanced), it is likely that the issue will be decided mainly on general political grounds. Such subordination of economics to politics fits in well with the long history of the quest for exchange rate stability in Europe, traced in the first part of this book. Recent developments in the monetary history of Europe cannot but remain a puzzle if we forget that a majority of European policy makers (and their constituencies) find the possibility of a permanent regime of flexible intra-EU rates utterly inconsistent with their policy preferences, whatever their roots (historical wisdom, sound economics, or unwarranted preconceptions).

Of course, monetary union represents a rather extreme solution to the policy problem of currency instability. A regime of narrow target zones, such as the ones implemented in Europe both during the Bretton Woods and the ERM eras, would on paper guarantee stable conversion rates without any drastic revamping of the institutional architecture of Europe. However, at least since World War II, no government has been able to enjoy the luxury of focusing monetary and fiscal policy exclusively on the defense of the external value of their currency. Absent a lexicographic utility function with the maintenance of the parity in the lead position, any commitment to a fixed parity is vulnerable and will be tested by the markets. In the absence of constraints on capital mobility, any fixed exchange rate regime that is not irrevocably fixed – that is, anything short of monetary union[35] – will collapse.

Governments (including benevolent, optimizing, and competent ones) that attempt to maintain exchange rate stability but are unable to commit to a fixed exchange rate policy in a credible way may choose to abandon their exchange rate target for a number of virtuous or opportunistic reasons. For instance, they may find themselves in a suboptimal position in their strategic interaction with the private sector (domestic and/or foreign) or with other governments. In these games, some equilibria involve a devaluation "move" that is rational from the standpoint of the country, while being inefficient from the standpoint of the system as a whole. In some other equilibria, the choice to devalue is optimal for both the "home" country and the other countries in the exchange rate system. We have presented examples of these equilibria in Chapter 8.

Under full capital mobility, currency and financial markets will typically anticipate, enhance, and perhaps overreact to economic problems and policy tensions that could motivate a devaluation. Historical evidence does not seem to support the opposite view, that currency crises are nothing but the outcome of the intrinsic instability of the financial markets, unrelated to fundamental tensions in the system.[36]

35. It is true that even monetary union is not irreversible. The Maastricht Treaty, however, does not have any provisions for a country leaving EMU after joining it. Indeed, neither the Rome Treaty nor the Maastricht Treaty has provisions for member states leaving any of the European institutions to which they have acceded.
36. See for example Bordo and Schwartz (1996).

Indeed, in this monograph we have forcefully reiterated the view that the ineluctability of the collapse of managed exchange rate systems does not depend on capital mobility per se. The central insight in our main theoretical chapters, Chapters 5 through 8, is that, any system of fixed but adjustable pegs will, sooner or later, be subject to disruptive forces that are comparable to those eventually leading to the ERM crisis in 1992–93.

Facing large and unusual shocks, the design of a common policy response to these disturbances brings about international tensions. Specifically, it raises the important issue of the distribution of costs and benefits from cooperative actions among the participating members. As the likelihood of uncoordinated actions at country level increases, rational market participants modify their expectations, adding to and magnifying the disruptive forces in the system. Free capital mobility increases the penalty paid by the policy makers for failing to reach an efficient and sustainable agreement on a coordinated response to the shock. In the absence of such a response (or when this response is too weak), the clash between fundamentals and pegged conversion rates quickly turns into a systemic crisis of the exchange rate regime.

In the light of this analysis, moving toward a currency union represents the only way to (re)construct a stable and lasting monetary system in which (current and future) conflicts between Center and Periphery, and within the Periphery itself, can be mediated and resolved rather than aggravated through the adverse dynamics of imperfect national credibility. To the extent that such a "shelter" makes monetary cooperation easier, a currency union is the logical – and definitive – solution to the problems of monetary cohabitation raised by the currency crisis in 1992–93.

In this perspective, the desirability of EMU as the systemic solution to the Europe-wide "quest for exchange rate stability" probably transcends its desirability on the basis of the "one money, one market" arguments. If the political tide towards greater European integration is halted or reversed, monetary union will go by the board, together with the effective chance of preventing the materialization of Europe-wide financial turmoils such as those from 1992–93 again. If European integration gets a second wind, much as it did in 1986 with the signing of the Single European Act, there will be a single European currency for most of the current EU members by the beginning of the next century. Only at that stage will the lessons of the ERM crisis become obsolete. It now seems certain that what began with politics will also end with politics. *Plus ça change...*

Appendix

This Appendix provides a formal treatment of the points raised in Section 10.4.2. Our argument requires a slight modification and extension of the model developed in Chapter 6 and used in Chapters 7 and 8. It is essential to model the domestic monetary equilibrium conditions explicitly, since the performance of a floating exchange rate in the face of "demand shocks" depends crucially on whether these shocks are IS shocks (shocks to the goods market) or LM shocks (shocks to money demand or money supply). The model of Chapters 6, 7, and 8, like most of the literature in this area, focuses exclusively on IS shocks. The simple model given below in equations (A.1)–(A.7) below distinguishes between goods market shocks and financial market shocks, but is the same as our earlier model in all other respects.

We deal with a small open economy model with perfect international capital mobility. All variables are in natural logarithms with the exception of nominal and real interest rates. Foreign variables and parameters are distinguished by a star superscript. All parameters are positive. m is the nominal money stock, p is the GDP deflator, q is the CPI, s is the nominal spot exchange rate (the domestic currency price of foreign exchange), y is real output, z is the real exchange rate, d is the stock of domestic credit, and ρ is the stock of international reserves. The money demand shock, the IS shock, and the supply shock are denoted λ^l, λ^d, and λ^s, respectively.

$$m_t - q_t = k(p_t + y_t - q_t) - \gamma i_t + \lambda^l_t \tag{A.1}$$

$$y_t = -v r_t + \delta z_t + \lambda^d_t \tag{A.2}$$

$$r_t \equiv i_t - E_t q_{t+1} + q_t \tag{A.3}$$

$$i_t = i^*_t + E_t s_{t+1} - s_t \tag{A.4}$$

$$q_t \equiv (1 - \beta) p_t + \beta \left(p^*_t + s_t \right)$$

$$y_t = (1 - \alpha)(p_t - E_{t-1} p_t) + \lambda^s_t \tag{A.5}$$

$$z_t \equiv s_t + p^*_t - p_t \tag{A.6}$$

$$m_t = \theta d_t + (1 - \theta) \rho_t \tag{A.7}$$

203

Assume for concreteness that the objective of policy is to stabilize real output around its full-information natural level λ_t^s.[37] Basically, nominal exchange rate flexibility is desirable when faced with IS shocks. Nominal exchange rate flexibility is definitely undesirable in the face of domestic financial market shocks (say, liquidity preference [money demand] or shocks to the domestic money supply process). The relative merits of fixed versus floating exchange rates are qualitatively ambiguous and depend on the relative magnitudes of key behavioral parameters for supply shocks and foreign interest rate shocks. Without going through a rather tedious full-blown Poole-style analysis, we can still be precise about the case of monetary shocks.

With a floating exchange rate, $\rho = 0$ (and for notational simplicity $\theta = 1$); the money stock, $m = d$, is exogenous. Since our economy takes the foreign interest rate as given and has perfect international capital mobility (as shown by the uncovered interest parity [UIP] condition in (A.4)), credibly fixing the nominal exchange rate (setting $s_t = E_t s_{t+1} = 0$, say) is equivalent to pegging the domestic nominal interest rate at the level of the foreign nominal interest rate. The now endogenous domestic money stock adjusts passively to shocks in the demand for money through endogenous variations in the stock of international reserves, ρ, even if the stock of domestic credit, d, is exogenous. Real economic activity (output, real exchange rate, and real interest rate) is perfectly insulated from domestic financial shocks λ_t^l. So is the domestic price level.

The presumption in favor of interest rate pegging, and therefore of fixed exchange rates, with perfect international capital mobility in the face of domestic financial shocks carries over in the multicountry version of this model. The particular system-wide monetary and exchange rate policy package that is optimal from the point of view of insulating real activity (and the price levels!) in all countries from the effects of monetary shocks is system-wide nominal interest-rate targeting. This means a fixed nominal exchange rate and an adjustment rule of the system-wide quantity of money that keeps common nominal interest rate constant at its target level in the face of monetary shocks, both global and country-specific.

---

37. Alternatively, the objective could be to stabilize output around its ex ante full-information natural level, zero. The optimal policy response to LM shocks and IS shocks is unaffected by this. The optimal policy response to supply shocks obviously would be.

References

Agénor, P.R., Flood R., and S. Bhandari, 1992. Speculative Attacks and Model of Balance of Payment Crises. *International Monetary Fund Staff Papers* 39, 357–394.

Akerlof, G.A., A.K. Rose, J.L. Yellen, and H. Hessenius, 1991. East Germany in from the Cold: The Economic Aftermath of Currency Union. *Brookings Papers on Economic Activity* 1, 1–87.

Alesina, A., and V.U. Grilli, 1993. On the Feasibility of a One or Multi-Speed European Monetary Union. *Economics and Politics* 5.

Artis, M., 1988. Exchange Controls and the EMS. *European Economy*, May.

Backus, D., and J. Galí, 1995. International Factors in the Recessions of the Early Nineties. New York University, Working Paper, October.

Banca d'Italia, 1992. *Economic Bulletin* 15, October.

Barro, R.J., 1979. On the Determination of the Public Debt. *Journal of Political Economy* 87, 940–971.

Barro, R.J., and D. Gordon, 1983a. Rules, Discretion, and Reputation in a Model of Monetary Policy. *Journal of Monetary Economics* 12, 101–121.

Barro, R.J., and D. Gordon, 1983b. A Positive Theory of Monetary Policy in a Natural-Rate Model. *Journal of Political Economy* 91, 589–610.

Basevi, G., 1988. Liberalization of Capital Movements in the European Community: A Proposal, with Special Reference to the Case of Italy. *European Economy*, May.

Bayoumi, T., 1995. Who Needs Bands? Exchange Rate Policy before EMU. Centre for Economic Policy Research Discussion Paper No. 1188, May.

Bayoumi, T., and B. Eichengreen, 1993. Shocking Aspects of European Monetary Unification, in F. Torres and F. Giavazzi, eds., *Adjustment and Growth in the European Monetary Union*, Cambridge, UK: Cambridge University Press.

Bayoumi, T., and P. Masson, 1994. Fiscal Flows in the United States and Canada: Lessons for Monetary Union in Europe. Centre for Economic Policy Research Discussion Paper No. 1057, November.

Bayoumi, T., and A. Thomas, 1995. Relative Prices and Economic Adjustment in the United States and the European Union: A Real Story about EMU. *International Monetary Fund Staff Papers* 42, 108–133.

Begg, D. et al., 1990. *Monitoring European Integration. The Impact of Eastern Europe.* London: Centre for Economic Policy Research.

Begg, D. et al., 1991. *Monitoring European Integration. The Making of Monetary Union.* London: Centre for Economic Policy Research.

Begg, D., and C. Wyplosz, 1993. The European Monetary System: Recent Intellectual History, in CEPR (1993).

Bertola, G., and L. Svensson, 1993. Stochastic Devaluation Risk and the Empirical Fit of Target-Zone Models. *Review of Economic Studies* 60, 689–712.

Bini-Smaghi, L. and S. Micossi, 1990. Monetary and Exchange Rate Policy in the EMS with Free Capital Mobility, in De Grauwe and Papademos (1990).

205

Bini-Smaghi, L., T. Padoa-Schioppa, and F. Papadia, 1994. The Transition to EMU in the Maastricht Treaty. *Essays in International Finance* No. 194, International Finance Section, Princeton University.

Bini-Smaghi, L., and S. Vori, 1993. Rating the EC as an Optimal Currency Area. *Temi di Discussione del Servizio Studi* No. 187, Banca d'Italia, January.

Blackburn, K., and M. Sola, 1993. Speculative Currency Attacks and Balance of Payment Crises. *Journal of Economic Surveys* 7, 119–144.

Blanchard, O., and L. Katz, 1992. Regional Evolutions. *Brookings Papers on Economic Activity* 1.

Blanchard, O., and P.A. Muet, 1993. Competitiveness through Disinflation: An Assessment of the French Macroeconomic Strategy. *Economic Policy* 16, 11–56.

Blanco, H., and P.M. Garber, 1986. Recurrent Devaluations and Speculative Attacks on the Mexican Peso. *Journal of Political Economy* 94, 148–166.

Bodnar, Gordon M., 1991. Capital Control Liberalization and Financial Markets in the European Monetary System: An Empirical Investigation. William E. Simon Graduate School of Business Administration Working Paper, University of Rochester.

Bordo, M., and A. Schwartz, 1996. Why Clashes Between Internal and External Stability Goals End in Currency Crises, 1797–1994. National Bureau of Economic Research Working Paper No. 5710, August.

Buiter, W.H., 1981. The Superiority of Contingent Rules over Fixed Rules in Models with Rational Expectations. *Economic Journal* 91, 647–670.

Buiter, W.H., 1983a. Measurement of the Public Sector Deficit and its Implications for Policy Evaluation and Design, *International Monetary Fund Staff Papers* 30, 306–49.

Buiter, W.H., 1983b. The Theory of Optimum Deficits and Debt, in Federal Reserve Bank of Boston, *The Economics of Large Government Deficits*, Conference Series No. 27, 4–69.

Buiter, W.H., 1985. International Monetary Policy to Promote Economic Recovery, in C. van Ewijk and J.J. Klant, eds., *Monetary Conditions for Economic Recovery*, Amsterdam: Martinus Nijhoff. Reprinted in W.H. Buiter, *International Macroeconomics*, Oxford, UK: Oxford University Press, 1990.

Buiter, W.H., 1986. Fiscal Prerequisites for a Viable Managed Exchange Rate Regime, in *Wisselkoersen in een Veranderende Wereld. Preadviezen 1986,* Leiden: Stenfert Kroese, 99–117.

Buiter, W.H., 1987. Borrowing to Defend the Exchange Rate and the Timing and Magnitude of Speculative Attacks. *Journal of International Economics* 23, 221–239.

Buiter, W.H., 1989. A Viable Gold Standard Requires Flexible Monetary and Fiscal Policy. *Review of Economic Studies* 56.

Buiter, W.H., 1995. Politique Macroéconomique dans la Période de Transition vers l'Union Monétaire. *Revue d'Economie Politique* 105, 807–46.

Buiter, W.H., G.M. Corsetti, and P.A. Pesenti, 1995. A Center-Periphery Model of Monetary Coordination and Exchange Rate Crises. National Bureau of Economic Research Working Paper No. 5140, June.

Buiter, W.H., G.M. Corsetti, and P.A. Pesenti, 1997. Interpreting the ERM Crisis: Country-Specific and Systemic Issues. Paper presented at the CEPR conference "Speculative Attacks on Foreign Exchange Reserves", Sesimbra, Portugal, 18–19 April.

Buiter, W.H., G.M. Corsetti, and N. Roubini, 1993. Excessive Deficits: Sense and Nonsense in the Treaty of Maastricht. *Economic Policy* 16, April, 57–100.

Buiter, W.H., and K.M. Kletzer, 1991. Fiscal Implications of a Common Currency, in A. Giovannini and C. Mayer, eds., *European Financial Integration*, Cambridge, UK: Cambridge University Press, 221–244.

Buiter, W.H., and R. Marston, eds. 1985. *International Economic Policy Coordination*. Cambridge, UK: Cambridge University Press.

Buiter, W.H., and M.H. Miller, 1985. Cost and Benefits of an Anti-inflationary Policy: Questions and Issues, in V.E. Argy and J.W. Nevile, eds., *Inflation and Unemployment: Theory, Experience and Policy-Making,* London: George Allen & Unwin, 11–38.

Bulow J., J. Geanakoplos, and P. Klemperer, 1985. Multimarket Oligopoly: Strategic Substitutes and Complements. *Journal of Political Economy* 93, 488–511.

Bundesbank Monthly Report, various issues.

Campa, J.M., and K.P.H. Chang, 1996. Arbitrage-Based Tests of Target Zone Credibility. Evidence from ERM Cross-Rate Option. *American Economic Review* 86, 726–740.

Canzoneri, M.B., and D.W. Henderson, 1991. *Monetary Policy in Interdependent Economy.* Cambridge, MA: MIT Press.

Casella, A., 1992. Participation in a Currency Union. *American Economic Review* 82, 847–63

Cavallari, L., 1996. The Cost of EMU: A Reconsideration of the Empirical Evidence. Working Paper, Dipartimento di Economia, Universitá di Roma La Sapienza.

Cavallari, L., and G.M. Corsetti, 1996. Policy Making and Speculative Attacks in Models of Exchange Rate Crises: a Synthesis. Economic Growth Center Working Paper No. 752. Yale University.

CEPR [Center for Economic Policy Research], 1993. *The Monetary Future of Europe.* Report of the Conference held on 11/12 December 1992 in La Coruña, Spain. London: Centre for Economic Policy.

Chamley, C., 1986. Optimal Taxation of Capital Income in General Equilibrium with Infinite Lives. *Econometrica* 54, 607–622.

Chen, Z., and A. Giovannini, 1994. The Credibility of Adjustable Parities: The Experience of the European Monetary System, in P.B. Kenen, F. Papadia, and F. Saccomanni, eds., *The International Monetary System,* Cambridge, UK: Cambridge University Press, 170–200.

Ciampi, C.A., 1995. Dall'Esperienza dello SME al Processo di Unione Monetaria Europea: Vincoli e Prospettive per la Politica Economica Italiana. *Rivista di Politica Economica* 5, 94–110.

Collier, I.L., 1991. On the First Year of German Monetary, Economic and Social Union. *Journal of Economic Perspectives* 4, 179–186.

Collins, S., 1988. Inflation and the European Monetary System, in F. Giavazzi, S. Micossi, and M. Miller, eds., *The European Monetary System,* Cambridge, UK: Cambridge University Press.

Commission of the European Communities, 1993. "The ERM in 1992." *European Economy* 54, 143–157.

Commission of the European Communities, 1994. *Annual Economic Report,* March.

Commission of the European Communities, 1995a. *Green Paper. On the Practical Arrangements for the Introduction of the Single Currency.* Brussels, May 31.

Commission of the European Communities, 1995b. *The Impact of Currency Fluctuations on the Internal Market.* Brussels, COM(95) 503 final, October 31.

Commission on the Role of Gold in the Domestic and International Monetary System, 1982. *Report to the Congress.* Washington, DC: Government Printing Office.

Committee for the Study of Economic and Monetary Union, 1989. *Report on Economic and Monetary Union in the European Community.* Luxembourg: Office of Official Publications of the European Communities.

Committee of Governors of the Central Banks of the EEC, 1993. *Annual Report 1992,* April.

Cooper, R., 1985. Economic Interdependence and Coordination of Economic Policies, in R. Jones and P.B. Kenen, eds., *Handbook of International Economics,* Vol. II. Amsterdam: North Holland.

Courchene, T.J., 1993. Reflections on the Canadian Federalism: Are there Implication for the European Economic and Monetary Union? *European Economy,* Special Issue No. 4, 23–166.

Currie, D., 1992. Hard-ERM, Hard ECU and European Monetary Union, in M. Canzoneri, V.U. Grilli, and P. Masson, eds., *Establishing a Central Bank: Issues in Europe and Lessons from the US*. Cambridge, UK: Cambridge University Press.

Currie, D., and P. Levine, 1993. *Rules, Reputation and Macroeconomic Policy Coordination*. Cambridge, U.K.: Cambridge University Press.

De Cecco, M., 1988. Il Sistema Monetario Europeo e gli Interessi Nazionali, in Guerrieri and Padoan (1988).

De Grauwe, P., 1994. Towards European Monetary Union without the EMS. *Economic Policy* 18.

De Grauwe, P., and L. Papademos, eds., 1990. *The European Monetary System in the 1990s*. London and New York: Longman.

De Grauwe, P., and W. Vanhaverbeke, 1991. Is Europe an Optimum Currency Area? Evidence from Regional Data, in P. Masson and M.P. Taylor, eds., *Policy Issues in the Operation of Currency Unions*, Cambridge, UK: Cambridge University Press.

De Kock, G., and V.U. Grilli, 1993. Fiscal Policies and the Choice of the Exchange Rate Regime. *Economic Journal* 103, 347–358.

De La Dehesa, G., and P. Krugman, 1993. Monetary Union, Regional Cohesion and Regional Shocks, in G. De La Dehesa, A. Giovannini, M. Guitian, and R. Portes, eds., *The Monetary Future of Europe*. London: Centre for Economic Policy Research.

Dixit, A., and R. Pindyck, 1994. *Investment Under Uncertainty*. Princeton, NJ: Princeton University Press.

Dornbusch, R., and H. Wolf, 1992. Economic Transition in East Germany. *Brookings Papers on Economic Activity* 1, 235–270.

Dowd, K., and D. Greenaway, 1993. Currency Competition, Network Externalities and Switching Costs: Towards an Alternative View of Optimum Currency Areas. *Economic Journal* 102, 1180–1189.

Drazen, A., 1985, A General Measure of Inflation Tax Revenues. *Economics Letters* 17, 327–330.

Drazen, A., and P. Masson, 1994. Credibility of Policies Versus Credibility of Policymakers. *Quarterly Journal of Economics* 109, 735–54.

Dumas, B., L. P. Jennergren, and B. Näslund 1993. Realignment Risk and Currency Option Pricing in Target Zones. National Bureau of Economic Research Working Paper No. 4458, September.

Economic Report of the President, 1971. Washington, D.C.: United States Government Printing Office.

Eichengreen, B., 1990. One Money for Europe? Lessons from the US Currency Union. *Economic Policy* 10, 117–187.

Eichengreen, B., 1992. Is Europe an Optimum Currency Area?, in Borner and Grubel, eds., *The European Community after 1992: The View from Outside*. London: Macmillan.

Eichengreen, B., A.K. Rose, and C. Wyplosz, 1994. Speculative Attacks on Pegged Exchange Rates: An Empirical Exploration with Special Reference to the European Monetary System. National Bureau of Economic Research Working Paper No. 4898, October.

Eichengreen, B., and C. Wyplosz, 1993. The unstable EMS. *Brookings Papers on Economic Activity* 1, 51–124.

Emerson, M., D. Gros, A. Italianer, J. Pisani-Ferry, and H. Reichenbach, 1990. One Market, One Money. *European Economy* 44, October. Also published by Oxford University Press, 1992.

Emminger, O., 1986. *D-Mark, Dollar, Nährungskrisen*. Stuttgart: Deutsche Verlags-Austalt.

Feldstein, M., 1993. Does European Monetary Union Have a Future?, in CEPR (1993).

Fischer, S., 1987. British Monetary Policy, in R. Dornbusch and R. Layard, eds., *The Performance of the British Economy*. Oxford, UK: Oxford University Press.

Flood R.P., J. Bhandari, and J. Horne, 1989. Evolution of Exchange Rate Regimes. *International Monetary Fund Staff Papers* 36, 810–835.

Flood, R.P., and P.M. Garber, 1983. A Model of Stochastic Process Switching. *Econometrica* 3, 537–551.

Flood, R.P., and P.M. Garber, 1984. Collapsing Exchange-Rate Regimes: Some Linear Examples. *Journal of International Economics* 17, 1–13.

Frankel, J., 1988. Ambiguous Policy Multipliers in Theory and in Empirical Models., in R. Bryant et al., eds., *Empirical Macroeconomics for Interdependent Economies.* Washington, D.C.: Brookings Institution.

Fratianni, M. and J. Von Hagen, 1992. *The European Monetary System and European Monetary Union.* Boulder, Colorado: Westview Press.

Froot, K.A., and K. Rogoff, 1991. The EMS, the EMU, and the Transition to a Common Currency, in O.J. Blanchard and S. Fisher, *NBER Macroeconomics Annual 1991.* Cambridge, MA: MIT Press, 269–317.

Garber, P.M., and L.E.O. Svensson, 1995. The Operation and Collapse of Fixed Exchange Rate Regimes, in G. Grossman and K. Rogoff, eds., *Handbook of International Economics,* Vol. III. Amsterdam: Elsevier.

Geadah, S., T. Saavalainen, and L.E.O. Svensson, 1992. The Credibility of Nordic Exchange Rate Bands: 1987–91. International Monetary Fund Working Paper.

George, E.A.J., 1995. The Economics of EMU. Churchill Memorial Lecture, February 21.

Gerlach, S. and F. Smets, 1994. Contagious Speculative Attacks. Centre for Economic Policy Research Discussion Paper No.1055.

Ghosh, A.R., and P. Masson, 1994. *Economic Cooperation in an Uncertain World.* Oxford, UK and Cambridge, MA: Basil Blackwell.

Giavazzi, F., and A. Giovannini, 1989. *Limiting Exchange Rate Flexibility. The European Monetary System.* Cambridge, MA: MIT Press.

Giavazzi, F., and M. Pagano, 1988. The Advantage of Tying One's Hand: EMS Discipline and Central Bank Credibility. *European Economic Review* 32, 1055–1075.

Giavazzi, F., and L. Spaventa, 1990. The New EMS, in De Grauwe and Papademos (1990).

Girardin, E., and V. Marimoutou, 1992. La Crédibilité de la Parité Franc-Deutsche Mark: Une Étude sur Données de Haute Fréquence pour la Période 1989–1992. *Economies et Sociétés* 9, 199–223.

Giscard d'Estaing, Valery, 1969. The International Monetary Order, in Mundell and Swoboda (1969).

Goldstein, M., D. Folkerts-Landau, P. Garber, L. Rojas-Suárez, and M. Spencer, 1993. *International Capital Markets. Part I. Exchange Rate Management and International Capital Flows.* Washington, DC: International Monetary Fund.

Goodhart, C.A.E., and S. Smith, 1993. Stabilization. *European Economy,* Special Issue, No. 5, 417–456.

Grilli, V.U., 1986. Buying and Selling Attacks on Fixed Exchange Rate Systems. *Journal of International Economics* 17, 1–13.

Grilli, V.U., 1989a. Exchange rates and seigniorage. *European Economic Review* 33, March, 580–87.

Grilli, Vittorio, 1989b. Seigniorage in Europe, in M. De Cecco and A. Giovannini, eds., *A European Central Bank? Perspectives on Monetary Unification After Ten Years of the EMS.* Cambridge, UK: Cambridge University Press, 53–79.

Gros, D., and A. Steinherr, 1991. Einigkeit Macht Stark: the Deutsche Mark also?, in R. O'Brien, ed., *Finance and the International Economy* 5. The Amex Bank Review Prize Essays. Oxford, UK: Oxford University Press, 52–67.

Gros, D., and N. Thygesen, 1992. *European Monetary Integration: From the European Monetary System to European Monetary Union.* London: Longman.

Guerrieri, P., and P.C. Padoan, 1988. *L'Economia Politica dell'Integrazione Europea.* Bologna: Il Mulino.

Hamada, K., 1976. A Strategic Analysis of Monetary Interdependence. *Journal of Political Economy* 84, 677–700.

Haq, N., I. Kaul, and I. Grunberg, eds., 1996. *The Tobin Tax: Coping with Financial Volatility.* Oxford, UK: Oxford University Press.

Hughes Hallett, A.J., and Y. Ma, 1995. Economic Cooperation within Europe: Lessons from the Monetary Arrangements in the 1990s. Centre for Economic Policy Research Discussion Paper No. 1190, June.

Ingram, J., 1969. The Currency Area Problem, in Mundell and Svoboda (1969).

Ingram, J., 1973. The Case for European Monetary Integration. *Princeton Essays in International Finance* No. 98, International Finance Section, Princeton University.

Ishiyama, Y., 1975. The Theory of Optimum Currency Areas: a Survey. *International Monetary Fund Staff Papers* 22.

Kenen, P.B., 1969. The Theory of Optimum Currency Areas: an Eclectic View, Mundell and Svoboda (1969).

Kenen, P.B., 1993. Comment on: The European Monetary System: Recent Intellectual History, in CEPR (1993).

Kenen, P.B., 1995. *Economic and Monetary Union in Europe. Moving Beyond Maastricht.* Cambridge, UK: Cambridge University Press.

Kenen, P.B., M. Mercurio, and P.A. Pesenti, 1996. Forecasters on the Spot: Explaining the Forecast Variance and the Risk Premium for Six Currencies. International Finance Section Working Paper, Princeton University.

Keynes, J.M., 1936. *The General Theory of Employment, Interest, and Money.* Reprinted by Harcourt Brace Jovanovich, 1964.

Klein, M., and M.J.M. Neumann, 1990. Seigniorage: What is it and Who Gets it? *Weltwirtschaftliches Archiv* 126, 205–221.

Klein, M., and M.J.M. Neumann, 1992. The Distribution of Seigniorage. *Weltwirtschaftliches Archiv* 128, 352–356.

Kremers, J.J.M., 1990. Gaining Policy Credibility for a Disinflation. Ireland's Experience in the EMS. *International Monetary Fund Staff Papers* 37, 116–145.

Krugman, P., 1979. A Model of Balance-of-Payments Crises. *Journal of Money, Credit and Banking* 11, 311–325.

Krugman, P., 1990. Target Zones and Exchange Rate Dynamics. *Quarterly Journal of Economics* 106, 669–682.

Krugman, P., 1992. Second Thoughts on EMU. *Japan and the World Economy* 4.

Krugman, P., 1993. Lessons of Massachusetts for EMU, in F. Torres and F. Giavazzi, eds., *Adjustment and Growth in the European Monetary Union*, Cambridge, UK: Cambridge University Press.

Krugman, P., 1996. Are Currency Crises Self-fulfilling? Annual Macroeconomics Conference. National Bureau of Economic Research. Cambridge, MA, March 8–9.

Kydland, F.E., and E.C. Prescott, 1977. Rules rather than Discretion: The Inconsistency of Optimal Plans. *Journal of Political Economy* 85, 473–491.

Leeftinck, B., 1994. The Desirability of Currency Unification; Theory and Some Evidence. Tinbergen Institute Research Series No. 92.

Lewis, K., 1989. On Occasional Monetary Policy Coordinations that Fix the Exchange Rate. *Journal of International Economics* 26, 139–155.

Ludlow, P., 1982. *The Making of the European Monetary System: A Case Study of the Politics of the European Community.* London: Butterworths.

McKibbin, W.J., and J.D. Sachs, 1991. *Global Linkages. Macroeconomic Interdependence and Cooperation in the World Economy.* Washington, DC: Brookings Institution.

McKinnon, R.I., 1963. Optimum Currency Areas. *American Economic Review* 53, 717–25.

Mankiw, G., 1987. The Optimal Collection of Seigniorage: Theory and Evidence. *Journal of Monetary Economics* 20 (2), September, 327–41.

Mantel, S., 1994. The Prospects for Labour Mobility under EMU. *Economie et Statistiques*, Special Issue, 137–147.

Marston, R.C., 1995. *International Financial Integration. A Study of Interest Differentials between the Major Industrial Countries.* Cambridge, UK: Cambridge University Press.

Masson, P., 1995. Gaining and losing ERM Credibility: the Case of the United Kingdom. *Economic Journal* 105, 571–582.

Masson, P., S. Symansky, and G. Meredith, 1990. MULTIMOD Mark II: A Revised and Extended Model. *International Monetary Fund Occasional Paper* No. 71, July.

Masson, P., and M.P. Taylor, 1992. Issues in the Operations of Monetary Unions and Common Currency Areas, in Goldstein et al., Policy Issues in the Evolving International Monetary System. *International Monetary Fund Occasional Paper* No. 96.

Mélitz, J., 1991. A Suggested Reformulation of the Theory of Optimal Currency Areas. Centre for Economic Policy Research Discussion Paper No. 590.

Mélitz, J., 1994. French Monetary Policy and Recent Speculative Attacks on the Franc, in David Cobhams, ed., *The 1992–93 Upheavals in the European Monetary System*, Manchester, UK: Manchester University Press, 61–81.

Minford, P., 1995. Time-inconsistency, Democracy and Optimal Contingent Rules. *Oxford Economic Papers* 47, 195–210.

Molho, L.E., 1992. The Italian Lira in the Narrow Exchange Rate Mechanism Band: The Challenge of Credibility. *Giornale degli Economisti e Annali di Economia* 11–12, 501–525.

Muehring, K., 1992. Currency Chaos: The Inside Story. *Institutional Investor,* October, 11–15.

Mundell, R.A., and A. K. Swoboda, eds., 1969. *Monetary Problems in the International Economy.* Chicago, IL: University of Chicago Press.

Muet, P.A., 1991. Croissance, Emploi et Chomage dans les Années Quatrevingt. *Revue de l'OFCE* No. 35, January.

Muet, P.A., 1995. Ajustements Macroéconomiques et Coordination en Union Monetaire. Paper Presented at the Journées AFSE 1995, Nantes, 8–9 June 1995.

Mundell, R.A., 1961. A Theory of Optimum Currency Areas. *American Economic Review* 51, 657–75.

Nikolakaki, M., 1996. Is Europe an Optimum Currency Area? A Reconsideration of the Evidence. Working Paper, London School of Economics, April.

Nölling, W., 1993. *Monetary Policy after Maastricht.* London: Macmillan Press.

Obstfeld, M., 1986. Rational and Self-Fulfilling Balance of Payments Crises. *American Economic Review* 76, 676–81.

Obstfeld, M., 1991. Destabilizing Effects of Exchange Rate Escape Clauses. National Bureau of Economic Research Working Paper No. 3630, January.

Obstfeld, M., 1994. The Logic of Currency Crises. *Cahiers Economiques et Monétaires* 43, 189–213.

Obstfeld, M., 1995. Models of Currency Crises with Self-Fulfilling Features. *European Economic Review* 40, 1037–47.

Obstfeld, M., and K. Rogoff, 1995a. Exchange Rate Dynamics Redux. *Journal of Political Economy* 103, 624–660.

Obstfeld, M. and K. Rogoff, 1995b. The Mirage of Fixed Exchange Rates. *Journal of Economic Perspectives* 9, 73–96.

Ozkan, F. G. and A. Sutherland, 1994a. A Currency Crisis Model with Optimizing Policy Makers. Working Paper, University of York.

Ozkan F. G. and A. Sutherland, 1994b. A Model of ERM Crises. Center for Economic Policy Research Discussion Paper No. 879, January.

Padoa-Schioppa, T., 1985. Squaring the Circle, or the Conundrum of International Monetary Reform. *Catalyst* 1, Spring.

Padoa-Schioppa, T., 1994. *The Road to Monetary Union in Europe.* Oxford, UK: Clarendon Press.

Persson, T., and G. Tabellini, 1995. Double-Edged Incentives: Institutions and Policy Coordination, in G.M. Grossman and K. Rogoff, eds., *Handbook of International Economics,* Vol. III, Amsterdam: North-Holland.

Poole, W., 1970. Optimal Choice of Monetary Instruments in a Simple Stochastic Macro Model. *Quarterly Journal of Economics* 84, 197–216.

Portes, R., 1993. EMS and EMU after the Fall. *The World Economy* 16, 1–16.

Rose, A.K., and L.E.O. Svensson, 1994. European Credibility Before the Fall. *European Economic Review* 38.

Roubini, N., and G.M. Milesi-Ferretti, 1994. Optimal Taxation of Human and Physical Capital in Endogenous Growth Models. National Bureau of Economic Research Working Paper No. 4882, October.

Rovelli, R., 1994. Reserve Requirements, Seigniorage and the Financing of the Government in an Economic and Monetary Union. *European Economy* 1, 11–55.

Rubin, J., and N. Thygesen, 1996. Monetary Union and the Outsiders: A Cointegration/ Codependence Analysis of Business Cycles in Europe. Institute of Economics Working Paper No. 96-08, University of Copenhagen.

Sala-i-Martin, X., and J. Sachs, 1992. Fiscal Federalism and Optimum Currency Areas: Evidence for Europe from the United States, in M. Canzoneri, V.U. Grilli, and P. Masson, eds., *Establishing a Central Bank: Issues in Europe and Lessons cfrom the US.* Cambridge, UK: Cambridge University Press.

Salant, S.W., and D.W. Henderson, 1978. Market Anticipations of Government Policies and the Price of Gold. *Journal of Political Economy* 86, 627–648.

Salop, J., 1981. The Divergence Indicator: a Technical Note. *International Monetary Fund Staff Papers* 28.

Sargent, T.J., 1987. *Macroeconomic Theory.* II edition. Orlando, Florida: Academic Press.

Schlesinger, H., 1994. A Perspective from Germany: The Economy after Unification and a Look at the Progress of European Integration. The John Foster Dulles Program Lectures. Woodrow Wilson School. Princeton, NJ, October 19.

Sibert, A.C., 1994. The Allocation of Seigniorage in a Common Currency Area. *Journal of International Economics* 37, 111–22.

Sinn, G., and H.W. Sinn, 1996. *Jumpstart. The Economic Unification of Germany.* Cambridge, MA: MIT Press.

Söderström, H.T., 1993. Finland's Economic Crisis. SNS Occasional Paper No. 47.

Solomon, R., 1977. *The International Monetary System 1945–1976: An Insider's View.* New York: Harper & Row.

Spaventa, L., 1982. Algebraic Properties and Economic Improprieties of the "Indicator of Divergence" in the European Monetary System, in R. Cooper et al., eds., *The International Monetary System under Flexible Exchange Rates.* Cambridge, MA: Ballinger.

Svensson, L.E.O., 1991. The Simplest Test of Target Zone Credibility. *International Monetary Fund Staff Papers* 38, 655–65.

Svensson, L.E.O., 1992. The Foreign Exchange Risk Premium in a Target Zone with Devaluation Risk. *Journal of International Economics* 33, 21–40.

Svensson, L.E.O., 1993. Assessing Target Zone Credibility: Mean Reversion and Devaluation Expectations in the ERM 1979–1992. *European Economic Review* 37, 763–93.

Svensson, L.E.O., 1994. Fixed Exchange Rates as a Means to Price Stability: What Have We Learnt? *European Economic Review* 38, 447–468.

Tabellini, G., 1994. Comments on European Credibility Before the Fall by A.K. Rose and L.E.O. Svensson. *European Economic Review* 38, 1221–1223.

Temperton, P., ed., 1993. *The European Currency Crisis, One Year On.* London: Probus.

Thygesen, N., 1979. The Emerging EMS: Precursors, First Steps and Policy Options. *Bulletin de la Banque National de Belgique*, April.

Thygesen, N., 1996. The Euro and Other European Currencies. Alpbach Economic Forum. Alpbach, 28–30 August.

Tobin, J., 1982. A Proposal for International Monetary Reform, in J. Tobin, *Essays in Economic Theory and Policy*, Ch. 20, Cambridge, MA: MIT Press.

Triffin, R., 1960. *Gold and the Dollar Crisis*. New Haven, CT: Yale University Press.

Tsoulakis, L., 1977. *The Politics and Economics of European Monetary Integration*. London: George Allen & Unwin.

Van Ewijk, C., 1992. The Distribution of Seigniorage; a Note on Klein and Neumann. *Weltwirtschaftliches Archiv* 128, 346–351.

Van Rompuy, P., F. Abraham, and D. Heremans, 1991. Economic Federalism and the EMU. *European Economy*, Special Edition No. 1, 109–1354.

Van Ypersele, J., and J.C. Koeune, 1985. The EMS, Origins, Operation and Outlook. *European Perspective Series*. Brussels: Commission of the European Communities.

Velasco, A., 1996. When Are Fixed Exchange Rates Really Fixed? Working Paper, New York University.

Von Hagen, J., 1992. Fiscal Arrangements in a Monetary Union: Some Evidence from the US, in D. Fair and C. De Boissieu, eds., *Fiscal Policy, Taxes and the Financial System in an Increasingly Integrated Europe*, Deventer: Kluwer.

Von Hagen, J., and G.W. Hammond, 1995. Regional Insurance Against Asymmetric Shocks: An Empirical Study for the European Community. Centre for Economic Policy Research Discussion Paper No. 1170.

Willman, Alpo, 1988. The Collapse of the Fixed Exchange Rate Regime with Sticky Wages and Imperfect Substitutability between Domestic and Foreign Bonds. *European Economic Review* 32, 1817–1838.

Woodford, M., 1990. Learning to Believe in Sunspots. *Econometrica* 58, 277–307.

Wyplosz, C., 1988. Capital Flow Liberalization and the EMS: A French Perspective. *European Economy*, May.

Index*

anticipated inflation tax, 184
asymmetries
　in early 1990s, 135
　in EMS, 26–8
　in exchange rate policies, 148–9
Austria
　debt of, 54*t*
　deficit of, 54*t*
　exchange rates in, 45*f*, 46*f*
　inflation differentials against Germany, 44*f*
　interest differentials against Germany,
　　76*f*–78*f*, 80*f*
　output growth rate for, 49*f*
　seigniorage in, 183*t*
　trade balance for, 51*f*
　unemployment rate in, 50*f*

band
　mean-reversion within, 75
　widening of, 65–6, 175
base money
　definition of, 180
　government revenue from, 180
Basle Agreement (1972), 23
Basle-Nyborg Agreement (1987), 1, 29
Bath Meeting (1992), 56, 130, 169, 172–3
Belgian compromise, 26
Belgium
　debt of, 54*t*
　deficit of, 54*t*
　exchange rates in, 45*f*, 46*f*
　inflation differentials against Germany, 44*f*
　interest differentials against Germany,
　　76*f*–78*f*, 80*f*
　output growth rate for, 49*f*
　seigniorage in, 183*t*
　trade balance for, 51*f*
　unemployment rate in, 50*f*
beliefs updating, 127–30, 133
benign neglect, 52*n*
Black Wednesday, 59–60, 170
Bretton Woods system, 19–21

Bundesbank
　borrowing credibility from, 28
　credibility of, 7*n*
　decrease of interest rates by, 58–9
　discount rate adjustments by, 54
　and EMS, 30
　German reunification and, 39, 40–1

CAP. *see* Common Agricultural Policy
capital controls
　advantages and disadvantages of, 68
　functions of, 67–8
　interpretations of, 61*n*
　removal of, 35
capital mobility
　as argument for common currency, 196–8
　disruptive potential of, 67
　versus exchange rate flexibility, 193
　exchange rate stability and, 67
　and transition to union, 35–6
Cecchini Report, 178
Center country
　definition of, 175
　demand boom in, 107
　employment in, 96, 146
　interdependence with Periphery, 141–2
　objective function of, 97–9
　policy preferences of, 97–8
　reaction function in, 136–7
　real exchange rate of, 94, 104–5
　in system of exchange rates, 11
　target level of employment in, 98
　technology of, 94–6
Center-Periphery model, 93–107
　and EMU, 199–200
　interpretation of ERM crisis in, 168–75
　semireduced form of, 103–7
central bank(s)
　European. *see* European Central Bank
　and financial markets, 167*n*
　national, sovereignty of, 35
　reputation of, 75

*Italicized letters *f*, *t*, and *n* following page numbers indicate figures, tables, and footnotes, respectively.